Following the Guidon

GENERAL CUSTER AND HIS SCOUTS.   [*Page* 218.

Following the Guidon

By Elizabeth B. Custer

ILLUSTRATED

Introduction to the Bison Book Edition
by Shirley A. Leckie

University of Nebraska Press
Lincoln and London

Introduction to the Bison Book Edition copyright © 1994 by the
University of Nebraska Press

First Bison Book printing: 1994
Most recent printing indicated by the last digit below:
10   9   8   7   6   5   4   3   2   1

Library of Congress Cataloging-in-Publication Data
Custer, Elizabeth Bacon, 1842–1933.
Following the guidon / by Elizabeth B. Custer; introduction to the
Bison edition by Shirley A. Leckie.
p. cm.
"Bison."
Originally published: New York: Harper & Brothers, 1890.
Includes bibliographical references (p.   ).
ISBN 0-8032-6362-7 (pa)
1. United States. Army—Military life—History—19th cen-
tury. 2. West (U.S.)—Description and travel. 3. United States.
Army. Cavalry, 7th. 4. Custer, George Armstrong, 1839–
1876. 5. Custer, Elizabeth Bacon, 1842–1933. 6. Indians of
North America—Wars—1868–1869. 7. West (U.S.)—History—
1860–1890. I. Title.
F594.C983   1994b
973.8—dc20
94-14464   CIP

Reprinted from the original 1890 edition published by Harper &
Brothers, New York.

∞

TO

ONE WHO HAS FOLLOWED THE GUIDON

INTO THAT REALM WHERE

" The war - drum throbs no longer
And the battle - flags are furled."

INTRODUCTION

By Shirley A. Leckie

Early on the morning of July 6, 1876, Elizabeth Bacon Custer learned that her husband, Lt. Col. George Armstrong Custer, and five companies of the Seventh Cavalry had been killed on the Little Bighorn River. Their deaths had occurred during an engagement with the Sioux Indians and their Northern Cheyenne allies. Shivering despite the heat, Elizabeth donned a shawl as she accompanied Fort Abraham Lincoln's interim commander, the post surgeon, and another officer while they informed the other newly-widowed women of their losses. Later she comforted soldiers, wounded during Major Marcus Reno's attack in the same battle that had taken her husband's life.

Thus, despite losses that included her husband's brothers, Thomas and Boston, his nephew Autie Reed, brother-in-law James Calhoun, and close associates, Libbie, as friends knew her, was already displaying the resiliency that would enable her to rebuild her life. She needed it, for at thirty-four she had no immediate family save her stepmother, Rhoda Bacon. Elizabeth had lost her three siblings and her mother, Eleanor Sophia Page Bacon, before her thirteenth birthday. Her father, Judge Daniel Bacon of Monroe, Michigan, had died in 1866.

At first Elizabeth drew strength from accolades that poured into the post. Walt Whitman's "A Death Song for Custer" appeared in the *New York Herald* on July 10. Eight days later, Will County, Illinois, named its new town Custer. On July 28, the Texas legislature passed a resolution memorializing Custer's "bold and dashing operations against the Indians."

But if some saw Armstrong as a hero, others blamed him for defeat. In a confidential report, intercepted by the press and published in the *Philadelphia Inquirer* on July 7, Custer's superior, Gen. Alfred H. Terry, commander of the Department of Dakota, stated that he had told the lieutenant colonel to march south about twenty miles before turning north and west. Had he complied he would have arrived at the battle site a day later when Colonel John Gibbon's forces were nearby, thereby assuring victory. Shortly after, Samuel Sturgis, colonel of the Seventh Cavalry, having lost a son at the Little Bighorn, railed against Custer as a man "insanely ambitious of glory." Even worse, President Ulysses S. Grant termed the losses "wholly unnecessary" and brought on by Custer's insistence on forcemarching worn-out men.[1]

As controversy swirled around her, Elizabeth returned to Monroe and began collaborating with Frederick Whittaker, a writer of dime novels. She gave him access to her husband's papers and correspondence, and in November he published *A Complete Life of Gen. George A. Custer*. The book exonerated Armstrong of responsibility for the Little Bighorn disaster, largely by accusing Major Reno of "gross cowardice" for failing to sustain his separate charge. Equally important, by presenting the slain soldier as an unblemished hero, it laid the basis for the heroic Custer that appeared in stories, novels, poems, and paintings for the next half century.[2]

Nonetheless, Elizabeth still faced difficulties. In settling her husband's estate, she discovered that indebtedness far outweighed assets. Compelled to make a living, she moved to New York City. By summer 1877 she was employed as secretary for the Society of Decorative Arts, a charitable organization that marketed the household crafts of women. That fall, Elizabeth oversaw the reinterring of her husband's remains at West Point Academy.

The next few years proved disappointing. Early in 1879, a court of inquiry, investigating Reno's conduct at the Little Bighorn, found no grounds for court-martial. Soon after, Elizabeth learned that a committee, including journalist Thurlow Weed and financier August Belmont, had commissioned a Custer monument at West Point without consulting her. When three-thousand people assembled for the unveiling on August 30, 1879, the widow was nowhere in sight.

Later, as she read newspaper reports of a dismounted, long-haired soldier, brandishing pistol and sword, Elizabeth concluded that the statue invited ridicule. Turning first to Commanding General of the Army William Tecumseh Sherman, and later to Secretary of War Robert Lincoln, she campaigned relentlessly for its removal. By late 1884 West Point officials had stored the cavalryman in a warehouse. Afterwards, Elizabeth told a friend that she had "literally cried it off its pedestal."[3]

In March 1885, three years after an increased pension permitted her to leave employment, the widow produced her own "Custer Memorial." *"Boots and Saddles"; or, Life in Dakota with General Custer* described Armstrong as a solicitous commander who never gossiped, never held a grudge, and never harbored jealousy. More important, he was a devoted family man. As Elizabeth wrote her friend, Fanny Kingsley, the widow of the British author Charles Kingsley, her compatriots "love him anew because he was such a son, brother, husband, friend."[4]

Two years later, Elizabeth published her second volume, *Tenting on the Plains; or, General Custer in Kansas and Texas*. This work covered the Custers' adventures in Louisiana and Texas during Reconstruction. It also described sympathetically Armstrong's efforts to mold "incongruous elements" into a unified regiment at Fort Riley after he assumed the lieutenant colonelcy of the Seventh Cavalry in 1866. Soon after, the determination of the Plains Indians to protect their hunting grounds against further encroachment led to war, and Elizabeth chronicled her husband's involvement in General Winfield Scott Hancock's abortive campaign.

In July 1867, during this campaign, Custer left his post at Fort Wallace without authorization and rejoined his wife at Fort Riley. In 1875 his book, *My Life on the Plains,* explained his actions by stating that cholera had appeared among his men and Wallace lacked supplies. Elizabeth repeated her husband's claims in her own work.[5] More recently, however, Minnie Dubbs Millbrook examined War Department records and discovered that cholera had not yet appeared among Seventh Cavalry troopers when Custer left Wallace on July 15. Moreover, her investigation of post returns indicated that Wallace was supplied for a month.[6] Not surprisingly, Custer's actions led to his court-martial and suspension from rank and pay for one year.

Following the Guidon, the last of Elizabeth's three books, appeared in 1890 and covered the years 1868 and 1869 after Philip Sheridan had won remission of Custer's remaining sentence. As commanding general of the Department of the Missouri, Sheridan, annoyed with officers who chased Indians by ambulance, had decided to wage a different kind of warfare. In winter, when military action was least expected, the army would strike the Indians in their villages, destroying everything of value and forcing them on to reservations away from settlements and railroad construction crews. No one, Sheridan believed, could perform this assignment better than Custer, who had waged similar warfare against civilians in the Shenandoah Valley during the Civil War.

After a brief preface explaining military routine and calls, Elizabeth began her narrative as Armstrong, having rejoined his regiment, prepared for the winter campaign. When supplies arrived, the Seventh marched into Indian Territory. On the morning of November 27, Custer split his forces into four battalions and surprised a Cheyenne village slumbering along the Washita River. By mid-morning the village was subdued, and among those killed was the peace chief Black Kettle.

The Battle of the Washita established Custer as one of his country's foremost Indian fighters. Nonetheless, the victory proved problematical. Black Kettle had, hours before, returned from a meeting with Col. William B. Hazen, commander of the Southern Military District. Concerned that the depredations of young Cheyenne braves might bring retribution, he had sought to bring his people to Fort Cobb. Instead, Hazen had advised him to make peace with Sheridan.

Eastern humanitarians who championed the Indian cause characterized the battle as a "massacre." Both Armstrong and Elizabeth now learned that divisions in public opinion regarding Indian policy ensured a mixed response to the victory. Defensively, Libbie wrote her aunt, Eliza Sabin of upstate New York, "Surely you do not believe the current rumors that Autie [Armstrong's nickname] and others are cruel in their treatment of the Indians? Autie and others only do what they are ordered to do." Westerners, especially women taken captive, had suffered "degradations unspeakable."[7]

Written more than two decades later, *Following the Guidon* makes that point once more. Although the Battle of the Washita had resulted in the capture of Cheyenne Indian hostages, many of the Southern Plains tribes did not move to reservations but instead fled in terror. Thus Custer was forced to mount additional expeditions, and the final one, in March 1869, extended to the Texas Panhandle. On the banks of the Sweetwater, the Seventh discovered that Cheyenne Indians under Chiefs Little Robe and Medicine Arrows had in their midst two captives, Anna Brewster Morgan and Sarah White. The scene in *Following the Guidon* in which Custer's men and the Nineteenth Kansas militia free the women is highly dramatic and emphasizes their rescue from the proverbial "fate worse than death."

There is another side to this story. According to Capt. Frederick Benteen, some Seventh Cavalry officers sexually exploited the Cheyenne women they took captive. Moreover, Custer shared his bed with the Indian woman, Mo-nah-se-tah.[8] While Benteen's hatred for his commander undermines his statements, Ben Clark, who replaced California Joe as Custer's Chief of Scouts, gave similar testimony to Walter M. Camp. (A railroad engineer, who died before he completed his history of the Battle of the Little Bighorn, Camp conducted extensive interviews with officers and scouts who had served in the Seventh Cavalry.)[9] Finally, Cheyenne tradition holds that Mo-nah-se-tah saw herself as Custer's second wife and bore him a child, her second.[10]

Whether Elizabeth heard these accounts is unknown. Nonetheless, as her husband had done earlier in his book, she transformed Mo-nah-se-tah into a supporting character in her narrative. The Cheyenne woman became the Indian "princess" who assisted the white hero.

Furthermore, by characterizing the other Indian women as degraded and exploited "squaws," Elizabeth provided additional justification for the conquest of the indigenous people. Like many middle-class Americans of Victorian America, Libbie believed that women were morally superior to men and bore the primary responsibility for maintaining virtue. In turn, she expected even rough frontiersmen to accord females public deference and respect. In Chapter Twelve of *Following the Guidon,* she notes that one Ellsworth, Kansas, innkeeper brought order among ruffians by uttering "the talismanic name of lady to quiet them." By contrast, as Libbie saw it (knowing little about the actual status of women in various tribes), Indian men treated their wives contemptuously, forcing them to perform all the manual labor and denying them honor.

In this context, Elizabeth's praise of officers as romantic and chivalrous lovers who carried their sweethearts' portraits in their shirt pockets and wore their amulets without complaint takes on greater meaning. Through their regard for womanhood, these men showed themselves the worthy representatives of a more advanced "civilization." In a similar fashion, Elizabeth emphasizes the homage officers paid to motherhood. Here she becomes overly sentimental, and one scholar, Ralph K. Andrist, calls some of her statements "purest moonshine." It is nonsense, he argues, to believe that Custer marched his regiment around a meadowlark's nest or that officers avoided shooting buffalo cows during their hunts out of respect for maternity.[11]

If the first part of *Following the Guidon* concerns the Battle of the Washita and the winter campaign that followed, much of the remaining portion recreates the Seventh's days in camp along Big Creek outside Fort Hays. To recapture her memories, Elizabeth rented a cottage on the banks of the Pocono River near Stroudsburg, Pennsylvania, in the summer of 1889. During the day she wrote outside and at night slept in a tent. The strategy paid off, for her descriptions of camp life, complete with "animated zoo," are vividly drawn, as are her delineations of the servant Eliza and her irrepressible brother-in-law, Tom Custer. Armstrong, however, remains somewhat remote largely because he is referred to as "General Custer," his brevet title from the Civil War.

By the late 1880s, Americans were already celebrating their pioneering heritage in the Trans-Mississippi West, and Elizabeth sought new ways of tying her husband to frontier lore. She extracts the maximum drama from nearby Hays City, Kansas, characterizing it as a sordid place where constant gunfire felled new victims daily. She also introduces her readers to James Butler Hickok, better known as Wild Bill, the hero of dime novels. He scouted awhile for the army, thereby permitting her to claim that he and Armstrong were "fast friends, having faced danger together many times."

Elizabeth's enthusiastic description of Hickok displays both her literary skill and her eye for attractive men, especially one who reminded her of a "thorough-bred horse." She is not, however, the most reliable source for information. Although she gives Hickok's death as July 4, 1876, Jack McCall shot him almost a month later on August 2, as he played poker in Deadwood, Dakota Territory.

Libbie also reminds her readers of the sacrifices officers and their wives made by serving in the frontier army. For men, promotion was "very slow" since vacancies opened only when retirement, resignation, or death occurred. Simultaneously, their wives found it hard to maintain middle-class standards of domesticity at poorly supplied and crowded posts.

With the publication of three books, Elizabeth established herself as a noted author. By the mid-1890s she was a familiar figure on the northern and midwestern lecture circuit. The work paid well, and through shrewd investments in Bronxville, a suburb of New York City, Libbie achieved affluence.

During her long widowhood, she enjoyed other triumphs. In 1901, her friend Mary Burt edited her three books into a single volume, *The Boy General.* Charles Scribner's and Sons published it as a textbook that taught youth patriotic values. Nine years later, Elizabeth stood beside President William Howard Taft as he extolled her husband's contributions to westward expansion at the unveiling of the Custer monument in Monroe. Then, on June 25, 1926, the *New York Herald* reported that Elizabeth looked back on fifty years of widowhood with pride, believing that schoolboys had made "General Custer a symbol of courage which has helped to mold the soul of an entire generation." In a real sense, however, it was her writings that had established Armstrong's heroism in the public mind.

Elizabeth Custer died on April 4, 1933, four days before turning ninety-one. One year later, Frederic Van de Water published *Glory-Hunter,* a critical biography that began the reevaluation of Custer that continues to the present day.[12]

Still, while Custer has lost much of his former luster as a hero, even his severest critic has only to begin reading *Following the Guidon* to be swept back to the days when the Seventh camped along Big Creek. Among the narratives of army wives in the West this one has enduring value, chiefly for the telling details, literary charm, and author's voice, which assures you that she has taken you into her confidence and all that follows is undeniably true.

Welcome to the Kansas Plains and enjoy the adventure, but don't mistake this for unbiased history. It is the work of a partisan who knows that, while the reader finds her stories humorous, underneath is the ever-present poignant sense of losses to come. Thus Elizabeth Custer still weaves her magic despite the passage of time.

NOTES

1. *New York Herald,* 2 September, 1876; Robert Utley, *Custer and the Great Controversy: The Origin and Development of a Legend* (Pasadena, Calif.: Westernlore Press, 1980), 44–45.

2. Frederick Whittaker, *A Complete Life of General George A. Custer* (1876; reprint, 2 vols, with introductions by Gregory J. W. Urwin and Robert M. Utley, Lincoln: University of Nebraska Press, 1993, vol. 2, xii–xiv, 573–608).

3. Marguerite Merington, ed., *The Custer Story: The Life and Intimate Letters of General George A. Custer and His Wife Elizabeth* (New York: Devon-Adair, 1950; reprint, Lincoln: University of Nebraska Press, 1987, 327).

4. Elizabeth B. Custer to Mrs. (Fanny) Kingsley, 6 January [1886], Elizabeth Bacon Custer Manuscript Collection, Western Americana Collection, Beinecke Rare Book and Manuscript Collection, Yale University, New Haven, Connecticut.

5. George Armstrong Custer, *My Life on the Plains; or, Personal Experiences with Indians,* introduction by Edgar I. Stewart (Norman: University of Oklahoma Press, 1962), 114; Elizabeth B. Custer, *Tenting on the Plains; or, General Custer in Kansas and Texas.* (New York: Charles Webster L. Webster, 1887), 696–700.

6. Minnie Dubbs Millbrook, "The West Breaks in General Custer," *The Custer Reader,* ed. Paul Hutton. (Lincoln: University of Nebraska Press, 1992), 138.

7. Elizabeth Custer to Eliza Sabin, undated letter, Merington, *Custer Story,* 284.

8. Frederic Benteen to Theodore Goldin, 14 and 17 February 1896, John M. Carroll, ed., *The Benteen-Goldin Letters on Custer and His Last Battle* (New York: Liveright, 1974; reprint, Lincoln: University of Nebraska Press, 1991, 258, 271).

9. Ben Clark, interviewed by W. M. Camp, Ben Clark Field Notes, Box 2, Folder F, Walter Camp Manuscript, Lilly Library, Indiana University, Bloomington, Indiana.

10. Kate Bighead as told to Thomas B. Marquis, "She Watched Custer's Last Battle," in Hutton, *The Custer Reader,* 364; Mari Sandoz, *Cheyenne Autumn* (1953; reprint, Lincoln: University of Nebraska Press, 1992, xvii, xix, 21, 32, 215); Charles J. Brill, *Conquest of the Southern Plains: Uncensored Narrative of the Battle of the Washita and Custer's Southern Campaign* (Oklahoma City: Golden Saga Publishers, 1938), 22, 45–46; David Humphreys Miller, *Custer's Fall: The Indian Side of the Story* (New York: Duell, Sloan and Pearce, 1957; reprint. Lincoln: University of Nebraska Press, 1985), 67–68.

11. Ralph K. Andrist, *The Long Death: The Last Days of the Plains Indians* (New York: Macmillan, 1964), 178–79.

12. Frederic F. Van de Water, *Glory-Hunter: A Life of General Custer* (1934; reprint, Lincoln: University of Nebraska Press, 1988).

PREFACE.

Before beginning the story of our summer's camp on Big Creek, Kansas, I should like to make our bugle a more familiar friend to those who know it only by hearsay. It was the hourly monitor of the cavalry corps. It told us when to eat, to sleep, to march, and to go to church. Its clear tones reminded us, should there be physical ailments, that we must go to the doctor, and if the lazy soldier was disposed to lounge about the company's barracks, or his indolent officer to loll his life away in a hammock on the gallery of his quarters, the bugle's sharp call summoned him to "drill" or "dress parade." It was the enemy of ease, and cut short many a blissful hour. The very night was invaded by its clarion notes if there chanced to be fire, or should Indians steal a march on us, or deserters be discovered decamping. We needed timepieces only when absent from garrison or camp. The never tardy sound calling to duty was better than any clock, and brought us up standing; and instead of the usual remark, "Why, here it's four o'clock already!" we found ourselves saying: "Can it be possible? There's 'Stables,' and where has the day gone?"

The horses knew the calls, and returned from grazing of their own accord at "Recall" before any trooper had started; and one of them would resume his place in the ranks, and obey the bugle's directions as nonchalantly as if the moment before he had not lifted a recruit over his head and deposited him on the ground.

The horses were often better tacticians than the soldiers,

for it frequently happened that one of them had served our country through one enlistment of five years, and was well on through another when assigned to a recruit who had never before mounted. The intelligent beast, feeling himself insulted by being called upon to carry a green trooper, seemed in very scorn to empty the saddle. I sometimes thought the wise animals thus disposed of their riders and went back to the line, as if to say, "I'll teach that greenhorn that I know military life better than he does."

In large posts, like Fort Leavenworth or Fort Lincoln, there was a corps of trained buglers, and it was a surprise to strangers that such good music could be evolved from instruments with so few notes. On a summer's day the sound of the buglers came wafted to us from some divide over the plain, where they had gone to practise, and hoped to deaden the sound. Though the bugles might blow, they could not "set the wild echoes flying" out there, for we had neither the rocky fastness nor the hill and dale of Scotland or Switzerland. I should have liked to transport a band of our drilled buglers to the land of Roderick Dhu. The clans could have been summoned for miles by the clear reverberating notes, and there the stirring music, reproduced by enchanting echoes, would have been far finer than on our monotonous plains.

In the telling of this story of our summer's camp there is often reference to both the trumpet and the bugle. When I was first in the army the bugle was used for the infantry and cavalry, but later the trumpet was given to the mounted regiments. In this way it has occurred that the names have been used indiscriminately. The difference between them may be sufficiently indicated by calling the bugle the tenor and the trumpet the barytone of military music.

The soldiers, for no one knows how long, have fitted rhymes to the calls, and as the men pour out of the barracks to groom their horses for the morning or the evening hour a voice takes up the call, to be quickly joined by others, and after the bugles cease the humming of " Go to the stable," etc., continues until the sergeant gives the signal for work to begin with the curry-comb. A few of these jingles have been attached to the calls that were in most frequent use during the day. The words of these simple rhymes are just as familiar to military people as the household tales of infancy, and as indelibly impressed on an army child as " Twinkle, twinkle, little star," or " Now I lay me down to sleep."

The calls that are in almost daily use head the chapters throughout the book. Possibly a few of them may need some explanation. " Reveille " is the first roll-call of the day. The morning gun is fired as the first note sounds. The soldiers all come out of their quarters, and the sergeant calls the names alphabetically, and reports to the captain the whole company as " present, or accounted for," or certain ones as " absent without leave," etc. There are three of these roll-calls during the twenty-four hours—at Reveille, Retreat, and Tattoo. " Retreat" sounds at sunset, when the flag is lowered and the evening gun is fired at the last note of the call. "Tattoo" is sounded about nine o'clock, and soon after comes "Taps"—a signal to extinguish lights. "Assembly" is the signal for forming the company in ranks, and precedes the three calls described above. " The General" is the signal for packing up, striking tents, and loading the wagons for marching. " Boots and Saddles" is the first signal for mounting.

As there was a great deal of formality and "circumstance" about all these calls, and not the slightest infringement of the dignity of the routine was permitted, the rhymes which the soldiers made, in their rollicking off-hand fashion, were most violently in contrast with the solemnity of the martial forms to which they were attached.

The infantry mess-call evidently dates back a long time, as the soldiers' words to the drum-call for mess are " pease upon a trencher." " The dirty, dirty, dirty dough-boy "—the origin of which is referred to in *Boots and Saddles*—is also an infantry call.

It often happened that the soldiers changed their names in enlisting, and sunk their identity in the ranks of our army; but sometimes even there an irate wife, who had been deserted in the States, found out her culprit husband, and compelled him to send her money out of his pay for her support. Or, in another instance, though the man may have been angry enough, at the time of his enlistment, to feel that he would never return to his virago of a wife, he eventually melted when attacked with nostalgia, and confided to his comrades that he was married. It must have been on some such occasion that a scoffer suited these lines to the marching step in the drill, which begins " Left foot forward " always:

"Left—left—left my wife and seven small children behind me."

There is a legend that women never keep step. One of my friends, who is now a civilian, and the commanding officer of only one small woman, marshals his trooper out when husband and wife go for a stroll, repeating the old lines of volunteer days. I imagine that a sergeant who drilled the men was the original poet, for the order of march runs after this fashion:

" Left—left—left—had a good home and he left!"

Then, referring to the step:

" Now you've got it, d——n you, keep it—left—left—left!"

Some children having asked questions to which I could not reply, I was obliged, not long since, to visit the Astor Library to look up answers. I give a condensed summary of the results of my research. One of the old books I consulted had not had many readers, I imagine, for as I turned the mildewed, musty pages armies of tiny creatures chased each other to and fro in wild alarm, while bookworms were eating out the foundations of the volume. Still, unconsulted as

Grose's *Military Antiquities* seems to be, I found information there that must have some interest for a cavalryman.

The trumpet, of which our bugle is the sister, seems to antedate all musical instruments, as it appeared on the Egyptian bass-relief at Thebes, and was also used by the Israelites. The trumpets of the Romans were both straight and crooked. A shell bored at the end, and a horn with the point removed, were the most primitive forms of the instrument. The tuba, represented in the bass-reliefs of the triumphal arch of Titus, was a kind of straight bronze clarion, about thirty-nine inches long. Fra Angelico (1455) painted angels with trumpets with straight or zigzag tubes, the shortest being five feet in length. A change from the straight tube of the trumpet to one bent into three parallel lines was made about the middle of the fifteenth century. Luca della Robia represents the tube bent back in that way, and this shape was retained for more than three hundred years. A capistrum, or muzzle, was used by the ancients to preserve their cheeks in blowing the trumpet. Trumpets were in use during the crusade of 1248.

At one time the hautboy and kettle-drums were used in mounted regiments. There is, even now, one of the latter, captured from the English in the Revolutionary War, at the Military Museum on Governor's Island.

Hinde, in his *Discipline of the Light Horse*, says: "In the year 1764 his Majesty thought proper to forbid the use of brass side-drums in the Light Cavalry, and in their room to introduce brass trumpets; the trumpets are slung over the left shoulder and hang at their backs."

Grose says: "The banners of the kettle-drums and trumpets to be of the color of the facing of the regiment; the badge of the regiment or its rank to be in the centre of the banner of the kettle-drums, as on the second standard; the King's cipher and crown to be on the banner of the trumpets, with the rank of the regiment in ciphers underneath;

the depth of the kettle-drum banners to be three feet six inches; the length four feet eight inches, exclusive of the fringe; those of the trumpets to be twelve inches in depth and eighteen inches in length. The trumpets to be of brass; the cords to be crimson mixed with the color of the facing of the regiment; the King's Own Regiment of dragoons and the Royal Irish are permitted to continue their kettle-drums."

The chief beats of the drum formerly used by the infantry, according to Colonel Bariffe (1643), were a Call, a Troop, a Preparative, a March, a Bataille, a Retreat.

"By a Call, you must understand to prepare to hear present proclamation, or else to repair to your ensign; by a Troop, understand to shoulder your muskets, to advance your pikes, to close your ranks and files to their order, and to troop along with or follow your officer to the place of rendezvous or elsewhere; by a March, you are to understand to take your open order in rank, to shoulder both muskets and pikes, and to direct your march, either quicker or slower, according to the beat of the drum; by a Preparative, you are to understand to close to your due distance for skirmish, both in rank and file, and to make ready, that you may execute upon the first command; by the Bataille, or Charge, understand the continuation or pressing forward in order of bataille without lagging behind, rather boldly stepping forward in the place of him that falls dead or wounded before thee; by a Retreat understanding an orderly retiring backward, either for relief, for advantage of ground, or for some other political end, as to draw the enemy into some ambushment, or such like."

"The present different beats of the drum," says Grose, "for the infantry are these:

"The General: this is beat instead of the Reveille, when the whole camp and garrison are to march.

"Reveille: beat at daybreak to awaken the camp or garrison, after which the sentinels cease challenging.

"Assembly, or Troop: at this beat the troops fall in, the roll is called, and baggage loaded.

"Foot March: to march.

"Grenadiers' March: beat only to that company.

"Retreat: this is beat at sunset in garrisons and at gun-firing in camp, at which time the pickets are formed; in fortified places it is a signal for the inhabitants to come in before the gates are shut.

"Tap-too [our modern name is tattoo]: the signal for soldiers to retire to their quarters or barracks, and to the sutlers to draw no more liquor, from whence it derives its name. The tap-too is seldom beat in camp.

"To Arms: a signal to summon the soldiers to their alarm-posts on some sudden occasion.

"The Church Call (called also Beating the Bank): a beat to summon the soldiers of a regiment or garrison to church.

"The Pioneers' Call: known by the appellation of Round Heads, come dig. This is beaten in camp to summon the pioneers to work.

"The Sergeants' Call: a beat for calling the sergeants together to the orderly-room, or in camp, the head of the colors.

"The Drummers' Call: beat to assemble the drummers at the head of the colors, or in quarters, at the place where it is beaten.

"The Preparative: a signal to make ready for firing.

"The Chammade: a signal to desire to parley with the enemy.

"The Rogue's March: this is beaten and played by the fifes when a soldier is drummed out of the regiment.

"The Long Roll: for turning the regiment out in camp or garrison.

"There was in the King's household an officer titled Drum-major-general of England, without whose license no one could, except the King's troops, formally beat a drum."

The different sounds or signals given by the trumpet were, according to Markham, in his *Soldires Accidence*, as follows:

" The first is Butte Sella [modern Boots and Saddles], or put on your saddles, which, as soon as the souldiere heareth (in the morning or other times), he shall presently make ready his horse and his own person, trusse up his sack of neccessaries, and make all things fitting for his journey.

" The second is Mounte Cavallo, or mount on horse backe, at which summons the souldiere shall bridle up his horse, bring him forth, and mount his backe.

" The third is A la Standarde : goe to your colours, or standard, whether it bee standard, cornet, or guidon; upon which sound, the souldiere, with those of his fellowship, shall trot forth to the place where the cornet is lodged, and there attend until it is dislodged.   Also this sound, in the field or in service, when men are disbanded, is a retreat for the horseman, and brings him off being engaged; for as oft as he heares it he must retire and goe back to his colour.

" The fourth is Tuquet, or march; which beinge hearde simply of itself without addition, commands nothing but marching after the leader.

" The fifth is Carga, Carga, or an alarm, charge ! charge ! which sounded, every man (like lightning) flyes upon his enemy and gives proofe of his valour.

" The sixth and last is Aquet, or the Watch: which, sounded at night, commands all that are out of duty to their reste ; and sounded in the morning, commands those to reste that have done duty, and those that have rested to awake and doe duty ; and in these sounds you shall make the souldiere so perfect that, as a song he may lanquet or sing them, and know when they are sounded unto him."

The instruments used in battle are mentioned in a quaint ballad of King Edward III., made on the victory over the Scots at Hallidowne Hille, in which are these lines:

> " This was do with merry sowne,
> With pipes, trumpes, and tabers thereto,
> And loud clariones thei blew also."

In the prose account of the same battle we read : " Then the Englische mynstrelles beaten their tabers and blewers their trompes, and pipers pipe clene loude and made a great schowte upon the Skotles."

The guidon told the soldiers in color what the trumpet or bugle said in sound. If, after a long march, the men of each company detailed to carry the guidon were ordered to the front, the hearts of the weary troopers saw them depart with relief, for it meant that, after joining the commanding officer, the little band of men swinging aloft the fluttering pennants would take their place behind the color-sergeant carrying the guidon of the colonel, and after a brisk little gallop each standard-bearer would be posted at a given point to guide the company as it came up to the place where the tents were to be pitched for the night. The guidon is also posted as a line of march at guard mount, or at drill. The private flag of a general can be of his own design. It is placed in front of his tent or headquarters, or follows on the march or in battle. If the troopers value their general, and have faith in him as a dauntless soldier, they will rally round his flag in case the fight is so desperate as to endanger the colors.

Markham, an old authority, says : " The guidon is the first color any commander of horse can let fly in the field. It was generally of damask fringed, and usually three feet in breadth, lessening by degrees towards the bottom, where it was by a slit divided into two peaks. It was originally borne by the dragoons,* and might be charged with the armorial bearings of the owner."

The present cavalry guidon is a small United States flag sharply swallow-tailed, and mounted on a standard with a metal point, so that it can be thrust into the ground when in use as a marker.

---

* Troops trained to act on foot or on horseback.

CONTENTS.

ILLUSTRATIONS.

2

Garryowen.

Lively.

1. Let Bac-chus' sons be not dis-mayed, But join with me, each jov-ial blade; Come booze and sing, and lend your aid, To help me with the cho - rus.

Chorus.

In - stead of Spa we'll drink down ale, And pay the

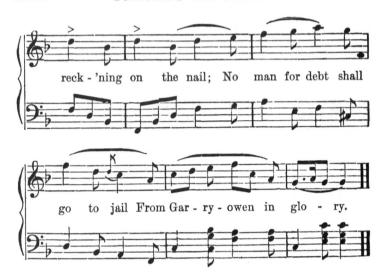

reck - 'ning on the nail; No man for debt shall
go to jail From Gar - ry - owen in glo - ry.

We are the boys that take delight in
Smashing the Limerick lights when lighting,
Through the streets like sporters fighting
And tearing all before us.—CHORUS.

We'll break windows, we'll break doors,
The watch knock down by threes and fours;
Then let the doctors work their cures,
And tinker up our bruises.—CHORUS.

We'll beat the bailiffs out of fun,
We'll make the mayor and sheriffs run;
We are the boys no man dares dun,
If he regards a whole skin.—CHORUS.

Our hearts so stout have got us fame,
For soon 'tis known from whence we came;
Where'er we go they dread the name
Of Garryowen in glory.—CHORUS.

FOLLOWING THE GUIDON.

The Assembly.

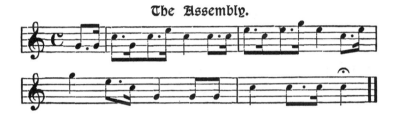

CHAPTER I.

THE MARCH INTO THE INDIAN TERRITORY.

AROUND many a camp-fire in the summer, and in our winter-quarters before the huge fireplaces, where the wood merrily crackled and the flame danced up the chimney, have I heard the oft-told tales of the battle of the Washita, the first great fight of the Seventh Cavalry. The regiment was still new, having been organized during the year after the war. It had done much hard work, and had not only accomplished some genuine successes in a small way, but its records of long untiring marches in the chill of early spring, during the burning heat of a Kansas summer sun, and in the sharp frosts of a late autumn campaign, were something to be proud of. Still, the officers and men had little in the way of recognized achievement to repay them for much patient work, and they longed individually and as a regiment for a war "record." This would not have been so powerful a desire had not the souls of our men been set on fire by the constant news of the torture of white prisoners by the Indians. History traces many wars to women; and women certainly bore a large though unconscious part in inciting our people to take up arms in attempts to rescue them, and to inflict such punishments upon their savage captors as would teach the Indian a needed lesson.

From the Department of the Platte, which has its headquarters in Nebraska, to the Indian Territory and Texas the trails of the regiment could be traced. It is customary to keep a daily record of each march, and a small pen-and-ink map is added. From these a larger one is made after the summer is over, and when the War Department issues yearly maps the new routes or fresh discoveries are recorded. One of these regimental journals lies before me. The map for each day marks the course of the stream, the place where the regiment encamped overnight, the "ford," the "rolling prairie," "high ridges," "level prairie," with dots to mark the line of the Pacific Railway, in course of construction; "small dry creek," "marshy soil," "level bottom," "stone bluff," etc.. One of the written records goes on to state where, as the days advanced, the troops encamped at night without water, and all the men and horses had to drink was got by digging down into the dry bed of a stream; or where, at another time, they found a "stream impassable," and "halted to build a bridge," together with such hints of experience as these: "struck an old wagon trail"; "marched over cactus-beds and through a deep ravine"; "made camp where there was standing water only"; "banks of stream miry—obliged to corduroy it"; "grass along the stream poor, sandy soil"; banks of next stream "forty feet high—great trouble in finding a crossing"; "obliged to corduroy another stream for each separate wagon"; "took four hours to cross twenty wagons"; "timber thick, grass poor"; "struck what is called by the Indians Bad Lands, being a succession of ridges with ravines fifty feet deep between; two wagons rolled over and went down one ravine"; "passed four ranches destroyed by the Indians and abandoned"; "left camp at 5 A.M.; so misty and foggy, could not see a hundred yards in advance;" "distance of march this day guessed, odometer out of order"; "marched up a cañon with banks fifty feet high"; "Company E left the columns to pursue Indians"; "all this day marched over Captain S——'s old trail"; "this was a dry camp, poor grass and plenty of cacti"; "found water-holes, the head of the river"; "total distance of march, seven hundred and four miles."

The names of the streams, the elevated points of ground, or the gulches were seldom taken from the musical nomenclature of the Indian; they seemed to have been given by the outspoken, irreverent pioneer or miner.

Evidently, if these first wayfarers had difficulty in making a crossing of a stream, they caused the name to record the obstacles. Our refined officers sometimes hesitated in their replies if asked by peace commissioners from the East, whom they were escorting to an Indian village, what the place was called. For instance, one of them said when he replied to such a question, "Hell Roaring Creek," etc. He looked out over the surrounding scenery till the effect of these shocking names had passed. A humorous Western paper, in commenting on this national idiosyncrasy, wonders, since the law requires that our national cruisers shall be called after cities, if "You Bet," "Hang Town," "Red Dog," "Jackass Gap," and "Yuba Dam" would answer. The worst of it all is that these names, given by a passing traveller with careless indifference to the future of the places on which they were bestowed, rest as an incubus upon localities that afterwards became the sites of places of prominence; and it is as hard for a town or region so afflicted as for the traditional dog to get rid of a bad name.

The brief itinerary of this one march, out of the many the Seventh Cavalry made, gives a faint idea of the daily history of a regiment. Concise as is the record, it served to point the way for many a tired pioneer who came after; for, on his map, compiled from these smaller ones, were the locations of places where he could stop for wood and water, as well as the warning where neither of these necessaries could be obtained.

Still, there was often a weary sigh among the youngsters who had no war record, and who longed to make some sort of soldier's name for themselves. Besides, they passed the dismantled, deserted home of many a venturesome frontiersman; they saw the burned stage stations; they met in forts or small settlements placed in a safe position ranchmen whose wives had been killed, or, worse still, made captives; they came upon the mutilated and horribly disfigured bodies of Lieutenant Kidder and eleven soldiers; everywhere on all its marches the regiment followed the trail of the Indian on his frightful career of rapine, murder, and outrage. Many a time the question was asked, what was the good of galloping after foes who knew the country thoroughly, who were mounted on the fleetest, hardiest animals in the world, that needed no grain, and who could go directly to rivers or streams where they could graze their ponies for a few days and start off refreshed for a long raid, and who each day could be bountifully fed on the game of the country without being hampered with a train of supplies. The odds were all against our fine fellows.

They had marched and countermarched over the country so constantly that the wit of the regiment said to the engineer officer who made the daily map: "Why fool with that? Just take the pattern supplement of the *Harper's Bazar*, and no better map of our marches could be found."

Much enthusiasm was felt when the announcement was made that a winter campaign was to be undertaken. "Now we have them!" was the sanguine boast,

The buffalo-hunting among the tribes was over for the year. Enough meat had been jerked or dried to keep them during cold weather, and the villages were established for the winter. In the summer the tribes travelled great distances. As soon as the grass in a river valley was exhausted by the ponies, everything was packed, the village moved, and another point was chosen. At certain seasons of the year there was a journey to timber lands, where lodge poles could be cut; another was made to certain clay-beds, where material for pipes was obtained; another to regions where the buffaloes were most numerous, and the winter's meat was prepared, or the hides dressed for robes or tepee covers. It is difficult to estimate the hundreds of miles that the villages traversed in the summer; but in the winter a remote spot was chosen, on a stream where the timber offered some protection from the winter storms, and the grass would last longest, and here the nomad "settled down" for a few months. It was such a village that our regiment was seeking.

The command starting into the Indian Territory was formidable enough, and had not the Indians been much emboldened by former successes, they would not have dared dash upon the rear-guard or rush in from a ravine to stampede the animals of the wagon train, as they often did on that march.

General Custer, in an unpublished letter to a friend in the East, describes the first attacks of the Indians after the march south began. "I had not been in my camp where I first joined two hours, when we were

INDIANS PREPARING TO MOVE.

attacked by a war party. I wish that you could have
been with us. You would never ask to go to a circus
after seeing Indians ride and perform in a fight. I
took my rifle and went out on the line, hoping to obtain
a good shot, but it was like shooting swallows on the
wing, so rapid were they in their movements. Their
object had been to dash into camp and secure some of
our horses. Disappointed in this, they contented themselves with circling around us on their ponies, firing
as they flew along the line, but doing no injury. As it
was late in the evening and our horses all unsaddled, I
prevented the men from going from camp to fight.
Sometimes a warrior, all feathered and painted, in order
to show his bravery to his comrades, started alone on
his pony, and with the speed of a quarter-horse would
dash along the entire length of my line, and even within three or four hundred yards of it, my men pouring
in their rifle-balls by hundreds, yet none bringing down
the game. I could see the bullets knock up the dust
around and beneath his pony's feet, but none apparently
striking him. We shot two ponies, however, in this way,
and may have inflicted greater damage; but in this as
in all things pertaining to warfare, the Indians are so
shrewd as to prevent our determining their losses. Occasionally a pony is captured. I have one now which
is white, with a tail dragging on the ground. We have
also captured an article of great value to them, an Indian shield. It is made of the thickest part of the buffalo-hide, adorned with rude paintings, and is usually
hung in front of a tepee to keep off evil spirits."

It gave the men excellent practice, this running fire on the march. The necessity for troops was so great that raw recruits were sent out, without taking time to drill them in target practice. It came to pass that many a soldier drew his carbine on an Indian in the first shot he had ever fired. A corps of forty sharpshooters was formed from men who day by day showed unusual skill in the use of fire-arms, and these were allowed some privileges, such as being marched as a separate organization, which of itself is a great favor. It is far from agreeable to submit to the irksome rules of a marching column. No guard or picket duty was expected from these sharp-shooters, so that they attained what is the supreme good of a soldier's life, "all their nights in bed." The soldier detailed for guard duty has two hours on and two off for twenty-four hours, and unless the command is large these times of duty come very often—in the estimation of the men.

In looking over some of the war poetry that filled the papers from 1861 to 1865, I came across a little jingle that describes a soldier's glory and grumbling, whether he be fighting the white or the red man:

"And how we fought and how we tramped,
　　Too long a tale perhaps I'll spin ye;
But, first and last, I think we camped
　　In every field in old Virginny!

"'Twas a gay old life, but Lord! 'twas hard—
　　No rest for the good, no peace for the wicked;
When you didn't fight you were put on guard,
　　And when you came off you went on picket,"

On the expedition the cavalry marched in a column of fours; then came a long wagon train, hauling the forage, tents, rations, and extra ammunition, and following all this was the rear-guard. The great struggle of the Indian when not actually ready for battle—which he never is unless all odds are in his favor—is to cut off the wagon train; this he tries to accomplish by frightening the mules. Sometimes the country admitted of the wagons being marched in four lines—an arrangement which required fewer soldiers to be deployed on either flank and in the rear for their protection.

In letters to his Eastern friend, from one of which quotations have been made, General Custer speaks with the greatest enthusiasm of the stag and fox hounds his correspondent had given him. The former were a new breed to him, and their feats, while only puppies, were daily marvels to their proud owner.

"Maida and Blucher both seized the first buffalo they saw while running, which was pretty plucky for pups, I think. The dogs have gone beyond my highest expectations. Three days ago Maida alone ran down a jack-rabbit and killed it, and they are the fleetest animals we have, except the antelope. Yesterday while looking for camp, accompanied by a few scouts and headquarters men, we jumped a prairie-wolf. Maida and Blucher, Rover and the other little fox-hound, started after it, the stag-hounds, of course, leaving the other two far behind. Blucher was the first to come up with the wolf; he had never seen one before. As soon as he reached it he seized it across the back, and never relinquished his hold until he had killed it, and this he did by breaking its backbone.   Blucher held on like a bull-dog.   A wolf is one of the ugliest animals a dog can handle.   Of the many dogs that are in this regiment there is but one that will attack a wolf, and he needs to be encouraged.   Don't you think that is pretty good for a pup?   The other day all the dogs went in chase after a jack-rabbit quite out of sight.   An officer mounted and started after them, and met the dogs, Blucher at the head carrying the rabbit in his mouth. What do you think of a stag-hound as a retriever?"

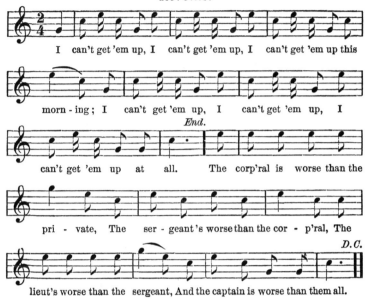

CHAPTER II.

GENERAL CUSTER'S LETTERS DESCRIBING THE MARCH.

I HERE make some extracts from many of my own letters from General Custer, in the belief that they will make the daily life on the march, and in camps which were established for unavoidable delays, on the journey into the Indian Territory clearer than it would otherwise be to the reader, who knows little of the progress of a military expedition.

FORT HAYS, KANSAS, *October* 4, 1868.

I breakfasted with General Sheridan and the staff. The general said to me, "Custer, I rely upon you in everything, and shall send you on this expedition without giving you any orders, leaving you to act entirely upon your judgment."

The expedition will consist of eleven companies of cavalry, four of infantry, and two howitzers, accompanied by a large train.

FORTY-TWO MILES FROM FORT DODGE, October 18th.

We have been on the war-path but one week. I joined the regiment near our present camp a week since, and within two hours the Indians attacked camp. We drove them away, killing two ponies. That night I sent out two scouting parties of a hundred men each, to scour the country for thirty miles round.

I never heard of wild turkeys in such abundance. We have them every day we care for them, and there are five dressed in the mess chest now. All the men have them, and in one day eighty were killed. Tom shot five in a few moments.

Now I want to tell you about my splendid stag-hounds. The other day Maida caught a jack-rabbit alone. Yesterday she and Blucher took hold of a buffalo, and to-day, as we came into camp, Blucher started a wolf and caught it alone. Within half an hour a jack-rabbit was started near camp. My three stag-hounds, Flirt, Blucher, and Maida, and two greyhounds, went in pursuit.

We could see the chase for nearly a mile, and it was a pretty sight; then they disappeared over a hill. The officers are constantly trying to buy the stag-hounds of me.

I wish that Eliza* was out here to make some nice rolls instead of the solid shot our cook gives us.

Tell Eliza she is the "awfulest" scold and the most " quar-

---

* Eliza was our colored cook who was with me at Fort Leavenworth.

relsomest" woman I ever met. She and the man who waits
on the table have constant rows.*

TWELVE MILES FROM DODGE, *October* 22*d.*

We will probably remain here ten days before moving
towards the Washita mountains. Some of the officers think
that this may be like others before it—a campaign on paper;
but I know General Sheridan too well to think that he will
follow any such example; he does not readily relinquish an
idea. The general has sent to the Osage Indians to employ
them on our side; they will be a profitable assistance.

October 24, 1868.

The general has finally decided upon a winter campaign.
If we cannot find the Indians, and inflict considerable injury
upon them, we will be on the wing all winter. We are going
to the heart of the Indian country, where white troops have
never been before. The Indians have grown up in the belief
that soldiers cannot and dare not follow them there. They
are now convinced that all the tribes that have been committing
depredations on the plains the past season have gone south,
and are near each other in the vicinity of the Washita mountains. They will doubtless combine against us when they find
that we are about to advance into their country.

To-day I gave the regimental saddler directions how to
make me a large pair of saddle-bags. They will contain

---

* This cook was the only woman on the expedition. She had
been a camp woman many years, and was tanned and toughened
by "roughing it." She was perfectly fearless, but the life had sad-
ly affected her temper. Even her brave husband (that is, brave in
battle) approached her guardedly if anything went wrong. When
the expedition was attacked at one time, she was cooking by a
camp-fire, and was heard to mutter when a bullet passed her by,
" Git out, ye red divils ye," and went on with her work as if nothing were happening.

3

nearly all that I desire to carry, and can be put on my led-horse.

The men are at target practice, and it sounds like a battle. All the officers of the regiment are now learning signals. Books have been furnished us from Washington. I found all the line-officers to-day in the classes. Most of the officers can now converse quite readily as far as they can see the signals. This is just the country for signalling, Nature having formed admirable signal stations over this part of the territory. General Sheridan, in his letter yesterday, said furloughs would be given to every enlisted man who would do well.

CAMP "SANDY" FORSYTH, *November 3d.*

You see I have named our camp after the brave "Sandy." I suppose that you have seen considerable excitement to-day over the Presidential campaign. I do not presume that of the many hundreds of men here a dozen remembered that to-day is Election Day, so little is the army interested in the event. I have been quite busy coloring the company horses. Don't imagine that I have been painting them; but I have been classifying all the horses of the regiment, so that instead of each company representing all the colors of the rainbow by their horses, now every company has one color. There are pure bays, browns, sorrels, grays, and blacks.

This morning I ordered "Phil" saddled, and rode up the valley looking for a new camp.* I was accompanied by my inseparable companions, the dogs (except Flirt, who is lame). When about three-quarters of a mile from camp, I discovered a large wolf lying down about half a mile beyond. Calling the four dogs—Rover, the old fox-hound, Fanny, the little fox-hound, Blucher, and Maida—I started for the wolf.

---

* When the earth becomes much trodden, and it is difficult to keep camp clean, it is customary to move on for a short distance to fresh ground.

When within a quarter of a mile he began to run. The two stag-hounds caught sight of him, and away went the dogs, and away went Phil and I, full chase after them. The fox-hounds, of course, could not begin to keep up.

Before the wolf had run three-quarters of a mile Maida had overtaken him. She grappled with him at once and threw him over and over; before he could regain his feet or get hold of Maida, Blucher dashed in upon him, and he was never allowed to rise afterwards. These two puppies killed the wolf before Rover and Fanny could reach the spot. I had put Phil to his mettle, and was near at hand when the wolf was caught. Blucher and Maida were perfectly savage; each time they closed their powerful jaws I could hear the bones crunch as if within a vice. There did not seem to be a bone unbroken when the dogs had finished him. All the officers and men were watching the chase from camp.

We started a jack-rabbit just at evening, and all the dogs joined in. I never saw any race so exciting. The dogs surpass my highest expectations. All four are lying on my bed or at my feet. I have a pair of buffalo overshoes, the hair inside, and I am to have a vest made from a dressed buffalo calf-skin, with the hair on. When we were encamped near Dodge I sent the tailor, Frank, in to buy some thread and buttons. He came home very "tight," and when I asked him if they kept thread and buttons in bottles at the sutler store, he answered me in droll broken English that made me shout with laughter.

November 7th.

I want to tell you something wonderful. A white woman has just come into our camp deranged, and can give no account of herself. She has been four days without food. Our cook is now giving her something to eat. I can only explain her coming by supposing her to have been captured by the Indians, and their barbarous treatment having rendered her insane. I send her to-night, by the mail party, to Fort Dodge. I shall send by the paymaster a live pelican, to be presented to the Audubon Club in Detroit. It is the first I ever saw. It measures nearly seven feet from tip to tip, and its bill is about ten inches long. One of my Cheyenne scouts caught it in the river near camp. He first struck it, and stunned it long enough to effect its capture.

CAMP ON BEAVER CREEK (100 Miles from Dodge), *Nov.* 21, '68.

The day that we reached here we crossed a fresh trail of a large war party going north. I sent our Indian scouts to follow it a short distance to determine the strength and direction of the party. The guides all report the trail of a war party going north-east, and that they evidently have just come from the village, which must be located within fifty miles of us in a southerly direction. Had the Kansas volunteers been here, as was expected, my orders would then have allowed me to follow the back trail of the war party right to their village ; and we would have found the latter in an unprotected state, as their warriors had evidently gone north, either to Larned or Zarah, or to fight the Osage or Kaw Indians, who are now putting up their winter meat. We did not encounter an Indian coming to this last point, which proves that our campaign was not expected by them. To-night six scouts start for Dodge with our mail and despatches for headquarters.

November 22d.

It lacks a few moments to twelve; reveille is at four, but I must add a few words more. To-day General Sheridan and staff, and two companies of the Kansas volunteers, arrived. I move to-morrow morning with my eleven companies, taking thirty days' rations. I am to go south from here to the Canadian River, then down the river to Fort Cobb, then south-west towards the Washita mountains, then north-west back to this point, my whole march not exceeding two hundred and fifty miles. Among the new horses sent to the regiment I have selected one, a beautiful brown, that I call " Dandy." The snow is now five or six inches deep and falling rapidly. The general and his staff have given me a pair of buffalo overshoes, a fur cap with ear lappets, and have offered me anything they have, for winter is upon us with all its force.

As a winter's campaign against Indians was decidedly a new departure for our regiment, and, indeed, at that time for any troops, and as this one ended with a notable victory for our people, it was the subject of many conversations on the galleries of our quarters, at the fireside, and around our dinner-tables for years afterwards. Certain ludicrous affairs fastened themselves on officers seemingly for all time. For instance, one night during the winter, when the regiment was away from its base of supplies, tents, and luggage, except what could be carried on the horses, the troops were obliged to sleep on the ground, and blankets were so scarce that everybody took a " bunkey," officers and all, in order to double the bedding. One very small officer rolled himself against the back of a huge man, six feet four inches high, who on other windy nights had served as a protection; but he did not combine every virtue, and when it was both windy and cold he had the inhumanity to turn in the night, and leave the poor little dot of an officer entirely uncovered. This is never thought to be an agreeable thing for a bedfellow to do, but on a bitter winter night, when the only awning over the victim was the starry sky, it was such a trial that the manner in which the sufferer told of his woes the next morning made him the laughing-stock of his comrades all winter and long afterwards.

Officers will run almost any risk to get a bath, but the way in which two of our brave fellows retreated from their toilet was also for years kept as a standing subject of jesting. I believe that it was their first and only retreat. In going into the Indian country the officers sometimes relaxed vigilance for a time. Perhaps days would pass with no sight of Indians. At such a time these two daring fellows went down the stream some distance to bathe, and to their delight found water deep enough in which to swim. They forgot everything in the enjoyment of clear water, for many of the streams west of the Mississippi are muddy and full of sand. Their horses saved their lives. Their attention was called to the telltale ears, quivering and vibrating, the nervous starts and the snorts that many old cavalry horses give at sight of Indians or buffaloes. Heeding these warnings, the bathers sprang to the bank. Within a few hundred yards of them Indians approached. There was no pause for clothes or for saddles. Unfastening their horses, and with a leap that would have done credit to a circus rider, they sprang upon the bare backs of the terrified horses, and digging their naked heels into the sides of the animals, they ran a race for life. Fortunately, the Indians came from a direction opposite that of the camp, but they had the temerity to follow with all the speed of their swift ponies until almost within sight of the troops. Our officers'

INDIANS ON THE WAR-PATH.

perfect horsemanship and the fright of the animals saved their lives. As the Indians yelled behind them, and finally sent their almost unerring arrows whizzing about the ears of our two men, they had little idea of escape. When they entered camp, if there had been a back way, an alley, a tree-bordered walk, through which these lately imperilled men could have reached their tents, it would have been a boon; but everything in military life is *en évidence*, and the camp is often laid out in one long line. Past all these tents, where, at the entrance of each, appeared at once the occupants, on hearing the unusual sound of horses' flying hoofs within the company street, and in the face, indeed, of all the regiment, these nude Gilpins reached their own canvas, and flinging themselves from their foaming horses, darted under cover. Then came the scramble for other clothes, which was a very difficult affair, as few officers carried extras, save underclothes, and the quartermaster's supplies were at Camp Supply, far in the rear. But every one shares freely with a comrade on the frontier, and a pair of pantaloons from one, a jacket from another, a cap from a third, fitted out the unfortunates.

Later a misfortune happened to one of these same men, our brother Tom, which bade fair to oblige him to adopt the costume of his red brethren—a blanket and a war-bonnet. His favorite dog, Brandy, the most tenacious of bull-dogs, refused to let go of a polecat that he had chased, with the dog delusion that it was a rabbit. Colonel Tom plunged into the fight in an effort to drag Brandy off, when the animal used the defence that nature has provided, and Colonel Tom's clothes were gone the second time. He realized that with this adventure added to his late aquatic episode, which had been followed by a deluge of jokes from his brother officers, there would be no mercy shown him, and he quickly decided to share with the others his unsought baptism. It was nearly dark; the tents were closed, the candles lighted, the pipes at full blast. Captain Hamilton, whose sense of fun was irrepressible, started out with the victim of misfortune to pay visits. Several of the tents were crowded, but both of the visitors being jolly men, room was made for them; but soon there was a general sniffing around and forcible expletives used about the dogs. "They've been hunting on their own hook again," was said, "and pretty close here, you bet;" and hands were stretched out for something with which to drive the creatures out. The guests having made sure the aroma Tom carried had become sufficiently apparent, departed, only to enter another crowd farther on. A tent is supposed to be well ventilated; but fill one with officers whose tobacco, obtained far away from a good base of supplies, is, to say the least, questionable, add the odor of rain-soaked clothes, the wet leather of troop boots, a dog or two with his shaggy, half-dry coat, and one can well imagine that Colonel Tom was the traditional "last straw."

When the pair had been in the second tent long enough to have the joke take effect, they bolted out into the night, roaring with laughter, and then went on to a third. The jeers of the officers next day were some-what toned down because of the evening episode, but poor Tom was around, begging for clothes again, and soon every one knew that his own outfit lay "without the camp" for all time.

Arrests are not at all unusual in military life, and the discipline is so strict it often happens that this punishment is inflicted for very small delinquencies. Sometimes, of course, it is a serious matter ; a set of charges is preferred, and a trial by court-martial and sentence ensue. Still, to be in arrest is so common that it is not in the least like the serious affair of civil law. If an officer was missed from the line that win-ter, and inquiries made by his comrades for him, his messmate or captain, laughing lightly, replied, "Why, don't you know he's leading the pelican?" and this ex-pression, as a synonym for being in arrest, stayed by the regiment for a long time after the bird had gone.

The pelican General Custer refers to in the letter already quoted was a rare specimen, and all the com-mand had great curiosity about it, considering it was unusual in the country where it was captured, and it was also the first specimen most of our command had seen. The bird was carried in a box in the wagon train that always travels at the rear of a column, and as an officer or soldier is condemned to this ignominious po-sition also, when deprived of his place with his com-pany, it became the custom to describe arrest as "lead-ing the pelican."

A perfect fusillade of wit was always being fired at

men to whom accidents had happened or on whom
jokes had been played. One unfailing subject for bad-
inage was the matrimonial opportunities neglected in
the winter's campaign. After the battle, the old squaws
were as full of admiration for the successful troopers as
they were for their liege lords, and the willingness to
part with their daughters was quite equal to that of
the predatory mother in the States, who is accused of
roaming from one watering-place to another in search
of game. But the primitive mother and father resort
to no subtle plan; they offer their daughters outright.
One officer was proffered a dusky bride by her father,
and a cup of sugar was asked for in exchange; while
the commanding officer, after hearing a mysterious
mumbling going on near him, found himself already
married, before any formal tender of the girl had been
made by the parents. It was with difficulty that the
fathers and mothers were made to understand that
among white people a man was required by our laws
to content himself with one partner at a time.

There were many references to the scouts in General Custer's letters, and the subject was an unfailing
source of interest to me, so much romance attends the
stories of these men's lives. Osage Indians were employed, being not only at peace with us, but imbittered
against the Indians by the marauding of hostile tribes
on their herds of ponies and their villages.

I find a few words about these friendly Indians in a
letter General Custer wrote to a friend at that time:
"Yesterday my twelve Osage guides joined me, and

they are a splendid-looking set of warriors, headed by one of their chiefs called 'Little Beaver.' They are painted and dressed for the war-path, and well armed with Springfield breech-loading guns. All are superb horsemen. We mounted them on good horses, and to show us how they can ride and shoot, they took a stick of ordinary cord - wood, threw it on the ground, and then, mounted on their green, untried horses, they rode at full speed and fired at the stick of wood as they flew by, and every shot struck the target."

CHAPTER III.

WHITE SCOUTS.

THE scouts and friendly Indians were an independent command that winter, and afforded much interest and variety to the whole regiment. They each received seventy-five dollars a month and a ration, and whoever took the regiment to an Indian village was to receive one hundred dollars additional.

A half-breed Arapahoe boy was the beauty of the command. He was nineteen years old; his eyes, large, soft, and lustrous, were shaded by long lashes. I had been amazed at the tiny feet of the Delawares the summer before, but this lad's feet were smaller, and the moccasin showed them to be perfect in shape. His hair was long and black. He was educated, but it was a disappointment to me in hearing of him to find that he called himself Andrew Jackson Fitzpatrick. With the ardor of a novel reader, I should have preferred at that time that he should lift the fringes of his soulful eyes in response to a Claude or a Reginald. Indians not only lose their picturesqueness when they encounter the white man, but they choose the most prosaic names in place of their own musical appellations. Think how "Running Antelope," or "the Eagle that flies," or "Fall Leaf" would have suited this boy.

One of the scouts had a nickname that ought to have pleased the most romantic, but the trouble in his case was that he did not fit the name. His real name was Romero, for he was a Mexican, and the officers soon dropped into calling him Romeo. His short, stocky figure, swarthy skin, and coarse features made him a typical "Greaser," and quite the replica of many we had seen in Texas; but Romeo had lived with the Indians and spoke Cheyenne.

Another scout was a New Yorker by birth, who emigrated to Michigan in 1836, thence to Texas, and finally to Kansas. He was over fifty, and gray-headed. It is surprising how wonderfully men no longer young endure the hardships of this life. There is something remarkably preservative about the air of the plains.

When we read now of the reunion of the Forty-niners,
and learn what jovial hours they are capable of enjoying even after their years of privation, we are forced
to conclude that a life sheltered from the rigors of climate and spared all deprivation is not the longest, and
surely not the merriest. When a man's entire possessions are strapped in a small roll at the back of his saddle, and his horse and outfit constitute his fortune, he
is not going to lie awake nights wondering what are
safe investments for capital.

After the campaign I saw the scouts, and though the
winter of 1866 was the time of California Joe's first
appearance among us, it was not long before I was introduced to him. It was not my privilege to hear him
talk for some time, as he was as bashful before a woman as a school-boy. The general arranged a little plan
one day by which I could hear him. I was sent into
the rear tent and specially charged to keep quiet, as
Joe could not talk without interlarding his sentences
with oaths, many of them of his own invention, and
consequently all the more terrible to me because so unfamiliar. A new oath seems much more profane and
vastly more startling than those one hears commonly
about the streets. At the time I listened to him surreptitiously he had been called to attend court at the
capital of Kansas, and had made his first journey on a
railroad. He complained bitterly of the hardships of
railway travel. The car was too small, too warm, too
fast, too everything to suit him. The officer who encountered him at Topeka said that Joe seized upon him

CALIFORNIA JOE.

with ardor, as being a link with his real life, and that he "never wanted to board them air keers agin, and was durned sorry he hadn't fetched his mule; he would a heap sight ruther go back on the old critter." He was too much dissatisfied with civilization for any one to doubt for one moment that he would willingly have taken the four hundred miles on horseback in preference to "them air wheezing, racing, red-hot boxes they shet a man in." After his return he came to our tent dressed in what the officers call "cit's" clothes, which he termed "store clothes." His long, flowing hair and shaggy beard were shorn, and his picturesqueness gone. One cheek was rounded out with his beloved "terbaccy," and he told the general he had "took his last journey on them pesky keers"; and when asked if he didn't like the States, said, "D——n a country where you have to wear a shirt-collar." He told us that he had been West forty years, and much of the time beyond the Rockies. He considered Kansas so far East that he "reckoned his folks would be thinking he was on his way home if they heard of him in there." At that time we were in the midst of such a wilderness it did not seem to us sufficiently far eastward to induce any one to think we were anywhere but on the stepping - off place. It was only to show off that he came in his travelling costume. The buckskin and flannel shirt soon appeared, but it took some time before his hair and beard grew out long enough to make him look natural.

When California Joe first joined the general in the

Washita country he studied him pretty thoroughly. In his rough vernacular, he wanted to "size him up," and see if he was really soldier enough for him to "foller." The contrast between a plainsman's independence and the deference and respect for rank that is instilled into a soldier is very marked. The enlisted man rarely speaks to his superior unless spoken to, and he usually addresses an officer in the third person. The scout, on the contrary, owns the plains, according to his views, and he addresses the stranger or the military man with an air of perfect equality; but long acquaintance with their ways taught me that at heart these men were just as full of deference for any brave man they served as is the soldier. In coming to an understanding with the general regarding his giving his services as scout, Joe asked his commander a few pointed questions about himself. He wished to know how he intended to hunt Indians. There had been some officers whom he had known who had gone to war in a wagon; the troopers called them "feather-bed soldiers." So Joe said: "S'pose you're after Injuns, and really want to hev a tussle with 'em, would ye start after 'em on hossback, or would ye climb into an ambulance and be hauled after 'em? That's the pint I'm headin' for." After putting the general through such a catechism, he decided to let himself be employed, as it was evident from his own impressions, and from what he had heard, that there was not much doubt that the chief was, in his own language, "spilin' for a fight" just as much as he himself was.

Joe was made the chief of scouts at once; but honors did not sit easily upon him, for in celebrating his advancement he made night hideous with his yells. The scout gets drunk just as he does everything else—with all his might. Living all his life beyond the region of law and its enforcement; being a perfect shot, he is able, usually, to carry out his spree according to his own wishes. He tells the man who might express a wish for a peaceful, quiet night that he had better not "tackle" him, and emphasizes his remark by drawing out of the small arsenal that encircles his body a pistol, which, pointed accurately, renders the average man quick to say, "It's of no consequence," and retire. I do not even like to say that the scouts were ever drunk, for they were profoundly sober when they went off on their perilous journeys with despatches; and when I think how all our lives were in their hands when they were sent for succor, and how often they took messages across country to put troops or settlements on their guard, or of a hundred other daring deeds of theirs, I prefer to remember only the faithful discharge of duty, not the carousal that sometimes followed the reaction caused by overstrained nerves and the relief from hours and days of impending death.

Anticipating a little, I remember that California Joe was selected for the most important scouting duty of the winter, which was nothing less than the transmission of the despatch announcing the success of the battle of the Washita. The command was then far away

4

from Camp Supply; it was midwinter, and the Indians were thoroughly aroused and on guard. It was not known how great the distance was that he must traverse, but the troops had taken four days to accomplish it. Joe was asked how many scouts he would like to take, and after going off to deliberate, returned, with the reply that he "didn't want no more ner his pardner, fur in this 'ere bizness more is made by dodgin' and runnin' than by fightin'." At dark he started, without giving the slightest evidence that he regarded the perilous undertaking as anything more than a commonplace occurrence.

One peculiarity of these men was their evident inability to feel surprise; the most extraordinary occurrences made so little impression upon them that it would seem as if they must have had a previous existence, and become familiar in another life with the strange events which made us gasp with astonishment. How often I have heard the officers refer to the variety these men made in the tedium of the march, by their stories of adventure, their wit, and their fearless and original expression of views! It was conceded that they "drew a long bow" sometimes, but the tales of their own lives were startling enough without the least necessity for exaggeration.

One story from the mines was told me, and may have lost nothing in the telling. An Irishman who was pretty drunk fell into a shaft sixty-five feet deep. He picked himself up unhurt, but partially sobered, and seeing a passage leading into the open air, he made his way out to the side of the mountain. Then he walked up till he reached the shaft, and looking down into its depths, was heard to say, "Be gorry, and I'm thinking it would kill me if I was to fall down there agin."

The scouts and frontiersmen were not slow to express their opinion on the few women they encountered, and a tale was told of a family consisting of a mother and several strapping daughters who lived in a cabin on the route over which cattle were driven to market. The " gals," as the Western man terms them, took care of some cows, and the narrator of the story stopped there to get milk. As he sat near the fire smoking, the raw-boned, shrivelled old mother bent over the fireplace puffing at a clay pipe, perfectly stolid and silent, until one girl came in and silently stood at the fire trying to dry her homespun dress. Without raising herself, and in a drawling tone, the mother said, presently, " Sal, there's a coal under you fut." In no more ani-mated tone and without even moving, her offspring replied, "Which fut, mammy?" The girl had run bare-foot all her life over the shale and rough ground of that country, and the red-hot coal was some time in making its way through the hard surface to a tissue that had any sensitiveness.

The widow of a miner, who kept boarders, was also on the scant list of female acquaintances of one of the fron-tiersmen, who describes a person called the "bouncer," who seems to be a well-recognized functionary in such establishments. He is always big and strong, and his duties consist in bringing to time people who neglect to pay their bill, and for this service he is boarded without charge. An Eastern man, a "tenderfoot," on one occasion asked some one to pass the gravy, whereupon the bouncer placed his pistol on the table and quietly remarked, "Any man as calls sop gravy has got to eat dust or 'pologize."

At that time we all returned to civilization with a goodly collection of frontier stories that had not found their way into the omnivorous newspaper, and our talk was full of allusions to jokes among ourselves, or to portions of these way-side tales that we had appropriated, because they fitted into our daily life so well. We believed, and there was no reason why we should doubt it, that the amusing or venturesome stories of these men were their own experiences, and I need not dwell upon the zest it gives to the listener when the hero of a tale is present as he tells it.

Another relief to the weariness of a march was hunting game, which was so plentiful that no one need run the risk of straying far from the command in search of it. The wild turkeys were the greatest treat of all, that winter, and there were so many of them that the soldiers' messes had all they wanted while the command remained in the locality they frequented. A former officer of General Sheridan's staff has been only recently reminding me of what a feast they were. In the vicinity of the Antelope Hills the trees were black with these wild-fowl.

One of the officers afforded great amusement at the time, and gave opportunity for many a sly allusion during the winter because of an attack of "buck fever." At sight of a tree weighed down to the ends of the branches with turkeys, he became incapable of loading, to say nothing of firing, his gun; he could do nothing but lie down, great strong man as he was, completely overcome with excitement. At one point where General Sheridan and his staff came upon an immense number of turkeys, they sent videttes on the neighboring hills to keep watch for Indians, and then began to shoot the fowls. Between half-past five and half-past seven they killed sixty-three with rifles. The place where they first came upon this game is now marked on the map as "Sheridan's Roost." This officer remembers to have seen General Custer cut the head from a turkey with a Spencer repeating rifle at two hundred yards. The poor soldiers, armed only with their short-range carbines, of course saw many a shot go foul, but if they happened to be the selected orderlies of the officers they were often permitted to use the rifle, and in a case where an officer had two, the soldier riding behind his commanding officer proudly carried the second best. I know that when General Custer and his orderly returned from a hunt, their eyes like coals, so brilliant were they, and with every evidence of suppressed excitement, yet neither, as is the custom of the army, speaking a word, I used to accuse the commanding officer of only waiting to get beyond the first bluff that separated him from the camp before he forgot to be military, and fell to talking with the enlisted man. There is so much in common among enthusiastic sportsmen!

The soldiers knew how to make the best of their short-range guns, and many of them became such accurate marksmen that they could select the particular part to be hit, and not tear the game into shreds with their large bullets. The best shots in a company were allowed to leave the column and bring in game for the rest. At night, when the troops were bivouacked, the fires lighted for the soldiers' suppers, the men hovered around the coming dinner, rejoicing in its savory smells, suggesting to the company cook their ideas of how game should be prepared, and calling out triumphantly to any neighboring mess whose hunters had not been so fortunate as their own. Think what it must have been to vary the frugal bacon of daily use with rump steaks of the buffalo or toothsome morsels of wild turkey! The men needed no sauces or jellies to whet the appetite or improve the flavor; that would have been "painting the lily" in their eyes. There has been much criticism regarding the destruction of the buffalo, but in the case of our soldiers it was often a health measure, as the use of salt meat and absence of vegetables produced scurvy.

All this hunting, joking, story-telling on the march, and around the camp-fire, lost some of its charm, however, as winter really set in. Although it is the custom of soldiers to make light of hardships, there were new features in this winter's campaign which needed all their fortitude to meet and endure.

Charge!

CHAPTER IV.

BATTLE OF THE WASHITA.

The orders for moving towards the Indian Village were issued on the evening of November 22d. It began to snow, and our men stood round the camp-fire for their breakfast at five o'clock the next morning, the snow almost up to their knees. The Seventh, consisting of nine hundred men, were to leave General Sheridan and the infantry, and all the extra wagons and supplies, and strike out into this blinding storm. General Sheridan, awake with anxiety at reveille, called out to ask what General Custer thought about the snow and the storm. The reply was, "All the better for us; we can move, the Indian cannot." The packing was soon done, as every ounce of superfluous baggage was left behind, and forward our brave fellows pushed into the slowly coming dawn.

The air was so filled with the fine snow that it was perilous to separate one's self even a short distance from the column. The Indian guides could not see any landmarks, and had it not been for the compass of the commanding officer, an advance would have been impossible. The fifteen miles of the first day's march would have been a small affair except for the snow; but the day dragged, and when at night camp was made in some timber bordering a creek, the snow still fell so fast that the officers themselves helped to shovel it away while the soldiers stretched the small amount of canvas that was spread. Fortunately, even at that late season, fresh meat was secured for all the command, for in the underbrush of the streams one out of a group of benumbed buffaloes was easily killed.

In crossing the Canadian River, the quicksands, the floating snow and ice, were faced uncomplainingly, and the nine hundred wet soldiers started up the opposite side without a murmur.

Finally the Indian trail, so long looked for, was struck, and the few wagons were ordered to halt; and only such supplies as could be carried on the person or the horse, consisting of rations, forage, and a hundred rounds of ammunition for each trooper, were taken. The detail of the officer to remain with the train (always assigned according to turn) fell to one of the finest of our officers. But Captain Hamilton was not to yield his privilege of being in a fight so readily. He appealed to go, and finally the commanding officer thought out a way by which it might be accomplished, for he was thoroughly in sympathy with the soldier spirit of this dauntless young fellow. If another officer could be found to take his place, he could be relieved from the odious detail. One of the Seventh was suffering from snow-blindness, and to this misfortune was Captain Hamilton indebted for his change of duty. In the long confidential talks about the camp-fires he had expressed an ardent desire to be in an Indian fight, and when the subject of death came up, as it did in the wide range of subjects that comrades in arms discussed, he used to say, "When my hour to die comes, I hope that I shall be shot through the heart in battle."

The first hours of following the trail were terribly hard. Men and horses suffered for food, for from four in the morning till nine at night no halt could be made. Then by hiding under the deep banks of the stream, fires were lighted, and the men had coffee and the horses oats; but no bugle sounded, no voice was raised, as the Indians might be dangerously near. The advance was taken up again with the Indian guides creeping stealthily along in front, tracing as best they could the route of their foes. The soldier was even deprived of his beloved pipe, for a spark might, at that moment, lose all which such superhuman efforts had been put forth to gain.

After what seemed an interminable time, the ashes of a fire lately extinguished were discovered; then farther on a dog barked, and finally the long-looked-for Indian village was discovered by the cry of a baby. General Custer in his accounts stops to say how keen were his regrets, even with the memory fresh in mind of the atrocities committed by Indians, where white infants' brains had been dashed out to stop their cry-

ing, that war must be brought to the fireside of even a
savage.

The rest of the night was spent in posting the command on different sides of the village, in snatching a
brief sleep, stretched out on the snow, and in longing
for daybreak. Excitement kept the ardent soldiers
warm, and when the band put their cold lips to the
still colder metal, and struck up "Garryowen," the
soldiers' hearts were bursting with enthusiasm and joy
at the glory that awaited them. At the sound of the
bugles blowing on the still morning air—the few spirited notes of the call to "charge"—in went the few
hundred men as confidently as if there had been thousands of them, and a reserve corps at the rear.

All the marching scenes, hunting experiences, the
quips and quirks of the camp-fire, the jokes of the officers at each other's expense, the hardships of the winter, the strange and interesting scouts, are as familiar
to me as oft-told tales come to be, and in going back
and gathering them here and there in the recesses of
memory, aided by General Custer's letters, magazine
accounts, and official reports, the whole scene spreads
out before me as the modern diorama unrolls from its
cylinder the events that are past. Often as this battle
has been talked over before me, I do not feel myself
especially impressed with its military details; woman-
like, the cry of the Indian baby, the capture of a white
woman, the storm that drenched our brave men, are all
fresher in my memory, and come to my pen more readily, than the actual charging and fighting. I therefore

RECONNOITRING THE SITUATION.

make extracts from General Custer's very condensed official report, instead of telling the story myself.

HEADQUARTERS SEVENTH CAVALRY,
CAMP ON WASHITA, *November* 28, '68.

On the morning of the 26th, eleven companies of the Seventh Cavalry struck an Indian trail numbering one hundred (not quite twenty-four hours old) near the point where the Texas boundary line crosses the Canadian River

When the Osage trailers reported a village within a mile of the advance, the column was countermarched and withdrawn to a retired point to avoid discovery. After all the officers had reconnoitred the location of the village, which was situated in a strip of heavy timber, the command was divided into four columns of nearly equal strength. One was to attack in the woods from below the village. The second was to move down the Washita and attack in the timber from above. The third was to attack from the crest north of the village, while the fourth was to charge from the crest overlooking the village on the left bank of the Washita. The columns were to charge simultaneously at dawn of day; though some of them had to march several miles to gain their positions, three of them made the attack so near together that it seemed like one charge. The fourth was only a few moments late. The men charged and reached the lodges before the Indians were aware of their presence. The moment the advance was ordered the band struck up "Garryowen," and with cheers every trooper, led by his officer, rushed towards the village. The Indians were caught napping for once. The warriors rushed from their lodges and posted themselves behind trees and in deep ravines, from which they began a most determined resistance. Within ten minutes after the charge the lodges and all their contents were in our possession, but the real fighting, such as has been rarely, if ever, equalled in Indian warfare, began when attempting to drive out or kill the warriors posted in ravines or ambush. Charge after charge was made, and most gallantly too, but the Indians had resolved to sell their lives as dearly as possible. The conflict ended after some hours. The entire village, numbering (47) forty - seven lodges of Black Kettle's band of Cheyennes, (2) two lodges of Arapahoes, (2) two lodges of Sioux—(51) fifty-one lodges in all, under command of their principal chief, Black Kettle—were conquered.

The Indians left on the ground (103) one hundred and three warriors, including Black Kettle, whose scalp was taken by an Osage guide. 875 horses and mules were captured, 241 saddles (some of fine and costly workmanship), 573 buffalo-robes, 390 buffalo-skins for lodges, 160 untanned robes, 210 axes, 140 hatchets, 35 revolvers, 47 rifles, 535 pounds of powder, 1050 pounds of lead, 4000 arrows and arrow-heads, 75 spears, 90 bullet moulds, 35 bows and quivers, 12 shields, 300 pounds of bullets, 775 lariats, 940 buckskin saddle-bags, 470 blankets, 93 coats, 700 pounds of tobacco; all the winter supply of dried buffalo meat, all the meal, flour, and other provisions; in fact, all they possessed was captured, as the warriors escaped with little or no clothing. Everything of value was destroyed. 53 prisoners were taken, squaws and their children; among the prisoners are the survivors of Black Kettle and the family of Little Rock. Two white children, captives with the Indians, were captured. One white woman in their possession was murdered by her captors the moment the attack was made. A white boy, 10 years old, a captive, had his entrails ripped out with a knife by a squaw. The Kiowas, under Satanta, and Arapahoes, under Little Raven, were encamped six miles below Black Kettle's village. The warriors from these two villages came to attempt the rescue of the Cheyennes. They attacked the command from all sides, about noon, hoping to recover the squaws and the herd of the Cheyennes.

Though displaying great boldness, about three o'clock the cavalry countercharged, and they were driven in all directions and pursued several miles. The entire command was then moved in search of the villages of the Kiowas and Arapahoes, but after an eight-mile march it was ascertained that they had taken fright at the fate of the Cheyennes, and fled.

The command was then three days' march from the train of supplies, and the trail having led over a country cut up by ravines and other obstructions, difficult even for cavalry, it was impossible to bring the wagons on. The supplies which each man carried were nearly exhausted, the men were wearied from loss of sleep, and the horses in the same condition for want of forage. About 8 P. M. the return march was begun, and continued until the wagons were reached. In the excitement of the fight, as well as in self-defence, some of the squaws and a few children were killed and wounded ; the latter were brought on under medical care. Many of the squaws were taken with arms in their hands, and several soldiers were wounded by them. In one small ravine 38 warriors were found dead, showing the desperation of the conflict. Two officers, Major Elliott and Captain Hamilton, were killed, and 19 enlisted men. Captain Barnitz was seriously wounded.

The command marched through snow-storms and rough country, sleeping without tents; and the night before the attack the men stood for hours by their horses awaiting the moment of attack, when the thermometer was far below freezing-point. No one complained, the one regret being that "the gallant spirits who fell were among the bravest and best."

Many of the squaws and children fought like the Indians, darting in and out and firing with cool aim from the opening of the tepees. Some of these squaws

followed in the retreat, but there were some still pru-
dent enough to remain out of sight. While the fight
was going on they sang dirges in the minor key, all
believing their own last hour had come. Captain
Smith was sent round before the fight was ended to
count the tepees for the official report. The squaws
and children fired away at him so fast that he told his
wife afterwards, " The first count of those lodges was
made pretty quick, as the confounded popping kept
up all the time."

The attention of Captain Yates was attracted to the
glittering of something bright in the underbrush. In
a moment a shot from a pistol explained that the glis-
tening object was the barrel of a pistol, and he was
warned by his soldiers that it was a squaw who had
aimed for him, and was preparing to fire again. He
then went round a short distance to investigate, and
found a squaw standing in the stream, one leg broken,
but holding her pappoose closely to her. The look of
malignant hate in her eyes was something a little worse
than any venomous expression he had ever seen. She
resisted most vigorously every attempt to capture her,
though the agony of her shattered limb must have
been extreme. When she found that her pistol was
likely to be taken, she threw it far from her in the
stream, and fought fiercely again. At last they succeeded in getting her pappoose, and she surrendered.
She was carried forward to a tepee, where our surgeon
took charge of her.

As soon as the warriors were driven out, " Romeo,"

who spoke the dialect, was sent by the commanding officer to set the fears of the self-imprisoned women at rest, and they were then all gathered in some of the larger lodges. Two of the squaws had managed during the mêlée to mount and reach one of the herds of ponies, but in the flight, while driving the property off, California Joe had captured women, ponies, and all, and he came into camp swinging his lariat and wildly shouting.

Before leaving the battle-ground it was necessary, if our troops hoped really to cripple the enemy and prevent further invasion, to destroy the property, for it was impossible to carry away much of what had been captured. The contents of the village were collected in heaps and burned. The ponies were crowded together and shot. It took three companies an hour and a half to kill the 800 ponies. This last duty was something the officers never forgot. Nothing but the exigencies of war could have driven them to it. There were the several grades of animals as the Indian uses them: the ponies for marching, those for pack-animals to carry the luggage, the hunting-pony, and finally the best, truest, and swiftest, for battle alone. But the value of the animals was not what affected the officers; it was that, mute and helpless as they were, they must be sacrificed. But they could not be driven away in the deep snow, and with so small a command it was impossible to spare men to even attempt such a rescue. Besides, the presence of such a herd would still more strongly have tempted the constantly menacing Indians to follow and recapture so much valuable property. There was little time to deliberate, for one of the captured squaws reported, what afterwards proved to be true, that along the Washita, for twelve miles, were scattered many other villages. In this comparatively sheltered valley all the southern tribes had congregated. It was a hundred miles outside the reservation, but the timber, water, and grass were favorable for winter camps.

There was still one detachment from which no news had come. Men were sent out for two miles in the direction taken by Major Elliott, but no clew to his whereabouts was obtained. Officers and men felt the imminent danger that surrounded them. Nine hundred men so far from a base of supplies, exhausted from a long fast, and with horses worn out with a difficult march through the snow, were in no condition to risk the lives of the whole command in further search for their dead comrades. Not till the regiment returned to the battle-ground, a short time later, were the bodies of the brave officer and his men found.

In order to escape from the situation, which was most threatening, for the Indians were assembling constantly on the bluffs overlooking the command, General Custer put on a brave front, and ordered the band to play " Garryowen," and the colors to be unfurled; the skirmishers were sent on in advance, and the command set out in the direction of the other villages. I have often thought what nerve it required to assume so bold an attitude and march towards an enemy scattered for twelve miles in advance; the horses and men so exhausted, the ammunition low, and Indians outnumbering them three to one. The Indians, perceiving not only the determined advance, but appreciating that every sign of past victory was apparent, supposed the triumphant troops were about to march on the villages below, and they fled before the column. After dark the order to countermarch was given, and as rapidly as possible the tired troopers rode back to the train of supplies that had been endeavoring for days to make its way to the regiment.

In General Sheridan's letter to General Custer, after the battle, he says, in congratulation: "The Battle of the Washita River is the most complete and successful of all our private battles, and was fought in such unfavorable weather and circumstances as to reflect the highest credit on yourself and regiment."

The following extracts are from General Custer's letters to me:

The sad side of the story is the killed and wounded. Major Elliott and six men, who charged after two Indians, and Captain Hamilton, are gone. I had Captain Hamilton's body brought to this point (Beaver Creek, supply depot), where we buried him with full military honors. Eleven companies of cavalry and three of infantry followed him to the grave. The band played the dead-march; his horse was draped in mourning, carrying his boots, sword, etc., and followed his body. We intend to take the remains back with us when we go to Leavenworth. Colonel Barnitz was wounded by a rifle-ball through his bowels. We all regarded him as mortally wounded at first, but he is almost certain to recover now. He acted very gallantly, killing two Indians before receiving his wound. "Tom" had a flesh-wound in his hand.

FORT COBB, INDIAN TERRITORY, December 19th.

Here we are, after twelve days' marching through snow, mud, rain, and over an almost impassable country, where sometimes we made only eight miles a day. We have been following an Indian trail, and three days ago we overtook the Kiowas; but in order to get the whole tribe together, as well as not to frighten the Apaches and Comanches, who were also with the Kiowas, we refrained from attacking, but permitted Satanta and Lone Wolf, and many other chiefs and warriors, to come into our lines. We find it almost impossible to hurry the Indians much, they have so many powwows and ceremonies before determining upon any important action.

A few moments ago one of the chiefs, Kicking Bird, came in with the news that the entire Kiowa village was hastening in to give themselves up. The Cheyennes and Arapahoes are sick of war since the battle of the Washita. Five miles below the battle-ground, in a deserted Indian village, the bodies of a young and beautiful white woman and her babe were found, and I brought them away for burial at Arbuckle. The woman was captured by Indians—I think, near Fort Lyon, as she was recognized by several of our command.

FORT COBB, January 2d.

The last remaining tribes of hostile Indians have sent in their head chiefs to beg pity from us.

Yesterday a grand council was held near my tent. All the head chiefs of the Apaches, Kiowas, Comanches, Cheyennes, and Arapahoes were assembled. I was alone with them, except one officer, who took stenographic notes of the speeches. A line of sentinels had to be thrown around the council to keep back the observers, as there were crowds of officers, soldiers, and employés of the quartermaster's department.

INDIAN PRISONERS ON THE MARCH.

The council lasted for hours. The arrogance and pride is whipped out of the Indians; they no longer presume to make demands of us; on the contrary, they have surrendered themselves into our keeping. We are left to fix the terms upon which they may resume peaceful relations with the Government.

MEDICINE BLUFF CREEK, *January* 14, '69.

I want to tell you about the courage of one of the guides. Last evening, about two hours before dark, a soldier came running into my tent, and said a man nearly naked was mounted on a mule and riding through camp. We rushed out, and sure enough there was the man. " It's Stillwell," we both said simultaneously. He is one of my couriers, sent on the 4th with the mail to Camp Supply, and whose return with our mail we were anxiously awaiting. He had just returned, and this was the first we saw of him. I began calling to him in my delicate (?) tones, and we soon had him in my tent. After pouring a gill of whiskey down him that I directed the surgeon to administer, he was able to speak. Heavy rains for several days have filled all the streams to overflowing. We are encamped on the south bank of this creek, and it is impassable at any point except by swimming, and even then at great risk to both horse and rider, as the current is both rapid and powerful. Stillwell, with his party, and their pack-mules bearing the mail, reached the opposite bank about a mile above camp, found the stream impassable for the loaded mules, as they thought; so he plunged in with his horse and swam the stream, and being nearly frozen with the ice-water, he was making his way to the scouts' fire as rapidly as possible. He decided that, owing to the rapid current, it was impossible to bring the mail over till morning, when it was hoped the water would fall and render swimming unnecessary.

The others submitted to this decision, but I said I knew

there were letters for me, and I was going to try for that mail, and read my letters, if I had to put a candle in my pocket and swim the stream. My tongue fairly rattled off the directions. "Bishop, bring me a horse; don't wait to saddle him." I ordered so many men to report to me with lariats, axes, etc.; to another officer I called out to gallop up the stream, and tell the scouts to bring on the mail until they shall see me on the bank.

Jumping on Bishop's horse bareback, I forded one branch of the stream, and sought the most available point to cross the mail over the main stream. Some of the officers came down at first and looked on, but it was too cold, and they returned to their tent fires. I found a place where we could roll a long log out some distance in the water, and from it a rope could be thrown across to the other bank and secured by the mail-carriers. The men had to strip off their boots and pantaloons, and work in the water. I encouraged them all I could, and had the doctor send them whiskey, which Colonel Cook distributed to them. Tom thought he could make his way over on horseback, and tried it; but the current carried him and his horse down, and he had to struggle to get back. Finally we got the rope over and secured on both banks. One of the men volunteered to strip off and make his way across, holding on to the rope. In he went, and soon called out "All right" from the other shore. Fastening a mail-bag to his neck, he jumped in, and hard pulling against a roaring torrent brought him across; strong hands were waiting to lift him and his precious load out of the water. All this was after dark. In again he went and called out, as before, from the other side, "All right." Seven times did that brave man breast the current. Cook held the bottle of whisky ready for him as he came out the last time. "Drink, my man, I don't care if you are drunk a week," was my greeting; then putting him on a horse, naked as he was the day he came into the world, I told him to gallop to his tent and wrap up well in his blankets. As each mail-bag was landed, Tom, wet and cold, received it, galloped to the adjutant's tent, where it was distributed to the camp as fast as possible.

Two lodges of the Cheyennes have come in, and they say that the Arapahoes and Cheyennes, whose villages were a hundred miles distant when our council took place the other day, are all moving, but owing to the bad roads and high water they travel slowly. I am as impatient as a crazed animal to have them come in, so that I can start on my homeward journey rejoicing.

Tell Eliza I have just the thing for her. One of the squaws among the prisoners had a little pappoose a few nights since, and I intend to bring it home to add to the orphan asylum she always keeps.

The baby referred to was the child of an Indian princess described in a subsequent chapter. Owing to its lineage, the new-comer was treated with every attention by the prisoners, but it was not so with a poor little infant who was not the descendant of royalty. The mother of the little "forlornity" was killed while fighting in the Washita battle, and the captive women were given charge of the baby. They took advantage of every opportunity to drop it in the snow on the march, and our officers had to watch vigilantly to see that the squaws did not accomplish their purpose of leaving it to perish on the way.

IN CAMP, MEDICINE BLUFF CREEK, 11.30 P.M., *February* 8, '69.

It has been several days since I wrote to you. I have made a long march since. I asked the adjutant to write you during my absence. I did not tell you of my intentions, fearing that you might be anxious; but I am now back safe and well.

We have been to try and bring in the Indian villages, and have had what some people would term a rough time; were gone sixteen days, without wagons or tents. Our provisions became exhausted, there was no game, and officers and men subsisted on parched corn and horse-flesh, the latter not even possessing the merit of having been regularly butchered, but died from exhaustion. Scarcely a morsel of it was left uneaten. You could hardly have helped being amused, even though it was so serious, to have seen the officers sitting around the camp-fire toasting strips of horse-flesh on forked sticks, and then eating it without salt or pepper. I had buffalo robes for my bed, slept soundly and comfortably on the ground, with no shelter except the large rubber blanket spread over me from head to foot, and the rain pouring down. One night my pack-mule did not reach camp, and my robes and overcoat were all with it. I had to sleep all night without either, but I enjoyed it all, and often thought of the song:

> "The bold dragoon he has no care
>   As he rides along with his uncombed hair."

I write briefly, as it is late, and one of the officers going to Leavenworth to-morrow will tell you all the news.

The Cheyennes have delayed their coming in so long that I cannot get home and take our leave of absence as we hoped.

In returning here from our late march, General Sheridan was anxious to hear the result of our trip as soon as possible. I took half a dozen men, and, mounted on a good mule, I rode eighty miles in sixteen hours, through mountains, and guided alone by the compass, taking the general and every one else by surprise by my sudden arrival in camp.

Funeral March.

CHAPTER V.

INDIAN TRAILS, COUNCILS, AND CAPTIVES.

MEDICINE BLUFF CREEK, I. T., *February* 17, 1868.

Yesterday we made peace with the Kiowas, and released their two head chiefs, Satanta and Lone Wolf. We are now waiting the arrival of the train with supplies from Arbuckle, when we will at once bid a final adieu to this part of the country, and set out in a westerly direction, intending to treat with the Cheyennes at some point west of here, then turn our faces northward to Camp Supply.

MEDICINE BLUFF CREEK, *February* 20*th.*

It is a bright and pleasant morning, such as we often had in Texas. The climate here is lovely, seldom a day that even a light coat is uncomfortable. We have mistletoe here as plentifully as in Texas. The scenery is sublime—picturesque in the extreme; the climate all that can be desired—not surpassed, I imagine, by Italy; and such lovely sunsets! ... I wish you could see with what awe I am held by the Indians. A sound drubbing, you know, always produces this. They have given me a name, Mon-to-e-te, which means Strong Arm.

I cannot write but a few lines this evening, as I am now using the last piece of candle which can be obtained any where in camp. So bountifully are we supplied with Gov, ernment stores that not an officer here, from General Sheridan down, has any light; nor have they had for several nights, nor will we have until the arrival of the train of supplies. How we shall spend the long evenings I do not know—sleep, I presume.

As soon as the train of supplies arrives, I expect to move west about one hundred miles, through the Washita mountains, to see if the Cheyennes are in that vicinity; then I turn northward to Camp Supply. Tell Eliza I am tired of living on roast horse and parched corn, as we have had to, and I will soon be at home, and want soup every day.

General Sheridan hastens to Camp Supply, and will start with a train of supplies to meet me somewhere in the vicinity of the Washita battle-field. You see I am telling you our plans, when not a single officer of this command dreams of our destination, and all are wondering when we are going. I am telling you just as if I were with you. Look on the map and find a point on Cache Creek about one hundred miles due west from Fort Arbuckle. That is where we now are. When we move it will be nearly due south-west, following the Red River. There we expect to accomplish the object of our western detour, and will then be nearly on a line due south from Fort Dodge. I am thus minute in order that you may see what a vast extent of country we will have visited since the beginning of my experience on the plains.

Once back to Camp Supply, nothing further can be accomplished for some time; our horses will be worn out, many of them now being unable to proceed that far.

The horses are being fed on grass alone, running loose night and day. They come in at the sound of water-call as regularly and promptly as if led. The men are living on half rations of bread.

No officers' stores for the coming march. I intend to have driven along with us one hundred and fifty head of

Texas cattle, so that we will not be compelled to eat horse-meat again. You know how Texas cattle can travel, equal to any horse. I also have plenty of salt, so my command will not suffer.

General Sheridan has been in on my bed talking over our plans. He said again, for the fiftieth time, that I could go east at the earliest possible moment; but I tell him, as I always have, that I would not go till the work was all done.

Last night, a few moments after I had laid away my unfinished letter and writing materials, and was sitting alone in my Sibley tent, I heard the clatter of several feet coming, as if horsemen were approaching. It was bright moonlight, and I stood peering out of a small opening in the tent trying to divine who it could be entering camp at that hour of the night.

Three muffled figures, human in shape, mounted upon mules and leading two pack-mules, rode up to my tent and dismounted. I could not recognize them, but said, "Come in, who is it?" "Why, general, we have the mail," was the reply. "Hurrah! is that you, Jack?"

(Jack Corbin, one of my most reliable scouts, whom I sent to Camp Supply a month ago.)

If they had been my brothers I could not have greeted them more warmly. Shaking hands all around and asking them to sit down by my sheet-iron stove and warm (we are having a terrible norther), I called the adjutant to distribute the mail they brought. Why was I so glad to see these daring men?—not purely for themselves, though they are good, very good men, but a bird whispered in my ear that there were letters for me. I could have hugged them when I thought that they had braved the perils of two hundred miles, through the Indian country, in order to bring to us, 'way out here, news from our loved ones.

I was right in thinking I had letters in the bag. There were eight. The last was dated the 12th of February, and I received it in ten days from date. Is that not remarkable time for courier mail? It has made the quickest time that any document, official or private, has reached this command. Nothing seems to be a sufficient obstacle to prevent our letters coming. It often happens that General Sheridan desires to send off couriers post-haste with important despatches and cannot burden him with mail matter, so no one is informed of his going; but he never fails to quietly notify me, so that I can get a letter to you by every opportunity.

MEDICINE BLUFF CREEK, *March* 1, 1869.

This is the last day of our sojourn here. In fact, it was to have been the day of our departure, but the Quartermaster and Commissary departments have disappointed us, and I am forced to wait another day for supplies. My command has been living on quarter rations of bread for ten days. General Sheridan has been worried almost to distraction by this cause. He went away with the impression, from what he heard, that we were going to have a large and heavily loaded train. I have received advance lists of all they contain, and I can barely get ten days' rations of bread for my command, and about fifteen rations of other articles.

The troops remaining here have scarcely any commissary stores, but they cannot starve, though compelled to live on beef alone: but even then they will have no salt. I wish some of those who are responsible for this state of affairs, and who are living in luxury and comfort, could be made to share at least the discomforts and privations of troops serving in the field.

I am going to march over a portion of the country to which every one is a stranger, and the distance unknown. I wrote you, however, our proposed movements. I shall be glad to get on the move again. I have remained in camp until I am tired of it. I seldom care to stay in one camp

DISTRIBUTING THE MAIL.

over two or three days. I am almost as nomadic in my pro-
clivities as the Indians themselves.

I send you a likeness which it may not occur to you is
the picture of your husband. How do you like the beard?
The costume is a very fine one, made of dressed buckskin
and fringed. The cap is the one without a visor, that I
have worn all winter. Frank, the tailor, is the maker of the
suit.* One of the officers said that he thought you would
not recognize it, but would think that it was the man from
California, the great hunter, who gave the President the
bear-skin chair.

You would not imagine that I was writing amid frequent
interruptions. The officers are constantly coming in inquiring about preparations for the march. Several Indian chiefs
have been in to "talk"—to them I talk, and continue my
writing at the same time, an interpreter being present. I
send you a likeness of four of my scouts. The one on the
right is "California Joe," mentioned in General Sheridan's
and my despatches. He is the odd genius, so full of origi-
nality, and constantly giving utterance to quaint remarks.
He has been everywhere west of the Mississippi, clear to the
Pacific coast. He has not seen any of his relations for fif-

---

* The morning that this letter came, enclosing the little tintype
of General Custer with a full beard and a buckskin costume, I had
a visit from the tailor's wife, to whom I have referred in *Boots
and Saddles* as old "Trouble agin," because it was the preface to
all her speeches to me. She entered with an open letter and a
tintype of the soldier husband whom after every beating she loved
more fondly.

He was dressed precisely as the general was, as I discovered
from the picture that came in my letter later in the day. This
mystified me for a time, but I found, after General Custer's return,
that Frank, not explaining the exact reason, had borrowed the
buckskin suit, hurried to have himself tintyped as the Great North
American Scout, and sent off his letter to show Mrs. Frank what
a smart soldier she had for a spouse.

teen years, and when asked the other day why he never visited home, replied, " Oh, to tell the truth, gineral, our family
never was very peart for caring much about each other."

The third scout in the group is my interpreter, a young
Mexican. Do you notice his long matted hair? Barnum
would make a fortune if he had him. His hair never made
the acquaintance of a comb, and his face is almost equally
unacquainted with water. Yet he is a very good and de-
serving person, in his way. We have a great deal of sport
with him. I threaten to put kerosene oil on his hair and
set it on fire. He speaks several of the Indian languages,
and is very useful. The fourth in the group is Jack Corbin, one of my most reliable scouts and couriers. He has
made frequent trips to Camp Supply and back with the mail.

WASHITA BATTLE-GROUND, *March* 24, 1869.

We arrived here yesterday, having marched three hundred
and fourteen miles. I will rest two days and then start with
my entire command for Camp Supply.

I have been successful in my campaign against the Cheyennes. I outmarched them, outwitted them at their own
game, proved to them they were in my power, and could and
would have annihilated the entire village of over two hundred lodges but for two reasons. 1st. I desired to obtain
the release of the two white women held captive by them,
which I could not have done had I attacked. 2d. If I had
attacked them, those who escaped, and absent portions of
the tribe also, would have been on the war-path all summer,
and we would have obtained no rest. These reasons alone
influenced me to pursue the course I have, and now, when I
can review the whole matter coolly, my better judgment
and my humanity tell me I have acted wisely. You cannot
appreciate how delicately I was situated. I counselled with
no one, but when we overtook the Cheyenne village, and
saw it in our power to annihilate them, my command, from

highest to lowest, desired bloodshed. They were eager for revenge, and could not comprehend my conduct. They dis· approved and criticised it. I paid no heed, but followed the dictates of my own judgment — the judgment upon which my beloved commander (General Sheridan) said he relied for the attainment of the best results. He had authorized me to do as I pleased, fight or not. And now my most bitter enemies cannot say that I am either blood-thirsty or possessed of an unworthy ambition.

Had I given the signal to attack, officers and men would have hailed it with a shout of gratification. I braved their opinion, and acted in opposition to their wishes, but to-day not one but says I was right, and any other course would have been disastrous. Many have come to me and confessed their error. The two women are bright, cultivated, and good-looking.

I now have the Cheyenne chiefs prisoners, and intend to hold them as such until their tribe comes in. I think we have rendered them sick and tired of war. We are delighted to find a large mail here. The paymaster is at Camp Supply waiting to pay the troops. One-half the command is dismounted, and what few horses we have could not go out again for two months.

General Custer refers in the letters written to me, from which quotations have just been made, to the rescue of the two white women. It was brought about after unending parleyings, delays, and excuses on the part of the Indians, by threatening to hang the three chiefs, Big Head, Fat Bear, and Dull Knife, who had been captured by our people with a view to holding them until all the white captives then with the hostiles were released. Indian messengers were sent to the tribe to report the danger to their chiefs, and finally, after long and weary watching of the hills over which the detachment from the village must come, a group of horsemen appeared. While they traversed several miles that separated them from our troops, the whole command watched with breathless interest. The young brother of a captured woman had been with the command all winter, and moving daily among our men, had kept their sympathies alive to the atrocity that had been perpetrated. All the troopers were watching this half-grown man, suddenly matured by anxiety and trouble, as he kept his eyes on the approaching Indians. The hearts of the soldiers beat faster and faster as the lad grew paler and more anxious. "The bravest are the tenderest," and that day proved it, for our rough men had scarcely any thought but for the suffering youth among them. Finally the Indians came near enough for an officer to perceive with his glass that there were two on one pony. A little nearer and they reported that they were women. The poor boy had no reason to be sure that one of them was his sister. To the Indian his captive is nameless. The chiefs had confessed that they had two white squaws, but by no means in their power could our people ascertain who they were. Finally the two figures descended from the pony, left the Indians, who were at a halt, and began to walk towards the waiting troops.

General Custer, by the aid of his powerful field-glass, told young Brewster that one of the figures coming was short and stout, the other taller. As soon as any observation was made by General Custer regarding what his glass revealed, one listening soldier told it to another, and a tremor of excitement spread from one end of the long watching line to the other.   As Brewster looked through the glass lent to him and saw the women, he began to believe that one of them was his sister, as she was of about her height, and he implored General Custer for permission to go to her.   It was hard to refuse, but he was obliged to do so, fearing the boy's horror at the change in her would make him forget the necessity for caution, and attempt revenge before the prisoners had really reached our lines.

The regiment of Kansas Volunteers had been or ganized to revenge some of the outrages to the border people, and with the hope of rescuing white prisoners, so General Custer gave them the privilege of first greeting their two States women.   Three ranking officers went forward to meet the poor creatures, who, even then, except for their white skin, could hardly be distinguished from the Indians, so strange was their dress. Hardly had the officers advanced a quarter of the way when the waiting lad darted from his place beside General Custer, and sped on before every one until he had reached the women.   As he clasped the taller of the two in his arms the soldiers knew that the sister for whom he had suffered so much was restored to him. The officers, in telling this story to us afterwards, always hurried over this part; they could not speak calmly.

They all crowded round the poor girls, eager to

shake their hands and welcome them; but the most daring, the most valiant among them, did not attempt to conceal the tears that rolled down their cheeks. Men who had laid the fair flower of chivalry, the loved comrade, Captain Hamilton, in the ground only so recently with tearless silence, now wept over the two captives. The longer they looked upon the poor creatures the harder it became to control their emotions. The young faces of the two, who not a year before were bright, happy women, were now worn with privation and exposure, and haggard with the terrible insults of their captors, too dreadful to be chronicled here. The rudely cut and scanty garment that barely covered them was made from flour sacks bearing the brand that our government purchases, thus proving that the Indians who captured them had been drawing rations from the United States Indian agency at the time. They had Indian leggings and moccasins, their braided hair and arms encircled with spiral wire, their fingers covered with brass rings, their necks with beads, were evidences that the Indians, by thus adorning their prisoners, hoped to mollify the wrath of the white man. Fortunately, the one woman on the expedition, who was General Custer's cook, and from whose temper, as I have elsewhere related, her soldier husband so often suffered, now forgot the rages and furies of her daily life, and gave the poor released creatures some of her clothing, clad in which they left in charge of the now happy brother for their homes when the first wagon-train coming with supplies went back to Camp Supply.

The story of their life among the Indians was one of barbarous treatment and brutality; one had no knowledge that the other was a prisoner, as they had been captured separately, until they met in an Indian village, and after being traded about from one chief to another, they at last came to be owned by the same warrior. While together, they planned an escape. They did not know where they were, but stole out at night, and, guided by the stars, started north. With great joy they at last reached a wagon-road lately travelled. In the midst of this delight a bullet whistled by them, and soon they saw their owner in hot pursuit. New insults were inflicted, and more laborious work was loaded on the two after their return to the village. The conduct of the squaws, always jealous of white women, was brutality itself. The chief finally sold the two apart. With the terrible physical labor required of them, in addition to revolting indignities, it was a wonder they lived. They were almost starved, some days only being allowed a morsel of mule-meat, not over an inch square at most, for an entire day. The squaws beat them with clubs when the Indians were absent, and once one of them was felled to the ground by a blow from these same jealous fiends.

After all this dreadful life, it would seem as if the two women might have looked for immunity from future trouble, but in one instance it was not to be. Two years after their rescue, two of our officers were

6

riding past a ranch and saw a little Indian boy playing before the house. Seeing him, they were too much
interested not to inquire who lived there, and found,
when the woman of the house came to the door, that
it was one of the captives, whose face, owing to the
tragic circumstances of the release, was fixed indelibly
on their memory. It was impossible for her to resist
detaining them a few moments, recalling again her
gratitude to the troops for her rescue. When they
asked if all went well with her, she could not help
confiding to them the fact that the husband whom she
had married after her return, instead of trying to make
her forget the misery through which she had passed,
often recalled all her year of captivity with bitterness,
and was disposed to upbraid her, as if she had been
in the least responsible for the smallest of her mis-
fortunes.

In the many letters which I have looked over to
obtain my few notes of a winter that was so eventful,
I have found only occasional allusions to the hardships
undergone; but, little by little, references were made
after the return of the command that gave some idea
of the self-denial and self-control which every one had
to exercise. If afterwards any one exhibited the slightest sign of obstinacy, some teasing voice was sure to
pipe up and say, "What can you expect of a man who
has dined on mule-steaks?" General Custer could not
eat mule or horse when they were all reduced to that
desperate strait, but in his hunger he told me he used
to think that he might, to save himself from starva-

tion, make up his mind to eat his dogs' ears; and as they trotted along in front of him, quite happy over their mule breakfast, he looked longingly at these devoted friends, but with a hope that he might be spared the necessity of mutilating them.

The soldiers bartered for everything. One came to General Custer to beg to trade some tobacco for a loaf of bread. He received the half of the last loaf, but the tobacco was declined, as it was not the habit of General Custer to use it. That night the remaining half of the loaf was stolen. A little sack of oats was carefully treasured in General Custer's tent for his favorite horse, and the hungry animals left loose to pick what grass they could under the edges of the snow, came at night sniffing and snorting around the oats in hungry search. The horses grew so expert in foraging for themselves that they learned to put one hoof on a fallen sapling and tear off the bark with their teeth, as a dog holds and picks a bone.

It was on that campaign that I first heard of a sack made of a buffalo-skin to sleep in, and not even then should I have learned that such an invention was known, had not the handsome Adonis who used this clever device been unmercifully teased for indulging in so much luxury.

Indeed, it was mostly owing to the tormenting spirit of raillery, that is the characteristic of officer and soldier, that many of the hardships endured came to my knowledge at all. When the attention of a group was called to some comical situation, reminding the bystanders of some desperate plight, either of danger or deprivation, in which an officer had been placed, I had an insight into what had been endured by them all.

I suppose that I never should have heard of several incidents of the winter, had it not been that the Kansas Volunteers afforded some amusement to our men, from the fact that they, though brave men, were inexperienced campaigners, and their complaints did not escape our men, who considered themselves scarred veterans in comparison. For years, if any one said, talking of a hoped-for leave of absence, or describing some one who was lonely, "I can see home just as plain," I knew that it referred to a volunteer who was heard by some of our men crying with homesickness, and confiding his woes to his "bunkey." At heart our men were sorry for them, as there were some pitiful instances of nostalgia among them; but when they whined like children they were apt to encounter ridicule.

At the time when the supplies were getting low and half-rations were issued, and still the expedition pursued a fresh trail, instead of returning to the wagon train, the commanding officer ordered the band to play the regimental tunes, "Garryowen," "The Girl I left behind Me," etc., after camp was reached, in the hope of raising the spirits of the men. Evidently the soul of the Kansas Volunteers was not attuned to music when assailed by the pangs of hunger, for they were overheard to grumble and complain that "Custer fed them on one hardtack a day and the 'Arkansaw Traveller.'"

The story of the military part of the rest of the winter, unmarked by any battle, but full of parleyings, ruses, subterfuges, councils, and promises of peace on the part of the Indians, who eventfully did come to terms, has been much better told by another pen than mine. I needed only to outline the battle of the Washita, that I might introduce the prisoners who formed such a feature of our life during the following summer at Fort Hays, and explain how it came to pass that the regiment was able to have a permanent camp instead of being all off on a campaign at once.

CHAPTER VI.

IN CAMP ON BIG CREEK.

EARLY in the spring the Seventh Cavalry found themselves again in Kansas, and with the cheering prospect of some degree of quiet. The same Big Creek on which they had been located two summers before was chosen for a camp; access was had to the regimental baggage, which had been stored, and every one prepared to make himself comfortable. Some of the officers took leave of absence, and after the year's separation from their families the rejoicing was great. Two of our number brought their wives back to camp. Others were deprived of that pleasure, because their wives could not endure the hardships, or their children were too young to bear the exposure. There was great exchanging of confidences concerning the experiences of the officers on their leaves, and much unreserved narrating of domestic scenes; for, full of railing as every one was, a man's family life was sacred, and he felt that he could speak of it freely; so it was indeed as if we were one family. Those who went home amused us, on their return, by their stories of how they had surprised the home people—stealing in at the backdoor, catching up their wives and swinging them in air, while the frightened servants, hearing the screams, ran from the

kitchen with hands covered with flour, and the coachman from the stable, still holding his curry-comb, all of
them ready to defend their lady against the imagined
burglar or assassin. One of our number reached home
in the evening while his little son was sleeping. He
was awakened in the morning by the vigorous application of a pair of little fists on his face, and an angry
demand from the little fellow, accompanied by some
terrible language that the youngster had learned at
the cavalry stables, to "get out of his mother's bed."
He had, in the year that had elapsed, entirely forgotten how his father looked, and not knowing he
was coming, he did not suspect the identity of the intruder.

Those officers who had no families were busy over
piles of love-letters awaiting them from the East, and
sought in vain places where they might read in peace,
for those who were not so fortunate as to have a sweetheart rallied the lucky ones, and interfered as much as
possible with the envied enjoyment. Still, it is a well-
known fact that a soldier is usually a lover. The old
saw, "Love rules the camp, the court, the grove," is
one that fits all nations and all eras. Officers are pretty fearless about their devotion; if not avowing it
openly, still wearing all sorts of love-pledges—chains
and lockets which with the open-throated shirt in a
campaign are easily seen, or keepsakes on the watch-
chain: perhaps a curious ring which could not be mistaken for a man's under any circumstances, or other
such things. I have even seen a bangle made large

enough to encircle the arm, and locked on, of course, by fair hands. A Catholic officer often wore an *Agnus Dei*, and I believe that many a man would have disfigured himself with an ear-ring if the girl he left behind him had asked to pierce his ear for that purpose. They did not hesitate to carry their sweethearts' pictures in their inner pockets, and around the camp-fire take them out and look at the loved faces by the firelight the last thing before sleeping. Imagine, then, with all these officers, most of whom were in love with women, either their wives or the girls they hoped to make their wives, what a time of rejoicing it was when partial civilization was again reached, and the cars of the railroad were almost in sight, meaning to them an opportunity to go East—or failing that, at least a daily mail! Every one's heart seemed to be merry; the sound of laughter and song rang out from the tents, and the soldiers danced in the company streets to the music of an Irish bagpipe (differing somewhat from the Scotch instrument, but with just as merry music) that belonged to a recruit newly arrived.

Our summer camp was between two and three miles from Fort Hays, on Big Creek. Sometimes the stream ran along for a distance with no timber or underbrush to border it, but the place selected for our tents was under a fringe of good sized cotton-wood-trees. It was most gratifying to have this protection, and after a hot ride on the arid plain we came under the boughs and saw, with a real home feeling, the white tents **gleaming in the shade. All about us the undulating** country stretched its naked, glaring surface; not even clumps of bushes survived the scorching sun or the fierce tornadoes of wind that swept unchecked over the great unbroken stretch of country.

Professor Hayden so clearly explains the peculiar formation of the plains that I here insert a few paragraphs from his account of the matter:

We believe that at the close of the cretaceous period the ocean rolled uninterruptedly across the area now occupied by the Rocky Mountain Ranges. Near the close of the cretaceous era the surface had reached an elevation so great as to form long lines of separation between the waters of the Atlantic, on the east, and those of the Pacific on the west; and thus this great water-shed began to rise above the surrounding country. Then, also, began the existence of the first of that series of fresh-water lakes which we now know was a most prominent feature in the physical geography of this country during the tertiary period.

During the cretaceous period there was a gradual, slow elevation of the whole country west of the Mississippi; that about the close of that period the crust of the earth had been strained to its utmost tension, and long lines of fracture commenced, which formed the nucleus of our present mountain ranges. At the close of the cretaceous period, in the early days of the tertiary, when the crust had been elevated to its utmost tension, it broke sometimes in long lines of fracture, which gave birth to these lofty, continuous ranges along the eastern portion of the Rocky Mountains, as the Wind River, Big Horn, Black Hills, or the basaltic ridges formed by outbursts of melted matter arranged in series of sharp peaks or sierras.

It is possible to trace the growth of the continent, step by step, from the purely marine waters of the cretaceous ocean and the period when the mountain ranges were elevated in well-defined lines above the waters, causing the ocean to recede to the eastward on the one side, and to the westward on the other. The Rocky Mountains formed immense watersheds, which gave birth to innumerable fresh-water streams, which fed those great tertiary lakes along the eastern slope, two out of the four or five, of great extent. We believe that one, the great Lignite basin, extends as far southward as California, possibly, westward over the mountains to Utah, and northward probably to the Arctic Sea, interrupted by the upheaval of mountain ranges.

It is chiefly remarkable for its fossil flora of fan-palms and other tropical plants, which points to the conclusion that along the shores of this great lake grew luxuriant forests like those in Central America and Brazil.

We who roamed the vast plains had every reason to corroborate all the investigations that the scientists made. The great trackless waste of land all about our camp was like nothing but the sea, and the rolling country we rode over day after day was as if the earth had been indented by waves of a powerful ocean. We came suddenly, on our marches, upon cañons that were sharp fissures in the earth extending for many miles. These chasms, in an otherwise comparatively level surface, could mean nothing but cracks in the cooling earth's crust, through which a mighty rush of water had once plunged, deepening and widening the gorge. If we halted for luncheon, and spread our simple meal on the stunted grass, we could reach about us and pick up the vertebræ of fish that had once glided through water where we then sat.

In geological research the officers of our army have been of incalculable use to their Government. They explored the Indian infested countries long before the colleges or Government sent out scientists for the purpose. The remains of fishes, serpents, birds, crocodiles, lizards, turtles, bats, etc., were gathered by our officers and sent to the East. It was a strange sensation to find ourselves monarchs in a land which once was given up to all forms of vegetable and animal life, many varieties of which are now forever gone from the earth. The moss-agate was as common as the pebbles along a country road, and we broke off large flakes of rough surface to find incased in its transparent tomb exquisite sprays of delicate foliage, which reproduced in stone the fairy, fragile flora of a by-gone time. There was nothing remaining of that time of exquisite herbage. The dull sage-bush, or grease-root, or the sparse buffalo-grass, were all that the sun spared from its scorching rays.

The understanding was that we should have a permanent camp during the summer. By that it was meant that the regiment would have a headquarters in the field, and scouting parties be sent out from it. As we were so near a post, it was not difficult to get all the canvas we wanted. Our regimental quartermaster made requisition for the tents, which would be returned to the post in the autumn. We felt very rich, for, by borrowing from our Uncle Sam, we had as many rooms as some houses have—that is, calling each tent a room. The sitting-room was a hospital tent which

is perhaps fourteen by sixteen. It was clean, and had
no association of illness to keep one awake with imag-
inings at night. These huge tents are really designed
for hospital purposes, but, fortunately, I never knew
them to be used except in one epidemic of cholera.
In the few cases of illness or injury occurring among
the soldiers the patients were sent to a garrison hospital, for most posts have a regular building for this purpose. Opening out at the rear of our sitting-room was
our own room, a wall tent ten by twelve. In pitching
these tents General Custer had an eye for a tree with
wide-spreading branches to shade us, and in order to
utilize it he put the tents on the side bank running
down to the stream. Of course it was necessary to
build up a rough embankment of stones and earth, and
that left the tent floor at the rear almost up to the
limbs of the tree. We then thought how foolish of
us not to continue the floor around the tree. The company carpenter built such a comfortable little platform,
with a railing, that we felt as if we had a real gallery
to our canvas house ; and sitting out there, Tom smoking, I sewing, and General Custer reading, we imagined
Big Creek to be the Hudson, and the cotton-wood,
whose foliage is anything but thick, to be a graceful
maple or a stately, branching elm. Our brother Tom,
while he enjoyed our arbor, refused to call it anything
but the " beer-garden "—but calling names did not destroy our delight. The floors of the tents were an especial luxury, for every board in that region counted,
as it was difficult to get lumber. The cotton-wood

warped before it was fairly nailed down, and a pine plank even now looks to me like rare wealth.

The canvas of our rear tent was cut and bound, and a roller of wood to keep it down in wind-storms was sewed in, so that when tied up it left a broad window, seven feet wide, opening on the platform and giving a fine circulation of air. A huge tarpaulin of very thick canvas, used to cover grain and military stores, for which there was not room in the storehouses, was spread over the large tent and extended far in front, so that we had a wide porch, under which we sat most of the time.

It was with great relief that I saw the holes dug in which to sink the poles at the four corners of each tent. These were usually young saplings with a notch near the top ; and across the two on either side was laid another long pole, to which the ropes were lashed so securely that no storm tore the tent down during all the summer. To have a whole summer of relief from fear that our cotton-house would blow over was a great boon, for a Kansas wind can do much havoc with canvas, and it is not comfortable to lie watching a swaying ridge-pole in a storm and imagine yourself crushed in its downfall.

We had, of course, only the barest necessities in the tents—a rude bunk for a bed, a stool, with tin wash-basin, a bucket for water, and a little shaving-glass for a mirror. The carpenter had nailed together some benches and a cumbrous table. These, with our camp-chairs, were our furniture. There was a monotonous similarity of construction in the chairs made by the carpenter. Each consisted of one long board rounded at the top, to which another shorter board was nailed for the seat, and another put on as a brace at the back. One of our friends had a chair of this pattern, and as her husband, coming home to the tent at dusk, saw this white-pine board gleaming through the twilight, he called out, merrily: "If you do 'turn up your toes to the daisies,' we can just set this up at your head, with the inscription, 'Died so-and-so'; it would make a beautiful tombstone." They were truly sepulchral-looking, but we were not inclined to be over-critical of the style. It never occurred to us that we wanted anything more; for if all the camp-chairs, benches, and stools were occupied, the young officers threw themselves down on the buffalo-robes, or smoked sitting, *à la Turque*, on a blanket spread under the fly. Several Indian articles of luxury had been given us, out of which we had much comfort. They consisted of a light framework of interwoven willow withes about the width of a chair-back, and were called head-rests. These were laid on the ground, raised at the farther end at a gentle inclination, and strongly propped at the back. They could be rolled into small compass for carrying, and were vastly superior in strength to anything we could buy. When the officers reclined on these primitive but comfortable affairs, smoking, they looked so at ease that we addressed them as "bashi-bazouk," or pacha, or by some Eastern term that suggested habits of luxurious indulgence.

On the right of our tent began the others—one for guests, another for the dining-tent, then the round Sibley, that General Custer had used during the winter, for the cook tent. This must have been modelled after an Indian tepee, as it looked much like it. At that time Sibley tents were not in use, but why, we could never understand, as the wind had so little purchase upon them, finding no corners to toy with, that this circular house could almost defy a hurricane. The fire was built in the centre, and the smoke escaped through an aperture at the top, which could be half covered, according to the direction of the wind, by pulling ropes attached to a little fly. The Indians had the same arrangement, only they managed the opening a little better.

Next to the Sibley was a veritable tepee, that General Custer had brought from an abandoned Indian village. It was made of tanned buffalo skins sewed together with leather thongs, and stretched over a framework of thirty-six lodge-poles. These poles are fastened together at the top, and extend out in all directions above the hide covering. They are a precious possession in the eyes of an Indian, as he is often obliged to travel hundreds of miles to procure them, in the heavily timbered part of the country, where strong, light, flexible saplings can be cut. The buffalo hides were covered with rude drawings representing the history of the original owner, his prowess in killing Indians at war with his tribe, the taking of the white man's scalp, or the stealing of ponies. Instead of the flap of the entrance opening down to the ground, the aperture began some distance up, so that one had to undo and pull out innumerable little sticks that were put through holes in the hide, and made quite a step up before getting into the tepee. As it was carefully staked down with picket-pins all about the edge, and a ditch was dug around to carry off the water, such a tepee could challenge almost any storm. In this house of the aborigine lived our Henry, a colored coachman, who had come with us from Virginia years before. Sometimes he was teased by having his possessions pilfered, sometimes some one borrowed and forgot to return; but after the general gave him the tepee to live in, and he had tied a dog inside, and fastened the flap with the wooden pins, his "traps" were secure, and he said: "'Tain't no kind or manner of use to try to lift* my plunder now; for, as the soldiers say, 'I got the bulge on all of em.'" Usually a small line was hung to a tree at the rear, proclaiming that all days were Mondays with Henry. He was very neat, and the clothes swinging in the breeze were his washing. He said to me one day: "The general jest tries to tease me about my washin'. I jest tell him, 'I ain't no Chinee, general, and can't wash any but my Government clothes, but those can't be beat.'"

We were living quite apart from the main camp, in a little curve in the creek. The two other officers who had brought their wives out joined us, and put their

---

* "Lift," a word meaning steal.

tents farther on in the bend. Nearer the prairie the parade-ground began, then the rows of tents of the companies and the picket-ropes for the horses. The soldiers lived in "A" tents, so called because they have no side walls, but slope directly from the ground to the ridge-pole which joins the two upright poles, one at either end. At the end of each company street stood a wall tent for the first sergeant, who, as ranking non-commissioned officer of the company, is a great personage with the enlisted men. At a little distance, facing the company street, were the tents of the captain and lieutenant of each company. The sutler's tent was farther on at the other end of the line. Nearer us was a great room put up by the soldiers for their own entertainment. It was built of a framework of logs and cotton-wood slabs, over which were nailed tarpaulins. It was dignified by the name of the Opera House. The sutler lent a billiard-table, and in this improvised hall the soldiers could give minstrel performances or concerts. There is always in the ranks much amateur and sometimes some professional "talent." There were the clog-dancers, who were the idols of our regiment. How they managed to carry their professional shoes and tights was always a secret. The soldier is only allowed his haversack for his food and his overcoat, inside of which he can squeeze a few things. The roll at the back of the saddle is made up very tight on parades and inspection days, but on a march an indulgent officer allows the bundle to expand so that it mounts halfway up the soldier's back. If the officer is strict, he

7

demands to see the inside of this roll and orders it reduced; then the soldier makes friends with the teamster who drives the one wagon with the company property, and the violin, accordion, banjo, or other extra,
like the clog-dancer's shoes, is slipped into the box under the driver's seat, and no one thinks of "inspect-
ing" him.

A teamster is rather an independent sort of being.
He swears and growls, and when his wagon is stuck in
quicksand, or up to the hub in mud, no one ventures
to enter into conversation with him. He has ways,
last resorts for stirring his animals from lethargy into
activity, but in emergencies he communes only with
himself or with them. The soldiers may be directed
to "man the wheels," and after fifty are tugging at
the ropes that are fastened to the axles, calling out
"Heave ho!" as sailors do at each new struggle, the
teamster's voice rises above all in invectives that are
startling to every one except the mules. But the big
hearts of these frontiersmen are something to remember. They are very apt to share everything they have
with whoever comes along. They hide and coddle a
little fyst dog, or make a soft place for a pet antelope,
and take care of these creatures like trained nurses.

During the war there were some splendid stories
told of army teamsters. Ferocious and blasphemous
as they seemed to be, they took many steps to aid the
freedman, and permitted the ragged, half-starved, foot-
sore children of the plantations—for they were, even
at sixty years of age, nothing but children—to share

their seats or their fare with them. The story that stays by me is of a burly driver who fearlessly tended a little negro baby, whose mother had abandoned it by the road-side. It is the sarcasm and bantering that makes all of us hide our good deeds, or prevents our doing any at all in public—but this tender-hearted man let hundreds of soldiers pass him as his wagon was being dragged slowly along by the tired mules, and heard, quite unmoved, the ribaldry and the keen wit which comes from a line of soldiers, and which sets the company into roars of laughter, while he held the little pickaninny with one arm and managed the reins with the other.

General Custer was genuinely attached to the Government teamster who drove his headquarters wagon during the campaign of the winter. He was very intelligent, and as some of our teamsters then were old stage-drivers, they had a fund of anecdote and valuable information about what they called the "lay of the land," the features of the country, etc. Our teamster was rarely moved to wrath, nor did he seem capable of becoming excited over any occurrence. By some rare mode of silent understanding the driver and the master became deeply attached to each other. If General Custer came with his orderly galloping up to the wagon at the rear with game, or with the head of an elk or a buffalo to preserve, the driver found a place for the article in his crowded wagon, and his own little camp-fire at night crackled as the buffalo, antelope, or venison steak given him dropped its fat from the stick on which he broiled his supper. When the summer was ended, and these two were about to part, General Custer asked for his picture, but what was his disappointment when he found the patched and picturesque clothes of the summer were replaced for the occasion by new "store clothes;" a thing which took all the naturalness away.

The pleasure of our camp life was greatly enhanced by our being so near the post. Fort Hays was commanded by General Nelson Miles, who had been but a short time on the plains, and though an infantry colonel, was at heart a true cavalryman, and entirely in sympathy with our branch of the service. The manner in which he welcomed our regiment, ragged and travel-stained from their long campaign, won all hearts. The band in full uniform was sent to accompany the regiment for a distance, and played the Seventh Cavalry tune, "Garryowen." General Miles rode at the head of the column, and all the officers came from their companies to join him for the short distance he rode with us. He did not hesitate to say that he envied the success of the regiment, and should emulate their successful mode of Indian fighting as soon as he had an opportunity.

Of course, with such a reception we knew that we were all quite welcome, and though we had little to offer them in the way of hospitality, it was always a pleasant sight to us when an ambulance from the post came in view round the bend, filled with ladies with cavaliers as outriders.

The post was about as dreary a spot as can be imagined. I do not remember a tree near it, and the sparse, stunted grass on the scorched parade-ground was scarcely green. The officers' quarters were almost as plain and bare as the soldiers' barracks, and were crowded. Two families, I remember, who were not friendly, were obliged to live in a double set of quarters. The hall was narrow, the rooms were small, and the walls so thin that every word spoken on one side could be distinctly heard on the other. The wife of one of our Seventh Cavalry officers was the occupant of the quarters on one side, and the wife of an infantry officer lived on the other. A swarm of little children prevented the cavalry officer's wife from coming to camp to live, but she consoled herself as best she could by the permit her husband received to spend from Saturday night till Monday morning of every week at home. The husband and wife were of different nationalities, and though sincerely attached to each other, they were of such decided natures that they disagreed on many points. When the children were all in bed on Saturday night it became necessary, as the wife told me, that the question at issue, whatever it might be, should be talked over—each endeavoring, I suppose, to convince the other that he or she was wrong. But, as the madame further explained, it was impossible, while her enemy was on the other side of so thin a wall, to enter into any animated discussion, lest she and her spouse should be accused of serious quarrelling; so, as she expressed it, "We were obliged to go out on the parade-ground and have it out there." Then, when the argument was done and the domestic air cleared, they returned to their cramped little quarters, the wife cooked her companion an excellent supper, and harmony reigned until the next difference of opinion. A government that deprives a man of the luxury of a Caudle lecture may have male supporters in plenty, but no one can uphold a parsimonious country in depriving a man and woman of the privilege of arguing—to put it mildly—and compelling them both to take to the open prairie to do the necessary convincing. In this small and uncomfortable post there was much happiness, harmony, and generous hospitality, and we joined in many a little merrymaking among the cordial people.

They scarcely realized what pleasure they gave us. We are told something of one who gives a cup of water to a thirsty man, but when in this case it turned out to be ice-water, those who were condemned habitually to drink the rather warm water of Big Creek were anxious to add a line to the blessing in token of gratitude. Our young officers sometimes came home at night from the post, after an evening's hospitality, full of boyish delight over a pie or a cake baked on purpose for them, and almost ludicrously grateful for the ministration to appetites long unused to dainty gratification.

Fatigue.

CHAPTER VII.

INDIAN PRISONERS.

THE one feature of great interest at the post was the presence of the Indian prisoners brought from the battle of the Washita. General Custer was obliged to go to them very often, as he had learned their sign-language, and his scout, who spoke their dialect, acted as interpreter. It happened, therefore, that we often rode up on horseback, or I drove in our large travelling carriage to take guests, who were constantly coming by the Eastern trains.

It was an unprecedented event to have sixty Indians from warlike tribes on whom we could safely look, or with whom we could actually visit. I cannot say that I mounted my horse with perfect tranquillity the first time General Custer took me up to see them, nor that the hand that held my Phil was quite steady.

Though there were but three chiefs among them, and those carefully guarded, I had a perfect knowledge of what desperate work the squaws and children had done in the battle; and our own General Gibbs described a charge he had made into an Indian village before the war, where he had seen an old squaw cease for an instant stirring her soup, snatch her knife from her belt, plunge it into a soldier who was unsuspicious of a woman as a warrior, resume her soup-stirring perfectly imperturbed, not even looking at the dead soldier at her side. All these, and many more such tales, from my friends who had been eye-witnesses, made the road from camp to Hays a purgatory to me, and for once my side of the conversation languished. General Custer understood that silence meant fright with me, as scarcely anything save fright kept me still, and he reassured me over and over again. He reminded me that every advantage was ours—that these were whipped and, consequently, peaceful Indians; but Indians were Indians to me, and no amount of explanation quieted my agitation.

To add to my fears, I found Phil trembling as we neared the high stockade which had been built next to the guard-house. Horses once thoroughly frightened by Indians never quite recover from their panic. Their sense of smell is so keen that they early begin to manifest their inward perturbation by the quivering ears, which express so much. I had all I could do to keep Phil from turning back to camp, and had not my reputation for horsemanship been at stake I should have liked to give him his head, for I wanted to go back just as badly as he wanted to take me in that direction. It was a relief to dismount and give the restless brute to the orderly, for as I was riding with a snaffle-bit to get a smoother gait, he had nearly dragged my arms from their sockets.

The stockade where the prisoners were confined was perhaps fifteen feet high, and made of perpendicular logs driven deep into the ground. Near the top ran a sentinel's walk around the whole corral. The enclosure was big enough to hold several large tents, and yet leave a good-sized vacant place where the children could play. We ascended the steps by which the sentinel reached his beat, and looked down upon the occupants, but this did not satisfy General Custer. He took me inside; and, as the crowd of women and children gathered around me, I almost felt knives penetrating my dress for a deadly stab, so great was my distress. I was introduced, and at once was an object of great interest, for General Custer had established confidence in them and they trusted his word. Moreover, there is no denying that a man who has once conquered Indians in battle commands the deepest admiration possible to their natures. When he told the squaws that I was his wife they made a sign to ask if I was the only one; and an expression of compassion came into their faces when he said yes, for among some of the tribes an Indian is always very much married if he is a chief of any consequence. Possibly they imagined that a white wife has the same amount of labor to perform for her hus-

band that a chief's squaws have, and they pitied me.
Polygamy has its advantages when it provides for a
division of the heavy labor done by the squaw wives.

The squaws came still closer, put their hands on my
shoulder, smoothing and caressing me. Others took
my hand in their horny old palms, the touch of which
moved me to pity, as it revealed the amount and kind
of work that they had done; but, worst of all, the
oldest, most withered and wizened of them laid their
cheeks against mine, after the manner of their kissing.
For once I was grateful that there are fashions in os-
culation as there are in everything else.

I kept my eyes furtively on the entrance, looked
stealthily towards the sentinel, and sought a reassuring
look from General Custer. The squaws and children
had many requests to make, and being busy with them,
he had no idea how tremulous were my steps, for after
reassuring me at the gate he supposed that my fears
had departed. Besides, he too was soon the centre of
a group of old hags, who drew his head down to lay
their parchment cheeks against his, and crooned some
gibberish over him.

It is strangely difficult to realize that deaf people
or foreigners do not understand us, and in speaking
of them in their presence we involuntarily lower our
voices. I asked under my breath why the old women
singled him out, and made him submit to the kind of
caresses they had invented, while the young and coy
faces were seen shyly hanging back on the outer limits
of the circle. He explained, in a word or two, that

among certain tribes it was deemed eminently proper for the grandmothers and elderly squaws to embrace strangers, but it was not permitted to the young girls either to receive or to offer such familiarities.

I forced a smile of feigned pleasure at all the attentions bestowed upon me, and so hid my tremors and my revulsion, but inwardly I wished with all my heart that the younger and prettier women had been detailed as a reception committee. The cunning and crafty looks of the antique ones kept me imagining that knives were hidden in the voluminous folds of their blankets, and that, quick as thought, they might plunge one into us as we stood there defenceless, for General Custer, to inspire confidence in these prisoners, entered the enclosure unarmed.

The old women were most repulsive in their appearance. The hair was thin and wiry, scattering over their shoulders and hanging over their eyes. Their faces were seamed and lined with such furrows as come from the hardest toil, and the most terrible exposure to every kind of weather and hardship, as the roving life took them sometimes to the bleak north, and again as far as the hot suns of Texas. The dull and sunken eyes seemed to be shrivelled like their skins. The ears of these hideous old frights were punctured with holes from the top to the lobe, where rings once hung, but torn out, or so enlarged as they were by years of carrying the weight of heavy brass ornaments, the orifices were now empty, and the ragged look of the skin was repugnant to me.

They wore one garment, cut in the most primitive manner, and over this a blanket, held in at the waist by the rough leather belt into which they had driven as many brass-headed nails as it would hold. As this blanket fell loosely over the belt, they made it a receptacle for every sort of utensil or household article, and were constantly thrusting their hands into its ample folds and bringing forth strange objects. It was at this opening of the garment that I gazed, expecting that each successive article would be the dreaded weapon with which to despatch me.

The bent old witches were curious beyond conception about every object I had on, and with an effort to suppress the terrified start with which I felt my hair being examined at my back, I made an effort to bend my head in politeness while the bird on my hat was fingered. They compared my hair to theirs, laying the two side by side, and generously giving mine the preference. The children were called to admire the military buttons on my habit, as on the plains our riding costumes were much gayer than the regulation habits we wore near or in a city. My hand was imprisoned, and the kid stroked and toyed with, while an inquiry was made, by signs to General Custer, asking what young animal ever wore that soft skin. While they bent over the hand General Custer said to me in a low monotone, for the purpose of teasing by frightening me, "They would admire those gloves, even to the point of possession, should they catch you alone outside the post!" It was all I could do not to snatch my hand away, and run as hard as I could to the exit of the stockade.

Even my feet were not neglected, and comparisons ensued; but they disapproved of my shoes, thinking their soft, pliable moccasins preferable. After all this careful inspection they turned to General Custer and gave their opinion of me, which amused him hugely; but I was denied a translation of their verdict.

Meanwhile the future warriors of the tribe danced around us, yelling and gesticulating like embryo chiefs. They played like other children in racing, catching each other, and scuffling; but their arrow shooting showed how truly the child is father to the man. It was done with the coolest, steadiest-handed, most "nervy" skill of a trained marksman. Even the tiniest, with his one little garment fluttering in the breeze, could handle a bow with the grace and dexterity of the matured boys. The latter were naked save for the cincture about their loins, but still the little girls, burdened with a blanket, belted on like their mothers', could fly over the ground as lightly and swiftly as the bronzed legs that followed them in pursuit. The pappooses came the nearest of anything in that strange place to making me forget my trepidation. Swathed in innumerable bandages wound tightly round the little form, as is the Italian bambino, it was a wonder that the bright, black beads of eyes looked out from the nest as contentedly as they did. If one unaccustomed to children trembles to hold a white infant because the sprawling arms and limbs seem to be dropping off, there is no such difficulty with a pappoose. It is gathered into a little cocoon-like roll that stays where you put it, because the limbs are lashed into absolute quietude. The brown mothers were just as susceptible to flattery concerning their babies as white women are, and understood as readily as if they spoke our language that everything we said was praise. We said, *sotto voce*, "Talk about a universal language, there *is* one, and it is flattery."

There was one little scion of the race in whom we felt extreme interest, because it had been born after the prisoners were taken at the battle of the Washita. Its mother deserves the first word. Her two names, Nav-a-rouc-ta and Mo-nah-se-tah, were so musical that they well became the comely squaw. The latter meant "The grass that shoots in the spring." She was the Princess, the ranking woman among them all, being the daughter of Little Rock, who, since the death of Black Kettle, in the battle of the Washita, was the highest in authority among the Cheyennes. During the winter her intelligence and judgment had been of service in the attempts that had been made to bring the tribes to surrender. When couriers from among the Indians, who had previously given themselves up, had been sent out to their villages to try to induce the others to come in, Mo-nah-se-tah had been consulted and her advice taken. Mah-wis-sa, sister of Black Kettle, had been a powerful ally in endeavoring to bring her tribe to terms of peace, but when she went on a journey to her village her people detained her, sending back the warrior who accompanied her with the messages.

Mo-nah-se-tah could be most useful in examining a trail, and the painstaking of her patient search was something wonderful to watch. The bones of the game killed by the party encamping, the fur or skin of the animals, the ashes of the camp-fire, all the small and apparently unimportant details were suggestions to her. The condition of the marrow in the bones told her the length of time the game had been killed, the ashes yielded up their testimony as to when they had been red with the glow of a camp-fire. Of course the troopers soon learned to trace a trail when ponies' hoofs and lodge-poles had beaten down the grass, but for subtle study of the smaller signs no one could equal an Indian, and above all a squaw, on account of her delicate touch and her untiring patience.

Mo-nah-se-tah had in many other ways made herself of service to the command. She was young and attractive, perfectly contented, and trustful of the white man's promises, and the acknowledged belle among all other Indian maidens. Until a girl is married her life with her tribe is one of ease. The older women wait on her, and no duty or labor is ever exacted. The idle lolling of the young girls about an Indian village is in strange contrast to the untiring industry of the married women. Work of the most exhausting kind becomes their portion after marriage. The game may be shot by the braves, but it is the women who ride out to the hunting-ground, bring back and prepare the animal for use, jerking the meat—that is, cutting it in strips and drying it on poles—and tanning the skin. I never heard of a buffalo-robe being dressed by an Indian man. The women tanned all of them. There is a great amount of work necessary to tan a buffalo-hide. It is, while still pliable, stretched on the ground and tacked down on the edge very closely with small wooden pegs. Then, day after day, the squaw bends over the skin, rubbing it with a very hard bit of stone that is kept for the purpose. When the hide is soft and quite white her lord often sketches his career on the surface. The figures are usually painted in red, blue, and yellow, and the pictorial history consists of the number of Indians at war with the tribe, or the number of white men the invincible has shot. Sometimes a buffalo hunt is added. It is almost invariably the chief's public life that is delineated: domestic detail seems to him too insignificant, and besides, it would elevate the servile squaw to a plane she is never allowed to reach. The hauling of wood and water, the pitching of tepees, the packing of camp equipage, and the braiding and embroidery of the war garments, tobacco-pouches, and gun-cases of the warriors, besides cooking the food and the care of the children, left no idle hour, and so the freshness of youth soon departed from the face of a bride.

Mo-nah-se-tah had not been married long enough to fade and grow old with manual labor. Her one matrimonial venture had not been successful. The Indian women, like the French, have their marriages arranged

INDIAN VILLAGE.

for them by the parents, as a rule. It is true there are elopements, and in some tribes if a brave can get his sweetheart away from the village for twenty-four hours it is equivalent to a marriage ceremony, and opposition ceases when he returns. Most of the unions are wholly practical, however. The young warrior has to show himself to be worth so many ponies or other commodities that constitute wealth with the red man. He buys his wife, in other words. The wife costs all the way from two ponies up. The real road to these dusky maidens' hearts is the reputation the lover bears for deeds of valor. These are never hidden under a bushel, for at every war-dance each warrior airs his record with entirely unblushing egotism. This prowess does not count, however, with the father in the dickering for his daughter.

The daily intercourse of men and women in an Indian family is not as free as in ours. The first son-in-law, the husband of the eldest daughter, takes precedence after the father. Should the latter die, all the questions of the family government are decided by this son-in-law, and no marriage is contracted but by his consent. The laws prevent his speaking to his mother-in-law, or even remaining in the tepee with her if they are alone. A sister and brother cannot speak together. The girls of some tribes are so carefully guarded that their only opportunity for love-making is perhaps when they go for water to the stream. The affection of Indians for their babies is a well-known trait. Even at a solemn council, when

8

General Custer was discussing some subject with them, the talking ceased when a babe far on the outskirts of the log-hut, where the band of Indians were staying near our post, began to cry. The mother, uneasy at the interruption her child had caused, gave it to the squaws near, to pass it on to the father, who was outside. The infant was handed on till it reached the council, the old chiefs each took it, giving it tenderly from one to another, till the father at the door received the little one and stilled its cries. While all this went on there was complete silence. General Custer remained watching the scene quietly, and the interpreter observed the event interestedly, all the Indians and squaws looking on; the council neither spoke nor moved until the pappoose was quieted.

Mo-nah-se-tah found the husband her father had chosen a very distasteful one, and being, I suppose, somewhat spoiled, owing to her exalted rank, she refused to do all the grovelling labor expected of her, and became unmanageable. Neither threats nor warnings moved her, and when her liege attempted to force her to submission she shot him, crippling him for life. There seemed to be no course open for them but divorce, which is such a simple affair among the Indians that the return of the eleven ponies by Little Rock to the irate husband constituted a quitclaim to the possession of his daughter. The birth of her baby after her capture, her high position, and the stories from the Indian scouts of the lofty manner in which she had reminded her husband of her superiority of birth, all

made me anxious to see her; and yet, when the soft
eyes smiled on me, I instantly remembered how they
must have flashed in anger when she suddenly, and to
her husband's surprise, drew the pistol from under her
blanket and did him the greatest injury, next to death,
that can happen to an active warrior. How could I
help feeling that with a swift movement she would
produce a hidden weapon, and by stabbing the wife,
hurt the white chief who had captured her, in what
she believed would be the most cruel way. Her dis-
cernment in taking from her hated husband all that
makes life valuable to an Indian warrior—that is, his
capacity to hunt or to fight—would perhaps make her
keen to discover equally effective means of harming
the foes who had triumphed over her.

But the baby disarmed me. "A little child shall
lead them," and so it did me. Mo-nah-se-tah, when
called, slid away from the outer circle of the crowd
and ran into a tent, dropped the ugly gray Government
blanket and threw about her a red one, coming forward
to us shyly, and modestly hanging her head. Her face
was not pretty in repose, except with the beauty of
youth, whose dimples and curves and rounded out-
lines are always charming. The features of the Indian
women are rarely delicate, high cheek-bones and square
jaw being the prevailing type. Mo-nah-se-tah let the
blanket fall from her glossy hair, her white, even teeth
gleamed as she smiled, and the expression transfigured
her, and made us forget her features. I missed the
paint that the beauties of the village usually lay on

with no sparing hand; for even though it is but a big blotch of color on either cheek, it certainly improves the brown skin. Of course we asked for the baby, feeling unusual interest in a captive born within our lines. Mo-nah-se-tah turned to a bent old crone who had the honor to be grandmother to this rather imperious granddaughter, and authoritatively ordered her to bring the child. It was a cunning little bundle of brown velvet, with the same bright, bead-like eyes as the rest. The mother saw a difference, doubtless. She was full of maternal pride, and ran into the tent again to bring a ferrotype of this young chieftain that had been taken by a travelling photographer who stopped at the post. We were amused and rather surprised at her quick observation, and at the perplexity in her face as she asked with signs why the pappoose was on the left arm in the picture while she had held it in her right when sitting. It was rather difficult for General Custer to explain the photographer's art to this woman, ignorant of any world outside the Indian village, and I think the mystified and superstitious look after he finished meant that she should continue to think as she did at first—that it was the intervention of the Great Spirit which changes a baby in its mother's arms without her knowledge. Though she was so proud and fond of the little creature, she offered it to us to keep until she should return to her people. I presume I should have accepted this somewhat embarrassing gift (from sheer fear of the consequences I dreaded if I declined) had not the other head of the house had the tact to assure the mother that we could not think of robbing her, however sincere her generosity might be.

Mo-nah-se-tah's hair was braided, and this fearless departure from the custom of the Indian women was due to her admiration for the Irish woman to whom reference has been made as having been a cook, and the only woman on the expedition during the previous winter. Another departure from custom was her acceptance of the name our brother Tom gave her. He gave up trying to pronounce the musical sobriquet, and took "'Sallie Ann,' for short," he said. Mo-nah-se-tah had no other feeling but pleasure at the exchange, and she was rarely addressed by any other name. Colonel Tom himself had been rechristened by the Indians, and though Mouksa sounds very well to the ear, the peculiar intonation the officers gave it betrayed a teasing significance, which the translation "Buffalo Calf" may explain.

Mo-nah-se-tah seemed to trust the word of our people from the first. She believed that in time the captives would be released; and, with this trust in the promises of those who had won the victory over her people, she made a most tractable captive; and as she was the highest in authority among the prisoners, her influence had weight with the rest of her people.

CHAPTER VIII.

CORRAL OF THE CAPTIVES.

W<small>HILE</small> we walked about the corral, waiting for the council for which the women clamored, we saw the three chiefs Fat Bear, Dull Knife, and Big Head being prepared for the solemn powwow. They were oiled and combed, the occasional stray hair on their beardless chins plucked out with tweezers—for Indians despise a beard—the vermilion laid on their cheeks, their gaudy beaded and embroidered garments fitted and smoothed upon them, their moccasins and leggings fastened, and the very pipes put into their indolent fingers by the usual valets of Indian warriors, the servile squaws.

The officers constantly made comparisons, and suggested changes in their domestic life in imitation, and roguishly affected to think that while we, as a people, might be in advance of the red man in some forms of civilization, we were not so in all.

Among the squaws that clustered around us was one who began a sign conversation with General Custer about the battle of the Washita. She walked away for a moment, returning with her two sons, striplings of boys, who, she asked General Custer to tell us, had lost their father in the fight. The tears ran down her cheeks as she talked on with her eager fingers, and though answering tears rose in mine, I could not but look at the promise of athletic strength in the children, and wish with all my soul that instead of these embryo warriors she might have had daughters, who would never be reared to go to war. It was strange how these little fellows reproduced their fathers as soon as they could toddle. When any of the hunting parties returned the prisoners had buffalo-meat served to them, and these tiny sons of braves cut strips from the raw meat and ate it, turning with wide-eyed wonder when we exclaimed at this evidence of barbaric tastes.

Among the tailless curs that scurried and skulked in and out of the tents there was a yellow one which was ill, and when our brother Tom came a second time he asked where it was. The squaws pointed nonchalantly to the iron dinner-pot, where the steam was rising from the poor dog's dismembered body, as it was being cooked for dinner. Tom in his quaint way bowed to the old frights, and promptly declined, most urbanely, an invitation to dine that had never been given, and which declination was of course all gibberish to the women.

Among the squaws was one who had holes shot through her blanket in the Washita battle. When we visited the corral she always held out the blanket and pointed to them, making a sound, "ping! ping!" to suggest what had occurred when the bullets went through.

There was another old creature whose little finger had been mutilated, as is the custom of Indians when mourning. She had taken all the flesh from it, and then blackened the bone in commemoration of the dead. The squaws sometimes give away all their clothes, as one manner of showing their grief at the death of one of their family, and another way of mourning is to cut off all their hair. Some of the southern tribes believe that the spirits of horses accompany the spirit of a dead man to the happy hunting-ground. In the death of Colorow, leader of the Meeker massacre, thirty or forty horses were shot by young braves.

Finally the three chiefs were pronounced ready, under the hands of their adorners, and we were signed to enter the tent, where the eager women, who had been all impatience, quickly followed. General Custer told me what an innovation it was to allow me to enter, and what an honor the three chiefs considered they had conferred upon me in shaking my hand; but I could have foregone the distinction, for, in the presence of these gigantic, fierce, and gloomy chiefs, my quakings began anew, and if the council could have taken place with both of us on the other side of the stockade, looking over, no matter how much such a position might have lacked in dignity, I should have been relieved. I took my place on the robe beside General Custer, who sat *à la Turque*, like the Indians. The usual solemn, silent preface to all councils ensued. The restless impatience of women and children, admitted on this rare occasion to a ceremony from which the chiefs usually excluded

them, was exhibited in the eager eyes, and the nest-
ling, nervous moving. A squaw lighted the inevitable
pipe of red clay, with its long wooden stem, at the end
of which beads were cunningly interwoven with the delicate, brilliant feathers of rare birds. The oldest of the
chiefs received it first, took a whiff, then the others followed with a prolonged inhaling of the fragrant kinni-
kinnic and it was passed to General Custer, who heroi-
cally followed the example. Even in this small council of four the Indian rules were rigidly observed, and
the seats were placed on a line from west to east, so that
all should face the south. The pipe is always handed
to the one nearest the east, and follows the course of the
sun, not going back, but being handed across.

Having been treated with so much honor as to be admitted to a council, I inwardly trembled for fear the
honors would not stop there; but, fortunately, the pipe
was kept circulating only among the four. It requires
infinite patience to wait for speech from these taciturn
beings. To be shut up in a Sibley tent with a crowd
of Indians on a warm day was not an experience that
one longed to repeat. Added to the odors and close-
ness, there was still a fire in the ground, in the centre
of the tent, where the squaws had been preparing the
dinner for the conquering heroes they served.

The kinni-kinnic saved our nostrils from what would
have been a still more insufferable infliction. It is a
mixture of willow bark, sumach leaves, sage leaf, and
tobacco, and this is thoroughly mingled with marrow
from buffalo bones.

In vain I buried my rebellious nose in my handker-
chief.   I seemed hopelessly permeated with the peculiar Indian odor, but etiquette forbade my going into
the open air.   When the silent trio at last signified
their willingness to talk, the squaws were reanimated,
for the subject of the conference was their exchange
and return to their village.   The utmost caution was
necessary not to hurt the feelings of the chiefs, and to
signify impatience or haste is, in their estimation, an
insult to them.   Many questions were put to General
Custer.   The replies, from first to last, were that as
soon as every white man, woman, and child was released
from captivity the Indian prisoners should be allowed
to return to their homes.   Grunts of satisfaction, further exchanges of the pipe, more hand-shaking, and we
escaped into the open air.

Our visits were quite frequently repeated.   Eliza, our
colored cook, who was introduced in *Tenting on the
Plains*, has recently given me her recollections of her
first visit with us to the corral.   We took her everywhere that it was possible to take her, in order to vary
the monotony of the life of deprivation she endured
for us, and we were always rewarded by enthusiastic
gratitude ; and her descriptions, afterwards given to
the home people in the States, were more graphic than
any we could furnish.   Here is Eliza's account of her
initiation into the mysteries :

"The ginnel asked me didn't I want to see Ingins.
You know, Miss Libbie, I had never saw one afo'.   I
went in the big gate with the ginnel.   You went up

the steps where the guard was, where you could look down on the whole sixty. Ginnel told them with his fingers who I was, and called me black squaw. Miss Libbie, they had never seen a colored person afo'. They felt of me, rolled up my sleeve to see if I was brown under my dress, they patted me on the shoulder. I went into a tepee, and was looking at how they lived, and at a pappoose that was strapped to a board and lay in a corner as quiet as a mouse.

"Well, to be cunning, the ginnel slipped out when I didn't notice it, and they was making ready to give me a pipe to have me smoke their tobacco, for kind of friendship like, among the old squaws. I looked around and found the ginnel gone, and I took one leap and lit out of thar in a jiffy. The ginnel was watching and laughing at me, and the squaws, when they saw I was so scared, they just shouted. Well, I *was* scared, and I hadn't got no use for them nohow. They clapped their hands and yelled to think the black squaw was so afraid of 'em. Pretty soon they all come right up round the ginnel and began to moan and cry, and move their hands slowly together, and make signs* to know how long it was before they went home to their people — how many moons — and

---

* *Extracts from Clark's Indian Sign Language:* — 1. MOON. *Conception:* Night sun.—Make sign for Night (see 2), and then partially curve the thumb and index of right hand, space of about an inch between tips, closing other fingers; then raise the hand in a direction a little to south of zenith and well up, the plane of the circle formed with index and thumb perpendicular to the line of sight from the eye, through the incomplete circle of thumb and

they made a pretty sign for moon. When the ginnel
made signs, ' right away,' by closing his palms, to tell
them the time was come, they rejoiced. Miss Libbie, I
never did see such hard old women. They looked like
they had been lashed with trouble ; they was bent and
wrinkled, and carrying such loads I don't know how
they did wag themselves along. This was when they
was leaving."

The squaws had some small sense of humor. When,
on one of our visits, an officer whom they knew well
took his wife in to see the prisoners, one of them asked
by a sign if that was his wife. He, being full of fun,
shook his head, and placing two fingers in his mouth,
made the Indian sign for " sister." The squaw carefully scrutinized the wife's face, she trying not to flinch
while the brown fingers passed over the skin ; when

---

index, to the position in the heavens where the moon is supposed
to be.

Some Indians, in making the circle which represents the moon,
use the index fingers and thumbs of both hands.

I have seen a half-month represented by forming a crescent with
thumb and index ; and usually the moon is represented as full,
gibbous, half, and crescent, by indicating such and such a portion
as dead or wiped out.

2. NIGHT. *Conception:* Earth covered over. — Bring extended
hands, backs up, well out in front of body, fingers pointing to front,
right hand very little higher than left, hands about height of breast
and several inches apart ; move the right hand to left, left to right,
turning hands slightly by wrist action so that fingers of right hand
point to left and front, left hand to right and front, terminating
movement when wrists are crossed. Darkness, as I have said,
seems to be considered a material thing by Indians ; it spreads
over the earth like two huge blankets. I have also seen sign made
to denote sun setting for night.

the examination was finished, the squaw made a sign that she knew the statement was not true, and, as she shook her head decisively, a gleam came into her eyes as if of triumph in her keenness of perception.

The buttons of the lady's habit, her whip, with a dog's head on the handle (at sight of which the squaw bow-wowed), and finally the visitor's curls were closely examined, and great curiosity and surprise were evinced when the hair was pulled straight and the curl resumed its form on being released.

After many visits to the corral, which really added greatly to the interest of our life, we came to feel at home with these dusky strangers; and even the woman who at first would only stand by the sentinel and look down, because, as she said, she chose to die some other death than that by disembowelling, summoned courage to enter the tents and look at the ever-interesting, ever-new object to a woman, the pappoose. I at last forgot the knife that at first, in my excited state, I had almost seen gleaming in the folds of the blanket, and we even stood quietly while the bent and odious old squaws crooned and smoothed our faces. The uniform kindness with which these prisoners had been treated had convinced them that the white man meant to keep his word. In the councils that were constantly held, General Custer gave them the news of the negotiations that were going on regarding the delivering up of white captives to our people, and they knew that each event of that kind hastened their release.

One day an orderly from the post rode hurriedly up

to our tent in camp, and dismounting, gave the compliments of the commanding officer of the garrisor, and asked that General Custer should come to the post at once, as the Indian prisoners had made trouble, and no one could understand their desires further than that they kept calling for "Ouchess," meaning "Creeping Panther," a name they had given General Custer some time before. The two miles were soon accomplished, and General Custer found a sorry state of affairs and intense excitement prevailing. The officers in charge explained that as constant rumors were circulated of parties of hostile Indians hovering around the post and the corral, with the intention of rescuing the captives, and as it was feared that the three chiefs were preparing to attempt an escape, it had been thought best to remove the latter from their tent to the guard-house adjoining. The sergeant and guard had gone to them, but being unable to make any signs that the Indians could understand, they had attempted to force them to go into the prison. With the suspiciousness natural to the race, the braves had resisted with all their strength. All the women and children, witnessing the encounter, surrounded the officer, who had joined the soldiers as soon as trouble seemed imminent, and while he and the sergeant and men were trying to make their exit with the three chiefs, a general fight had taken place. The chiefs quickly drew from the folds of their blankets the knives they had been allowed to eat with. These had been surreptitiously sharpened and polished, and they flashed right and left as the braves plunged to and

CAPTURED CHIEFS—FAT BEAR, DULL KNIFE, BIG HEAD—IN TRAVELLING COSTUME.

fro in their struggles. The squaws, similarly armed, threw themselves with wild fury upon the guard. An old squaw singled out the officer in charge, sprang upon him, and plunged her knife down the back of his neck with unerring aim. One of the chiefs leaped upon the sergeant and stabbed and gashed him in so horrible a manner that his life was despaired of. The remainder of the guard came to the rescue, but not before one chief, Big Head, had fallen dead, and another, Dull Knife, was mortally wounded by a bayonet thrust through the body. The third, Fat Bear, was felled by the butt of a musket, but was uninjured. The outside guard, by firing in, had quelled the mutiny among the women. When General Custer reached the corral the excitement was still intense, but he insisted upon entering the stockade alone, and talking with the prisoners. The women were running about, making frantic gestures, angrily and revengefully menacing the guard and the sentinel on his beat. As soon as General Custer appeared they closed around him, asking vehemently if they were all to be shot. He quieted them by his decision of manner, and his assurances that they were now safe, and asked what was the meaning of their violent conduct. They told him that they had asked again and again to have him as interpreter, for when the soldiers had come in to take the chiefs, they could neither understand nor be understood. They had supposed that the braves were being forced out to be hanged, and the special dread of an Indian is to die such a death. General Custer had learned to treat the

Indians with the patience that children require, and he told them, in endeavoring to conciliate and quiet the still agitated women, what the real intention of the guard was, how friendly the men had constantly been up to that time, and that their brusque conduct when resisted was not to be marvelled at, for that soldiers were drilled to quick, peremptory ways. The men had no intention, he assured them, of injuring any one; they only wanted to remove the three chiefs to the inside of the guard-house, and they could not talk with them, not having been out on the campaign the winter before.

This talk had at once a perceptible effect. Some of the older women crouched down to croon and moan over the dead, as is their custom; others walked about wailing and gesticulating in the expressive manner of the Indian. Many of them had gashed their legs horribly, in commemoration of the dead, and their leggings constantly irritated the wounds. One old squaw had been shot in the leg in the *mêlée*, and another exhibited her blanket with bullet-holes in it; but there was not much pity felt among the soldiers, whose lives had been imperilled, for these old viragos, who had fought so furiously.

General Custer went into the cell where the dying chief lay, and explained in the same manner the cause of the misunderstanding and disaster. The old warrior told the general how much they had wished, through all the imprisonment, that they had been confined within the limits of the cavalry camp, among the soldiers who had captured them, and who, during the past winter, had learned to talk with them by signs; he complained that the "Walk-a-heaps," as they called the infantry, who now had them in keeping, did not understand them at all.

After this unfortunate affair there was no more visiting the stockade on the part of the women. The very hands that had smoothed our faces and stroked our hair had too skilfully wielded the knives that we had all the time suspected them of carrying under their garments. They were now more dissatisfied, suspicious, and restless than ever, and when at last the news came that the white captives were released, and that they, in turn, would be sent back to their tribe, there was general rejoicing.

General Custer would not let me miss the departure, which he went up to arrange. The wagons that were to convey the Indians on their way to their village were drawn up in front of the corral when we arrived, and the company of cavalry which was to accompany them as escort stood at their horses' heads, awaiting the trumpet-call "Boots and saddles!" It seemed incredible that people who had come to us with nothing should depart with so much luggage. "All kinds of truck," to use the phrase with which the Western man designates a variety of possessions, was heaped in the big army-wagon by the willing soldiers, and the women and children mounted upon their property. Every one had given them a present—and nothing seemed to come amiss to them—though the donor

9

might be puzzled to imagine how they would ever use the gift.

Finally, Nav-a-rouc-ta walked out of the gate, her pappoose on her back, smiling and shy, and showing some regret at departure, for she had thriven in the idle life. The soldiers and by-standers called, " Good-bye, Sallie Ann," and she turned from the right to the left to receive the homage her sweet face elicited. Behind her, bent almost to the ground with a weight which we could scarcely believe concealed a human being, crept the old grandmother, carrying Mo-nah-se-tah's accumulated wealth. "Sallie Ann" came over to where we waited to say a special good-bye to us, and as she raised her liquid eyes coyly to smile and bid adieu, I could not realize that those same orbs could flash in anger, and the hand we took grow rigid in the madness of revenge; but her maimed husband, now limping through life, was a witness of her capacity for rage.

The old chief walked forth, too dignified to show joy at his release, but no amount of impressiveness of manner could subdue the soldiers and ourselves. Cries pealed out on all sides, " Halloa, Cardigan!" He had been relieved of his own title, Fat Bear, long before, and named for the Cardigan jacket that had been given to him, and that he evidently had never removed from the day of its presentation to the morning of his departure. An underling squaw carried his enormous pack as he stalked towards the wagon, she struggling on in the rear.

The prisoners, forgetting for once their stoicism, laughed and chattered their unintelligible gibberish, poking their heads out of the semicircle that the wagon-covers made at the rear, and went off with many a hearty cheer from their captors. The sentinel, relieved at the completion of the unusual duty, descended from his elevated beat to allow the stockade to be demolished, and with it departed all trace of the Indian captives, save the circles made by their tents in the soil.

CHAPTER IX.

PETS OF THE CAMP.

My first visit to our brother Tom's tent, after we made camp on Big Creek, will not become a dim memory during my life, I think, for I was so thoroughly frightened I shivered for days afterwards when recalling it. Of course, after all our arrangements for the summer were made, we very naturally wanted to exhibit our triumph over circumstances, our ingenuity at inventing conveniences, and to elicit praise from each other for doing so much with so little. Tom was not so proud of his tent as of his captures. At that time we all had many valuable Indian trophies—even Indian shields made of the toughest part of the buffalo-hide, and painted with warlike scenes; necklaces of the fore-claws of the bear; war-bonnets, with the eagle feathers so fastened that they stood out at right angles when worn, and extended from the head to the heels; and, alas for my peace of mind, there seemed to be scalp-locks everywhere! We had a warrior's jacket trimmed with them as fringe, with soft yellow child's hair among the rest. This was presented by an Indian, while some of the officers were offered other trophies in trade.

There was a captured scalp-lock, stretched over a small hoop made of a willow withe to keep it from shrinking, and this was hung to the belt in an Indian dance, or to the te-pee walls while they were not in full dress. Our brother Tom always had an ample collection of these Indian mementos, and it made his tent or quarters in garrison very uncanny, in my estimation. But if the war-bonnet, shield, or bear-claw necklace could be bought or traded for, or captured in an Indian fight, it was like possessing one's self of the family diamonds of an Indian, as these

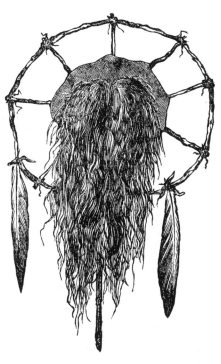

A SCALP-LOCK.

three heirlooms were handed down as we white people bequeath jewels, plate, or pictures.

Colonel Tom's next most valuable possession was a box of rattlesnakes. He was an expert in catching them. Being very agile and extremely quick, he never failed to bag his game. When he discovered a snake with seven or more rattles he leaped from his horse, called his orderly to take off his coat and tie up the end of the sleeve and hold it for the prisoner. Then, with a well-aimed and violent stroke with the butt of the carbine he pinioned the reptile near the head, and holding it down with one hand, seized it by the back of the neck, lifted it from the ground, dropped it into the sleeve, tied it again, and swinging into the saddle, joined the column as unconcerned as if the seven rattles were not threatening vengeance behind him. On my first meeting with him after a campaign he usually said, " Well, old lady, I have some beauties to show you this time, captured them on purpose for you," and I knew that my hour had come. I never passed for a fearless woman, and I did not hesitate to beg off, telling him I " appreciated the honor," but would see the reptiles " some other day," and resorting to any subterfuge to escape this form of hospitality. But I might as well have argued with the snakes themselves for all the good I accomplished. He came after me, and we started; in vain I dawdled by the way to delay the moment that was simply horrible to me; his cheerful "Here we are!" seemed to sound so soon. The insecure cages were patched-up hardtack boxes, and the snakes had to be lifted out to exhibit them.

Tom's bull-dog was always a terror to me, but in this new fright his ominous growls were forgotten. I only begged before the performance began to take up

my place on the bed—and oh, how I bemoaned the low-
ness of it! The agonizing thought was forced upon
me that at that very moment a snake might be lurking under the low camp-cot, or, worse still, wriggling
under the blankets on which my trembling toes then
rested. Then, with skirts gathered about me for a
sudden flight, with protruding eyeballs, I shook and
gasped as the box-lids were removed, and the great
loathsome objects stretched up to show their length,
a chance being given to each one to shake his rattles
in rage.

Words of regret from Tom awoke no answering
emotion in me when he found himself minus one
snake. What was a source of regret to him was an
occasion of horror to me; there was not a vestige of
the snake remaining; it had not escaped; it was a victim of reptile cannibalism, for the larger of the two
had eaten his smaller comrade, and not even a rattle
was left!

After this entertainment was over, and I was going
home, almost frisking with joy, over the plains that
separated us from the soldiers' and officers' tents, I
tried to argue with Tom that he should keep all of his
snakes together instead of in separate boxes; and I contended that this was nothing more than a measure of
justice to them, as they must miss the sort of companionship, a craving for which is said to exist throughout the animal kingdom; but he discovered my mo-
tive, and replied, "If you think, old lady, that after
all the trouble I have been to, to catch these snakes to

show you, I am going to make it easy for them to eat each other up, you are mightily mistaken." Some English tourists were so interested in Tom's daring mode of capture, and the snakes themselves were so novel a sight to them, that they persuaded him to send some specimens to the "Zoo" in London; and last summer I saw one of those who were our guests at that time (Dr. Townsend), and he told me that the snakes were still there. Tom's orderly might appear in this affair as an object of pity, but he was as much interested and as enthusiastic in the sport as his officer, and posed before the soldiers as a snake-catcher—a position not without honor among many daring men, who were willing to meet any sound of war except the threatening rattle of such a foe.

When we were encamped on Big Creek, buffaloes were all about us; the Kansas Pacific Railroad had been completed only to Fort Hays, and the herds were still roaming in immense numbers along the line. They frequently crossed the track in front of a train, but they were so intent upon getting away that the sharpest, most continued shrieks of the whistle did not turn them from their course; the leaders in a move are very faithfully followed by the herd as a rule. The engineer was often obliged to whistle down the brakes to avoid accident.

I remember standing among a group of officers at one time, resting after a charge into a herd. We were on a divide, where the horizon was visible in every direction. One of the group said to me, "Turn about,

Mrs. Custer, and notice that you are surrounded with buffaloes." It was as if the horizon was outlined with a dark rim. The officer continued, "You are looking now upon a hundred thousand buffaloes." I was rather incredulous of their stories when they were told to me, as I had been so often "guyed." I said: "Are you really in earnest? And can I tell this to the people in the East when I go home?" "Honor bright," he said; "I do not exaggerate."

I have been on a train when the black, moving mass of buffaloes before us looked as if it stretched on down to the horizon. Every one went armed in those days, and the car windows and platforms bristled with rifles and pistols, much as if it had been a fortification defended by small-arms instead of cannon.

It was the greatest wonder that more people were not killed, as the wild rush for the windows, and the reckless discharge of rifles and pistols, put every passenger's life in jeopardy. No one interfered or made a protest with those travellers, however. They were the class of men who carry the chip balanced very lightly on the shoulder, and rather seek than avoid its jostling. I could not for the life of me avoid a shudder when a long line of guns leaning on the backs of the seats met my eye as I entered a car. When the sharp shriek of the whistle announced a herd of buffaloes the rifles were snatched, and in the struggle to twist round for a good aim out of the narrow window the barrel or muzzle of the fire-arm passed dangerously near the ear of any scared woman who had the temerity to travel in those tempestuous days. Men are pretty patient with women's tremors if they try to keep them in control, and don't carry their shrieks too far; but when the delay was long enough to empty the car I felt intensely relieved. Sometimes the whole train was abandoned for a time, engineer and all going out for sport. There was no railroad competition then, and only one train a day was run—therefore, there was no attempt to keep a correct schedule. We rarely used the railroad, even if it was near, when once out in camp. Our own mode of travel seemed preferable.

In going on hunts the officers were not obliged to ride far before coming upon herds of grazing buffaloes, and sometimes the animals even came in sight of camp. Once, I remember, we were entertaining a distinguished Eastern journalist. He wanted to return with the record of a Nimrod, but he was too much exhausted from overwork to attempt riding, and he said, with regret, that he feared he would be obliged to go back without seeing a buffalo, and be unmercifully teased by his friends in the States into the bargain. Still he could not endure to lose for an hour the heaven of calm that his tired head enjoyed under the shade of our tarpaulin, where we begged him to lounge all day. Of course his enforced quiet was a boon to us. We plied him with questions as to Eastern progress, for, reading of new inventions put into use since we had come West, we could not quite understand from the newspaper accounts their practical application. I well remember how glad I was out there, when the first Elevated Road

was built in New York, to have it carefully explained
to me; for the papers, after all, take it for granted
that every one lives in the heart of civilization. As
our guest lounged under the shade one day we heard
a shout near, the dogs rushed barking to the stream,
the men ran at breakneck speed in the same direction,
and one of our own people called back, "Buffaloes!"
Here was a chance, for, when this Mohammed could
not go to the mountain, it bore down on him. The
stream was then low, so that with help we could go
over on logs and stepping-stones; and, standing on the
other bank, we saw a splendid chase. The officers, always ready to do what they could to entertain strangers, had driven the herd as near our tent as possible,
and the buffalo singled out to be killed was shot so
near us that we all saw it.

The air of Kansas was so pure that we had no difficulty in keeping meat; but our trial was the rapacity
of the dogs. They always seemed to be caverns, and at
no hour could we eat without being surrounded by a
collection of canines of all ages, which turned up their
large appealing eyes to us, contesting in this pathetic
manner every mouthful we took. In order to save the
buffalo-meat from their tremendous leaps, as they were
great thieves, it had to be strung far up in a tree, and
let down by ropes when the meat for dinner was to be
cut off. By violent "shooing," scolding, and throwing
of sticks at the waiting dogs, Eliza cut what was needed, and swung the rest back to its safe height. We
had then a pet wolf, or rather one that we would have

liked to pet; but the wolf is not an easy animal to tame. One of the soldiers, who was so devoted to General Custer that he would have lain down with a lion for his sake, kept the animal in his tent, and the chain allowed it to walk up and down, but, to my great relief, did not admit of a prowl of any considerable length.

The whole camp seemed like an animated "zoo," and each soldier or officer who owned a prized treasure boasted that his was superior to all others. There were besides wolves, prairie-dogs, raccoons, porcupines, wild-cats, badgers, young antelopes, buffalo-calves, and any number of mongrel dogs. Our wolf Dixie, being near the creek, could send his lonely cries at night over the still prairie on the farther side; and these appealing howls were often answered by other wolves, which we frequently saw in the moonlight, skulking along the bank on the opposite side.

By this time Eliza had been provided with a few chickens, which were the pride of her life; and it would be hard to give the reader a conception of how strange their domestic cackle seemed in that wilderness. Eliza's antipathy to the wolf was made a permanent memory, because her much-loved poultry suffered from his presence. Here is a report of one of her reminiscences touching the wolf and the other animals of the camp: "You know, Miss Libbie, our wolf Dixie. Well, I had to gain the good-will of him before I got up to him, or he would bite me sure if I didn't. He did bite me once, and I learned something from that. One

WARRIOR IN WAR-BONNET.

day I *heered* my chickies a-squalling and a-cackling at a great rate, and all of 'em up a tree. I cast my eyes at Dixie's house and he was gone! Miss Libbie, he had broken his chain, climbed up on some logs and into that tree, and was a-laying out on a limb as nice as ever you see anything in your life, watching chickens, and trying to get his chance to leap and catch one. I took hold of his chain and yanked him down, and Dixie was 'mad with me for two.' He used to chaw up the table-cloths and gnaw the sheets if we left 'em anywhere near him, and he was a terror, and I never could see why the ginnel would keep him. But, Miss Libbie, he wa'n't a showin' to that 'coon we had for long-headed mischief. He'd drag everything he could to the tin wash-basin, and fumble everything in the water, and all I could do the ginnel would just lie there and laugh at him. One day he got the ginnel's money out of his pocket-book, and rolled it into little wads. I ketched him, and I says, 'Ginnel, if you don't kill him *I will;*' but, lor', Miss Libbie, one of them pets was as precious as if it had been a gold-mine. Do you mind that time the 'coon nearly got killed, the time we just had an old colored man as waiter come to us? The 'coon got loose and mounted up on the tent, and the old man hadn't no notion it was a pet, and he licked and cut around there, and was a-pounding the 'coon, when the ginnel came out. Lord sakes, Miss Libbie! the old man cut and run the first word the ginnel said. He just hollered to him like as though he was going to leap through him, just to scare him, for fun, you know.

The old man just sprung to his feet like he was a young sparrow, and run back to him, for he liked him. Ginnel says, 'What are you doing?' 'Killing a 'coon, sah,' says the old man, and then he found out that all 'coons didn't belong to the colored folks. 'Well,' he says, 'if you haven't got anything to do but kill my 'coon, come in and wash my collars,' and then the old man primped up his mouth and went at it. Miss Libbie, I watched his face, and as they cum to pieces he prepared to cut again, for he had never seed paper collars. Some one had given the ginnel a box, thinkin' they would come handy on the march; but when they cum to pieces he just roared and shouted, and the old man found out, after all, that 'twasn't his fault that the collars didn't stay together."

Our tents were usually a menagerie of pets: the soldiers, knowing General Custer's love for them, brought him everything that they could capture. The wolf was the only one of the collection to which I objected. I was afraid of him, and, besides, he kept us, with his nightly howls, surrounded by his fellow-vagrants of the plains. Our own tent opened on the little platform at the rear, and, giving as it did a draught through to the front, made us comfortable during the warmest night. The dogs, of course, ran in and out at will; no one ever thought of repressing them. The best we had was not considered good enough for them. We knew them to be faithful and affectionate, and we kept them about us almost constantly. We knew their step, even, and could distinguish ours from the others

in the camp. One night I was awakened by the peculiar tread of some animal, and woke General Custer.
He said it was a large dun-colored dog from camp that
was roaming coolly from the fly to the platform; but to
make quite sure he rose to investigate, and came back
to take his pistol. This alarmed me, but he soon returned and said there was nothing more to be seen of
the intruder, and I went to sleep. Next morning I
was told that our uninvited guest was a large wolf;
but, thinking that if I knew it, it would effectually
end sleep, General Custer had reserved the information till day.

Harrison, the soldier who so adored his general that
he gladly kept the wolf near him, was a little discouraged one morning, and we learned through Eliza, who
was rewarding him with hot biscuit for perils passed,
that, awaking in the moonlight, he had found a wolf's
head just inside of his tent, and he "reckoned if he
kept Dixie much longer the hull tarnal lot of varmints
would think they'd got to visit him."

It was the only time I knew myself to be in such
proximity to wolves; but the calls of the pet animal,
added to the temptation offered by the odor of the
fresh meat hanging in the tree, made it more than possible that these ugly brutes wandered around our tents
night after night. Our dogs were often off on a predatory excursion of their own, and thus left the way
open for the strangers.

A camp is a very still place at night. Military rule
is so rigid that a soldier is not permitted to leave his

tent after taps without special permission. Of course there is always a daring set of men who do go to the nearest town; but they learn to skulk in shadows, and creep off so silently that the sentinel on his beat, no matter how vigilant, can be easily evaded. In one of the tents within call—that is to say, a loud call—of ours, we had a dear friend who was very plucky. She could fire a revolver, and as the officers added, "hit something, too," which was so significantly said that the dullest of us drew the conclusion that they thought it an impossibility for the rest of us ever to have an accurate aim. These tents, like ours, were near the stream, and domestic life went on there as happily as if the tent had been a palace. These friends were affectionately called the "Smithies"; that is, the husband was called "Fresh" Smith, to distinguish him from the sea captain in our regiment, who was "Salt" Smith, and the wife was Mrs. Smithy. Sometimes the head of the house answered if called "Pilgrim," which appellation, traced out, was found to have reference to the gray clothes he wore when he reported for duty, and also to be connected with some discordant notes he insisted upon singing, which, after much trouble, his jocular companions discovered to be an attempt at the hymn, "I'm a pilgrim and I'm a stranger." He was either musically unequal to the task, or he never was allowed to finish the "Do not detain me." It was an altogether unnecessary request, for no one thought of detaining him if he attempted to sing.

When he reported for duty in camp, before Mrs.

Smith joined him, he was met by our brother Tom, who was cordial and hospitable, as was his wont, urging the new-comer to go to his tent until his own was pitched, and help himself to anything that was needed. Tom, being on duty, could do no more than point out the way. Captain Smith was a brave soldier, as his disabled shoulder proved. After the war he had received an appointment in the regular army as reward for his services, and this was his first appearance on the plains.

The captain did not feel wholly at ease as he approached Colonel Tom's tent. A wolf was chained at the entrance, growling and walking his restless beat, as is the custom of that animal. He knew that it was regarded as a pet, but a wolf is a wolf, and do what you will, the familiar prowling gait of the jackal or panther is kept night and day, and the vicious eye roams from side to side in search of game upon which the beast can make his cowardly spring. Thinking of "Pilgrim's Progress," and the approach to the castle, the young stranger accomplished the entrance successfully, expecting momentarily that the wolf would set his teeth in his unprotected calves, only to be met with threatening growls from under the bed. The red eyes of Brandy, the greatest fighting dog of the regiment, glared at him, and a whole set of molars was lavishly exhibited. While the stranger stood irresolute in the centre of the small tent, the snakes in the boxes set up a rattling that was not to be mistaken for anything else. When Tom came hurrying in from drill, some time

10

after, his guest was prepared for a roar of merriment
at what he supposed was intended as a joke; but, on
the contrary, Tom having been accustomed to strange
room-mates, it had really not occurred to him that
there is always a first time for every one, and so
"Smithy" had passed alone through a part of his initiation.

Smithy was compelled to wait a short time for his
own tent, and Tom entertained him with an exhibition
of his snakes, and stories of the prowess of his dog. In
one of the contests illustrating Brandy's tenacity of
grip our bull-dog—Turk—had figured. So savage had
the dogs become that no ordinary means could separate
them. At last an officer knelt down and bit one of
Brandy's toes with all his might, but he did not relax
his grip in the least; then Colonel Tom seized a carbine, thrust it into the dog's collar, twisted it till Brandy gurgled and choked, and was compelled to drop
"the under dog in the fight." After that, if Tom was
separated from us, he would write, "Brandy sends his
love to Turk, 'his dearest foe;'" and when he came back
it became the study of every one to see that these im-
placable enemies should not meet. When Brandy's
record had been aired to Captain Smith, the history of
the snakes was narrated, and the wolf also had special
attention; but the pitching of his tent gave the new
officer an opportunity to regain the equilibrium that
had been so disturbed on his entrance into the new
life.

The Smiths themselves soon gathered a little collection of pets about them, and even a stupid little prairie-dog was partially tamed by their care. They had in time a buffalo-calf, which soon grew to be as much at home as if it had been a descendant of domesticated animals. Sometimes the soldier who cooked for them thought the calf altogether too familiar when he came galloping down to the cook-tent, knocking the camp-kettles about, butting at everything (the cook included) in the desire to exhibit a pair of growing horns.

The calf knew and was accustomed to officers and their uniforms, but one day one of them appeared in a spotless suit of white duck. It was warm, and the cool clothes were very aggravating to those who had none and were clad in woollen. The guest stroked the calf, petted and played with the apparently innocent animal, not noticing that the bushy little head dropped lower and lower. The spectators knew this ominous sign, but said nothing, trying even to hide the gleam in their eyes. In a flash the owner of the hated white duck was picking himself up from a neighboring mud-pud-dle, while the apparently innocent calf went on graz-ing as if he had not so much as thought of experiment-ing with his embryo horns.

There were animals that were not sought as pets, and naturally the "prairie dandy" was one. We were made aware that these animals were around us, for the dogs, in their zeal for game, made no distinction. After a successful chase of the polecat by themselves, they came bounding back to us in a most triumphant man-ner, sure of a welcome, and prepared to get on the bed, under it, in the camp-chairs, on my lap, anywhere they could be sure was the best and easiest place. Their look was full of surprise and reproach when all their friends started hurriedly to their feet, seized sticks, chairs, anything to hurl at them, shouting wildly, " Get out ! get out, you brutes !" while only that morning we had exhausted the vocabulary and coined words to tell them what darlings they were. Of course, followed by every available missile, they beat a retreat, but not for any great distance. Perfectly unconscious why they were not as acceptable at night as in the morning, they sat in a grieving semicircle some distance out in front of the tent, and reproved us by pitiful inquiring whines, by short interrogatory barks, by wagging tails and sinuous bodies, trying by their expressive motions to argue us out of our hard-heartedness.

There was another enemy that we did not cultivate living along the stream. We had a little cellar that the soldiers had dug in the side bank, making a roof of logs, and covering all with earth ; a rude door was cobbled out of drift-wood planks—for if you wait long enough on a Kansas stream you can almost count on any houses, fences, or household utensils you need being washed down to you, if there are any settlements above, so violent are the freshets. This cellar, being the first we had ever had, was a great possession to us, and we proceeded to get supplies from the commissary in some quantities, instead of, as usual, sending daily for enough to last twenty-four hours. The cellar was pronounced a grand success until it began to empty with such ra-

pidity that we mildly asked Eliza if we had not better
order the whole Commissary Department down at once.
We even lost some supplies for which we had been ex-
travagant enough to send to St. Louis.

Eliza says : " I used to hear a crawling near my tent.
There was an old fallen tree near, and the creeping
and crawling and sneaking 'peared to be right there.
I thought it was a snake. I just kept missing my things
out of the cellar right along. I was afraid to report
it, 'cause I was afraid it was somebody stealing. Finally I told the ginnel my potatoes was agoing so fast I
didn't know what was the cause of it. You know,
Miss Libbie, he was always a-teasing me, 'cause, he said,
I fed so many; so he says: ' I know the cause of it. Just
as like as not there's an orphan asylum started again
near my tent.' Next morning I had everything ready
to cook breakfast, and was running up the hill to wake
you and the ginnel. As I was a-passing that old hollow
tree I saw the biggest rat I ever did see, a-looking at
me as sassy as ever you saw anything. Well, I didn't
think it was a rat. I ran on to the tent and said, ' Ginnel, get right up and see the biggest rat you ever *did*
see.' He says, ' Rat! where ? who ever heard tell of rats
in the timber ?' But he jumped up and dressed, and
come down. Oh, my sakes, Miss Libbie! thar the rat
lay, with his paws sticking out, ready to run out of the
tree again. Well, he had carried out a load that night,
but he had lugged out a loaf of bread, and got stuck
on that, for he couldn't tug it into his den. The officers all come up, and every one had a shoot at it, but

the rat ran in, and they had to split open the tree before they could get at him. Everything* got together to have a look at him after he was killed, for he was a foot and a half long. He had in that old tree two buckets of potatoes, two candles, and a box of matches (the ginnel said he was fixing to get supper), a package of chocolate, beans, and lots of other things, as he was laying by stores for winter."

It was not pleasant to feel that we had such loathsome neighbors, but after I saw the rat I never felt sure that one like it would not dart through the tent, and every strange sound was attributed to them. But no such daring trespasser was found again on our doorstep almost—that is to say, what would have been a door-step if we had possessed a door.

---

* Eliza's expression "everything" meant everything human in camp—officers, soldiers, quartermasters, quartermaster's employés, and servants.

Stable Call.

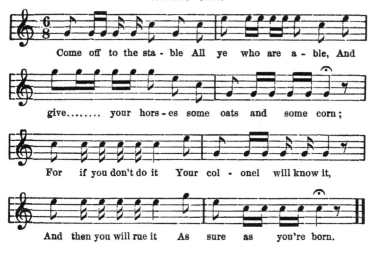

Come off to the sta - ble All ye who are a - ble, And
give........ your hors - es some oats and some corn;
For if you don't do it Your col - onel will know it,
And then you will rue it As sure as you're born.

CHAPTER X.

A SLOW MULE-RACE.

THE dislike I always had for horse-racing was somewhat abated when I learned, after my marriage, how
different an affair it is when conducted by gentlemen.
There were none of the usual obnoxious features of a
course. The officers rode their own horses; there was
no pool-selling; all the sport was within the Government reservation, or near camp, where no rough characters were admitted. We women were always expected to be present, and the rest of the spectators were the
soldiers, who rejoiced in an opportunity to vary their
dull lives, and though deprived of the privilege of
backing their captains or lieutenants with money, they

made up with boasts and applause. The officers, kept
down to a light weight by their active life, and learning to a nicety how to sit on their horses so as to favor
them as to weight, often got as much out of them as a
jockey could have done. We women felt that we would
gladly sacrifice the few seconds of time that a lighter
weight might make, to be permitted to look upon the
easy grace and fine physique of a gentleman as rider
instead of the wizened little monkey that the professional jockey seems when mounted.

The Seventh Cavalry spent several winters at Fort
Leavenworth, where there were comfortable quarters,
and the city, a few miles distant, offered a great variety
of privileges to men who were most of the year in the
field. There was a track on the reservation, where our
horses were timed, and many happy hours were spent
glorying in the speed, the beauty, the endurance of the
animals we owned. The track was on the side farthest
from the town, and perfectly retired. There was a
little stand for the group of ladies who accompanied
their husbands or their lovers, for there was much
sweethearting at that delightful post, and the joyous
cavalcade riding over the pretty road to the track made
music with their voices and happy laughter.

We had at one time sixteen horses ridden by their
owners at a hurdle-race, which was arranged only for
ourselves. The prizes were gold spurs and a silver-
mounted riding - whip. If our officers were not all
handsome, one was deceived into thinking they were,
for the brilliant eyes, the glow of health, the proud

carriage of the head, which is a soldier's characteristic, and, above all, the symmetry of their well-developed figures, gave one the impression that there was little to be desired in the general make-up of the men. These gentlemen riders were in gay jockey costumes, and the bright colors were reflected by knots of ribbon, or the scarfs about the pretty throats of the admiring women who looked on. The track was lined for some distance with the blue blouses of the excited soldiers, who were allowed to come *en masse*. It was decidedly a home-party, but none the less enthusiastic on that account.

The first hurdle was taken almost simultaneously by the sixteen riders, and as they vaulted into air rider and horse exhibited alike the greatest joy, and scarcely seemed to touch the earth before they shot off for another hurdle. All that wretched feeling of anxiety one experiences in looking on the set features and wild-eyed frenzy of the professional jockey, and on the absorbed, strained gaze of the by-standers when large sums are at stake on a regular race-course, was left out of our races. When money comes in, it is, to say the least, a disturbing element, and real sport can be had where gain is not in question. The familiar phrase which describes horse and rider as one is most perfectly justified when officers and soldiers ride thus in friendly rivalry. They not only sit the horse as if they really were centaurs, but the sympathy that exists between the animal and his master, after years of daily association, becomes almost human.

The officers spoke of the humor their horses were in as married people refer to the peculiar state of mind the circumstances or the day produces. For instance, riding beside us, they said: "I don't find Lulie or Peggy" (or whatever the name happened to be), "in first-rate humor this morning. I shall leave her to herself a while till she gets over her sulks;" or another would ask permission to leave the ranks, and the rest, looking after him, would say: "There goes —— to fight it out with his stubborn old brute of a Nero;" and after a while the subdued horse, carrying his triumphant master, returned to his place. Some one else, perhaps, observed: "My horse is teasing for a run, and bother it all, here we are, sandwiched in between the old jog-trotters at four miles an hour!"

Of course, when our men came to put their horses to their mettle, as in a race, they knew how to get their best out of them. They leaned forward, to throw their weight from the back as much as possible, and with their faces down almost on their horses' necks, they knew pet phrases and encouraging words that were secrets between master and beast, having been learned on many a lonely ride over the plains; and hearing these murmured in the sensitive ear, the animal instantly responded by increased effort.

Our hurdle-race ended suddenly by an accident to one of the officers. We resolved to discourage hurdle-jumping after that, when we saw the handsome head of one of our best riders in the dust. The group gathering round him, two of the riders returning, the soldiers carrying the insensible officer to an ambulance, made a sad and anxious spectacle for the little group of women, off by themselves, especially for each one who feared that the wounded man might prove to be her husband; it proved to be a bachelor officer instead. The horse, faltering, had rolled over him; but the breaking of an arm and a rib or two were light afflictions to him, and he was soon himself, making light of his accident, regretting with all his heart that he had proved a " spoil sport." The two riders who gave up their race to return to their fallen comrade lost their opportunity to win the prizes, and one of them, the best rider in the regiment, had every prospect of triumph when, with rare self-denial, he abandoned the contest to care for his friend.

While we were at Fort Leavenworth there was a mule-race arranged to be run on our track, and the preparations were most elaborate; hearing the arrangements so much talked of and studied over, we could scarcely wait for the day. A purse of fifty dollars was made up for the prizes. In the first place, the women were all tranquil in their minds. There would be no lofty leaps over dangerous hurdles, for reasons that the mule could offer; and as one of the conditions was that the slowest animal was to win, even the most timid woman need not dread reckless speed. The Government sent out from Fort Leavenworth, then the headquarters of the division, great trains of supplies for the far-distant posts; consequently there were many mules always in the quartermaster's corral. And they were not only many in number, but various in character, from the skittish little leaders to the ponderous wheelers. The latter were no one knows how old; they were stiff and lumbering, and their tough old sides seared and hairless, in long welts, where the harness had worn into the flesh in many a pull through sand or muddy river-bottom, or up the steep banks of streams.

It was over these antiques that the officers lingered. They sought out the dullest and the laziest, and were assured by the teamsters, when asking about their powers of lagging, that if it was laziness they were looking for, "that 'ere brute could beat the record." Poor, down-trodden animals, working all their dull lives in heavy harness, never in all their days so much as asked to go out of a walk, now suddenly to be launched upon the world as racers! Each officer, after his selection from the corral, had his mule conveyed to his own stable, and there in privacy he practised the art, new to all of them, of mounting mule-back. The animal, always taught to think that his mission in this world was to writhe and struggle through life under harness, had to be made acquainted little by little with a saddle. It was a long and dangerous instruction.

The mule General Custer selected never submitted to the discipline until the most marvellous harness was invented by the would-be rider, which so bound in every muscle, and subdued every kicking heel, that at last the saddle could be adjusted. General Custer, always brimming over with fun, had determined to add to the amusement of the day by selecting the animal that the entire quartermaster's department declared to be the most obstreperous. His record as a kicker was well known. Eliza described the mules that hauled our travelling-wagon along a quiet road as "the stupidest, stubbornest, most con*tra*ry animals ever I did see," and here was one that was renowned for being the most "con*tra*ry" of all that were used in the department.

The harness prepared extended from the tips of the mule's ears to the last hairs on the tail. There were huge blinders, consisting of a strap over his ears and broadening over the face like a mask. The whole body was a net-work of straps of leather, which bound the rebellious animal from head to foot. Even with the mask down, the orderly had to throw his coat over the entire head while General Custer leaped with the quickness of a cat into the saddle. The officers had heard something of the history of this mule from the quartermaster's employés, and when the time came for each officer to give up his mule and take another—for it was the rule that no one should ride his own animal— the one to whom the famous kicker fell was somewhat doubtful whether he might not be prevented by the animal from joining in the race at all. When General Custer, incited by the spirit of mischief, which was uppermost in a frolic, insisted upon taking his newly invented harness as well as his saddle to put on the mule he had drawn, there was a wild uproar and a general protest.

The thirteen gentlemen did not look like gentlemen,

for all, catching the spirit of the occasion, were attired in peculiar costumes, each flying a color or colors that were as infelicitous as the beasts they had selected. One of the young men was an object of ridicule because of his bald head. For some strange reason his hair had dropped out, and his head looked like a billiard ball. The fine curly wig, the *chef-d'œuvre* of the town barber, was wisely left at home, as there was a not unfounded idea that the kicking would almost dislodge well-rooted hair, to say nothing of wigs. The courage of this officer in appearing in so ridiculous a plight ought to have insured him immunity from the laughing taunts of his fellows; but for fear he should be assailed, he prepared his revenge in advance, and had his mule carefully covered with a thick coat of white paint; while the discussions preliminary to the race went on he rode unconcernedly among the riders, jostling every one, until he had left so much of the paint on his comrades that the mule's hide was quite visible again. Spurring their animals to get out of his way only put them in more fiendish temper, and the bucking, backing, and kicking were general.

It was plain that each mule was determined to protest against taking the track, and each objected in his own particular fashion. From the ladies' stand it looked like a conglomeration of hoofs, tails, fluttering ribbons, and flying coat-tails, legs vigorously digging spurs into ribs, arms swinging, whips waving, and every one talking at once, but not drowning the braying of the outraged animals.

A programme was prepared, in which some names were inserted that may not be understood, unless it is known that hardtack was issued by the commissary. "Eaton" was the name of the quartermaster who gave out the contracts; and "Card" was the name of another quartermaster, who had charge of the wagon train, muleteers, etc. The programme ran as follows :

UNITED STATES 🅾️ COURSE.

Fort Leavenworth, Kansas.

JUNE MEETING,

TUESDAY, JUNE 16th, 1868, 4 P.M.

MULE-RACE!

OFFICERS' PURSE - - - - - - - - - - $50

ONE—MILE DASH —— SLOW RACE.

1. General Custer enters Hyankedank, by Hifalutin, out of Snollygoster, second dam Buckjump, by Thunder, out of You Bet. Age, threescore years and ten. Colors, ring-ed, streak-ed, and strip-ed.

2. General McKeever enters Hard Tack, by Commissary, by Eaton (eatin'), second dam Contractor, by Morgan, out of Missouri. Age, forty years. Colors, purple, tipped with orange.

3. Colonel Parsons enters Symmetry (see me try), by Considerably, out of Pocket, second dam Polly Tix, by Nasby, out of Office. Age, seventeen years. Colors, uncommonly blue.

4. Captain Yates enters William Tell, by Switzerland, by Apple Tree, second dam Gessler, by Hapsburg, out of Austria. Age, eighteen years. Colors, apple green.

5. Lieutenant Leary enters Trump, by Card, out of Contractor, second dam Leader, by Mule-Teer, out of Wagon. Age, ten years. Colors, lemon.

6. Lieutenant Jackson enters Abyssinia, by Napier, out of Africa, dam Theodorus, by Solomon, out of Magdala. Age, thirty-nine years. Colors, scarlet, yellow spots.

7. Colonel Myers enters Pizzarro, by Peru, out of South America, second dam Cuzco, by Incas, out of Andes. Age, sixteen years. Colors, light brown.

8. Lieutenant Umbstaetter enters Skirmisher, by Picket, out of Camp, second dam Carbine, by Breech Loader, out of Magazine. Age, twenty-five years. Colors, dark blue, tipped with red.

9. Lieutenant Moylan enters Break-Neck, by Runaway, out of Wouldn't Go, second dam Contusion, by Collision, out of Accident. Age, fifty-six. Colors, sky blue.

10. Captain Huntington, enters Spavin, by Quartermaster, out of Government, second dam (not worth one). Age, twenty-one years. Colors, a-knock-to-ruin (an octoroon).

11. Lieutenant Howe enters Slow, by Tardy, out of Late, second dam Lazy, by Inactive. Age, three times 6, four times seven, twenty-eight and 11. Colors, queer.

12. Lieutenant Dunwoody enters Horatio, by Dexterity, by Taunt, second dam Estop. Age, fourteen years. Colors, tawney.

13. Captain Weir enters Revolutionist, by Hard Luck, out of Rib Smasher, second dam Blood Blister, by Can't-Stand-it, out of Let's Quit. Age, sixteen. Colors, black-and-blue.

Note.—The money accruing from this race is to be devoted to the support of the widows and orphans made so thereby.

If there is a reporter more energetic than another it is the Western man. The enterprise that drives him

West furnishes plenty of perseverance to penetrate wherever there promises to be novelty. The mule-race was unique, and the Leavenworth newspaper proved that there was a "chiel amang us takin' notes," which was, in reality, very easy to do, as the soldier, though he is silent on duty, cannot be muzzled when he gets furlough to go into town. The personal references in the following newspaper article were to officers who were either very large, very staid, or extremely quiet, and in one or two instances no longer young, which made the allusions extremely funny to us who knew them. The sensational exaggeration of Western journalism is sometimes got up to order now, in expectation of the instant appropriation of the wit by exchanges; but at that time it was spontaneous, and reflected the every-day habits of speech in the West:

THE GREAT SLOW MULE-RACE TO-DAY.

A FEAST OF REASON AND A FLOW OF SOUL.

INTENSE EXCITEMENT — THRILLING TIMES AHEAD.

Cato, a distinguished old grumbler, who resided somewhere some centuries ago, it is said, rebuked a good rider at a steeple-chase by telling him that his skill and ability were thrown away. Cato owed his publisher, hence Cato was sour and down on racing.

Gentle reader—that is to say, girls and boys—were you ever at a mule-race—a *slow* mule-race—a mule-race with Sheridan and Card and Gibbs and McNutt and Mills? If not, we advise you to go this afternoon.

11

THE RACE.

Every commissioned officer at this post has either to ride at the race this afternoon or pay a forfeit of five dollars. As money is scarce, and times tough at present, nearly all the officers will ride. At the call of time each rider is to mount his own mule, and parade before the judge's stand to show that he is not afraid. The judge then gives the order to dismount and "swap mules." At this command every rider mounts a strange mule—no one being allowed to ride his own. Then, at a signal, all start, each riding his darndest, and the mule that comes in *last* wins the race.

"SHERIDAN'S RIDE."

With feelings of deep regret we announce that the major-general commanding will not ride. This may be relied on as positive. He has paid his forfeit. He had bought him a little bob-tailed, blue, mouse-colored mule, and was training him like Sam Hill, when an idea struck him, to wit, that there were poets in Kansas. Suppose, thought he, that one of these fellows should get off a strain called "Sheridan's Mule-ride!" The thought sickened him, and, as aforesaid, he paid his forfeit. Buchanan Reid came near ruining Sheridan. After Jim Murdock first spouted the poem, every little girl and boy, every tough old maid, every big-paunched parson, every lawyer, every doctor, and everybody just *rode* Sheridan, until, from sheer exhaustion, he asked to be sent to the Indian country.

GIBBS WILL RIDE.

The gallant general commanding the post will ride—feather-weight. The general is said to be an accomplished mulist. General McNutt will also ride his trained mule Calamity, said to be one of the slowest mules in the department.

Card and Morgan have paired off, and paid their forfeits

like men. Both were raised on mules, as it were, and have ridden them from infancy, but the responsibilities weighing upon them were too great, and they were reluctantly forced to forego.

Dr. Mills won't ride, as he expects to be on hand to attend the wounded. He paid his forfeit like a Muncie chief. Dr. Brewer will be there, however, with his black-and-tan mule, Esculapius, and expects to get round if they will give him time enough.

The gallant Yates, with his massive three-deck jackass, proposes to go through on his own quarter-deck.

Both the Forsyths will appear above the horizon, and be visible to the naked eye, on gorgeous mules. Three friends are backing them against the field.

The chivalrous Parsons and the fiery Custer are practising on two mules. We saw them the other evening " rehearsing " in a ten-acre field, to the tune of " Benny Havens."* They propose to cross the last ditch, and as they are politeness itself, each will insist on crossing last.

The magnificent band from the Fort will be on hand to discourse sweet music. Boys, you'd better go and take the girls. These mule-races are fine places to study human nature. Every jackass, properly observed, contains a sermon— or perhaps two. Else why did Goldsmith write of the Vicar of Bray ?†

When McKeever rides everybody should be on hand. Talk of John Gilpin or Israel Putnam! They are nothing to McKeever on a graphic mule. McKeever's friends are taking odds on him. Boys, go!

When the race finally began each officer forgot personal appearance, ignored the ridiculous position into

---

* The West Point tune.

† The reporter's information concerning classic English literature seems to have needed some refreshing.

which he had put himself, and bent every energy of his body and mind to getting over that mile of earth. It was as ridiculous a sight as is not often seen. Men who prided themselves on having a perfect seat in the saddle, now doubled up in a heap, dug their knees into the animals' sides, and shouted as they tried to get the "dumb, driven" creatures into a gallop. Imagine how surprised the mules must have been to be lashed into a lumbering run! The officers' legs and arms were flying, the mules' long ears flopping in indignation, while their tails flew up in angry protest at every cut of the whip. These queer tails were shaved according to the fancy of the teamsters, only one little tuft usually being left on the end, like a lion's brush, while in some cases two rings of hair were spared at stated intervals to vary the plain surface. Whether tufted or plain, the animated tails expressed the mules' idea of the situation most graphically.

As each officer came straggling in by the judge's stand, quite done up with fatigue from his exertions in chastising his animal, he was greeted with applause; but when, after fifteen minutes, the last one entered, fagged and heated with the whacking he had administered to the unconscious and indifferent winner of the prize, all the company lifted up their voices in cries of excited merriment, while the beast that had won on his demerits and not on his gifts, if he had any, declined even to look around, but hung his dejected head and drooped his wide ears, and allowed the anger to depart from the much tufted and trimmed appendage, while he was decked with a gaudy ribbon as an emblem of victory.

Then our gay afternoon ended, and every one mounted spirited horses and started for home. First came the officers, eagerly talking over the race to the women who rode by their sides; then all the orderlies, riding at the regulation distance in the rear, disputing quietly, for fear of reprimand, over their especial views of the afternoon sport; while a crowd of vociferous, jolly soldiers, too far back to be heard and brought to order, laughed and shouted and rehearsed the events of the day in eager, buoyant tones, as pleased over the droll affair as if they had taken part in it, and each one boasted over the doings of the officer he especially liked, as if a vast sum of money and the reputation of thoroughbreds had been at stake.

The dews of evening were falling, and as our way for a time led through the rich bottom-land of the river, the flowers and the blossoms of the wild grape loaded the air with fragrance. It is seldom that so light-hearted and joyous a company of people is gathered together. They were light in pocket, it is true, but rich in health, in the keenest capability for enjoyment, in blessed fellowship for each other. Take envy out of a character and it leaves great possibility for friendship. Every one was so nearly even in the distribution of this world's goods and its gifts that there was little chance for that covetousness which eats like a canker.

If we had gone out with full purses, and had returned

with them empty, after the fashion of the race-course, the laugh would not have been so ringing, or the sound of merriment in the voices so free and fun-provoking. Delighting in contrasts, we drew pictures of the now distinguished - looking men as they had appeared in their grotesque attitudes and ridiculous energy over the " cattle " they had urged on to victory. The cavalcade was now something to rejoice in, and as the long line of horsemen wound through the wood and along the country road, the days of knight-errantry might seem, in the dim twilight, to have returned again in this nineteenth century.

Rogue's March.

Poor old sol - dier, Poor old sol - dier, He'll be tarred and feathered and sent to h—l, Be - cause he would - n't sol - dier well.

CHAPTER XI.

TALES OF SOLDIERS' DEVOTION AND DROLLERY.

By one of the changes that are constantly occurring in the line of duty, our brother Tom lost his tent-mate. There was no use in lamenting this apparently small circumstance, but still we could not help doing so, as the two had great comfort out of the intimate companionship; but there was another, and a ludicrous aspect of the change. Colonel Tom's tent-mate was afraid of snakes, and had good reason to be, as is subsequently explained. He had used Tom as a barricade on one side of the mattress spread on the ground, while the combined outfit of the two was heaped upon the other, as if it had all belonged to the younger officer, and thus he slept. This great, splendid fellow Tom, groaning over the exposed position he was destined to occupy alone in his tent, was an amusing sight; but his anxieties were very real, and nothing was too small in the way of a grievance for all of us to enter into it sympathetically in that circumscribed life. As the officer moving sat with us his man, an old Irish soldier named Hughes, kept travelling by carrying the "traps" of his lieutenant. Presently Tom cried out to the soldier: "See here, Hughes, it seems to me you're making a good many journeys, considering the condition of your lieutenant's wardrobe," and out he went to overhaul the load. Hughes, to reconcile his officer to leaving his tent-mate, and to supply some long-felt wants in the improvident lieutenant's outfit, had quietly extracted some of Tom's best things. When Tom came back with a bundle, of which he had relieved Hughes, he found even his tooth-brush and sponge in the parcel, and the laughing lieutenant, shaking with fun at Tom's indignation, said, calmly : "Hughes is so provident I never seem to need anything; I never ask how it happens that my holey socks are replaced by good ones, and my ragged underclothing in a single night comes out whole, if I happen to have a guest, but I do draw the line at a second-hand supply of tooth-brushes and sponges. There are limits even to friendship, and those two commodities I prefer shall be new."

It is, and has been for all time, a characteristic of army servants that however immaculate their honesty may be where they themselves are concerned (and they can be trusted with everything), they relax when it comes to setting up the officer they serve with what they think a suitable outfit.

Once at Winchester, during the war, we entertained General Sheridan and his staff. It was a cold night, and the officers did not all take an orderly, as is their custom, not liking to expose the men to the bitter air. While we were welcoming and entertaining our guests in the old Virginia house used as headquarters, our men in the stable were doing the same with the orderlies. As the pipes went round, and the canteen of whiskey was tipped, one soldier, conspiring with his comrades, slipped out of the circle and replaced all the shining bridles, and some of the fresh saddle-cloths and stirrups, with our well-worn property. In the dark, and in the excitement of departure, these changes were not noticed; but next morning a friendly note came with very pointed remarks about the cavalry thief being the most unscrupulous and adroit in the service, and the first that General Custer knew of the "lifting" was the announcement that General Sheridan made. No one could help laughing, however, at the shameless audacity of our men, who thought a major-general's outfit just as available for looting purposes as that of a second lieutenant, when the replenishing of their own officers' outfit was in question.

The devotion of the soldiers to their officers was so great that they were capable of such self-sacrifice as is seldom known outside of the army. They kept the purse sometimes, and when their spendthrift master demanded money, if he happened to be not quite himself, the faithful soldier refused to give it, or declared that it was all gone; but afterwards, when the mess bill was to be paid, the necessary funds were forthcoming.

I remember that General Custer and I were paying a visit at the tent of an Irish officer who had turned himself over to his man for safe-keeping. Literally, he had given himself up to be directed as Finnigan willed —not, of course, in official affairs, but in every-day doings. He even enjoyed declaring that he had no further responsibility in life. Finnigan kept track of his purse, his clothes, his outfit, his debts. He did not know where anything was, and he did not propose to inquire. Wishing to show us some decorations he had received in foreign service, he called to his man. Finnigan, clean, respectful, unspoiled by the familiarity and dependence of his master, produced the orders from his own little " A " tent at the rear. This captain, proud as Finnigan was of him, sometimes became so hopelessly boozy, the man concluded that the safest place for the valuables and the family funds was in his own quarters. As we held these precious possessions, admiring their beauty, and drawing their owner out to tell us of the field on which they were won, the subject turned upon the Pope. Finnigan visibly swelled with pride to think his master had once been in the service of that magnate. His straight back became straighter, and his expressive face spoke volumes. I sometimes thought the enforced silence of a soldier taught him to use his body as well as his face in expressing thought, and made them both take the place of speech. Suddenly

there was a limp look about him, his military spinal
column seemed to have hollowed out and to droop, and
his face looked reproof and disapproval. In trying to
account for this change I attributed it to the conversation. It was, if I am not mistaken, the summer when
the doctrine of the infallibility of the Pope was agitated.
The captain was a Romanist, but not an ultra one, and
Finnigan had looked remonstrance when the laughing
officer said to us, "Why, I have had so many notices of
excommunication I feel strange if I waken and don't
find one waiting for me every morning now."

The wit among these men was fully appreciated by
all of us, and very clever remarks filtered through the
kitchen which we never would have heard otherwise.
If an old soldier was addressed by an officer he replied
as briefly as possible, in obedience to the instructions of
his sergeant. Consequently, they habitually condensed
their replies, having so little chance at speech with the
officers, and no one tried to keep a straight face when
some of the Irishmen made answer. The higher the
rank the more the officer spoke with his men, those of
higher grade having reached that point in exaltation
where silence was not necessary to compel respect, as
in the case of the raw lieutenant. A ranking officer of
the Seventh said to an old soldier who was married to a
camp woman, and had lately been presented with twins,
"Well, Scott, I hear you've got a couple of recruits at
your quarters." A most pompous military salute was
given, accompanied by a pleased grin, and the reply,
"No, sir, a recruit and a laundress."

The mistakes of the raw recruits came around also by way of the kitchen tent to us, and afforded us many a laugh. For instance, a company drawn up in line is the severest type of exactitude. Each soldier stands like a statue, and if he does bend out in front, or his shoulders stoop the least bit, the sergeant claps the back of his sabre on the offending outline, and it straightens in a twinkling. The men, drilled to this immobility, stand without swaying while the roll is called. A certain sergeant, who had been promoted from the ranks of recruits for soldierly conduct, had not yet learned to distinguish accurately between official and social affairs. He seemed to think domestic as well as military news must be officially set forth, and on one occasion he reported his company "present, or accounted for," and, without pausing to take breath, continued, "Mulligan's baby's dead, sir."

Another incident illustrative of army life may be mentioned. An infantry officer was calling on a cavalry general, and they fell to discussing the discipline of the two arms of the service, each claiming for his own corps the more advanced state of military perfection. While they conversed a cavalry orderly brought a despatch, and before he could dismount his horse stumbled and threw him over his head, landing him in front of the officers. In an instant the man was on his feet, and saluting, he handed the paper to his officer with undisturbed face. The infantry officer was astonished at this quick recovery, and prompt compliance with military etiquette; but turning to his companion, he met a perfectly immobile countenance, as, with a wave of the hand, the cavalry commander said, "That's the way they always report."

In military life it is rather difficult to approach the commanding officer, for were it not so the men would run to him, like a lot of school-boys, with every trifling complaint. The soldier is therefore required to speak to his sergeant, he in turn to his captain, and the latter gives permission to the enlisted man to carry his request or complaint in person, if it proves to be of sufficient consequence. Rather an elderly man had come on as recruit, and he, not knowing the " divinity that doth hedge " a commanding officer, said to his troop commander, "See here, cap'n, where's the old man? I want to have a talk with him." After that General Custer went by the name of " the Old Man " among his brother officers when off duty.

The town of Hays City, near us, was a typical Western place. The railroad having but just reached there, the " roughs," who fly before civilization, had not yet taken their departure. There was hardly a building worthy of the name, except the station-house. A considerable part of the place was built of rude frames covered with canvas; the shanties were made up of slabs, bits of drift-wood, and logs, and sometimes the roofs were covered with tin that had once been fruit or vegetable cans, now flattened out. A smoke rising from the surface of the street might arrest your attention, but it indicated only an underground addition to some small " shack," built on the surface of the earth.

The carousing and lawlessness of Hays City were incessant. Pistol-shots were heard so often it seemed a perpetual Fourth of July, only without the harmlessness of that pyrotechnic holiday. The aim of a border ruffian is so accurate that a shot was pretty certain to mean a death, or, at least, a serious wound for some one. As we sat under our fly in camp, where all was order, and where harmony reigned, the report of pistol-shots came over the intervening plains to startle us. The officers, always teasing, as is so apt to be the case with those who are overflowing with animal spirits, would solemnly say to us, "There goes a man to his long home;" and this producing the shudder in me that was expected, they elicited more shivering and sorrowful ejaculations by adding, as the shots went on, "Now, there goes a woman; two were shot last night." Our men knew so much of the worthlessness of these outlaw lives that it was difficult to arouse pity in them for either a man's or a woman's death in the border towns.

It was at Hays City that the graveyard was begun with interments of men who had died violent deaths, and there were thirty-six of their graves before we left. The citizens seemed to think no death worthy of mention unless it was that of some one who had died "with his boots on." There was enough desperate history in the little town in that one summer to make a whole library of dime novels. I should not have heard much about these things had not the men delighted to shock the three women in camp with these tales of bloodshed; and, besides, it was rather difficult to keep us in ignorance of much that occurred in the town, as our soldiers were, unfortunately, engaged in many an affray with the citizens. No matter if our men were as much to blame as the rest, it was quite natural that we should be interested, and disposed to defend our own.

Soldiers seem always capable of escaping the vigilance of the sentinel, and after waiting till taps had long sounded, and the camp was still, they stole away, and no one was the wiser, for they were at reveille in the morning. If one of them got drunk, bruised, or wounded, the rest brought him home and propped him up to report at reveille; or, if he was too much intoxicated, they hid him until he was sober. If two or three men of a company were worsted in some encounter in town, they had only to come back and tell their version of the story to their comrades; the company would take the matter up, and such valiant partisans were they that even the sober, law-abiding ones would set out the next night to " clean out the town." When such a night came it seemed to us that an engagement was going on, for as many shots were fired as in a skirmish with a military foe. Next morning our men, if victors, revealed where they had been; but if they were driven off the enemy's ground, the vanquished kept sullen silence.

There was an officer of the guard each day, whose duty it was to remain at the guard-tent throughout the twenty-four hours. It was odious duty, but every kind of precaution was taken to keep the men from leaving camp. It was pretty solemn business when the detail came to either of the two officers whose wives were with them; but when they obtained permission to bring their wives to the regiment, it was with the understanding that their presence should not interfere with any duty. With such a stipulation it goes without saying that we three women made as little trouble as possible. With a whole camp of faithful soldiers who, no matter what they did outside, would never harm their own, the wives of the two lieutenants were perfectly safe; still they quieted themselves, if left alone, one with her pistol beside her at night, the other with her husband's sabre. We all laughed at a huge lock one of them had put on a door which was made of some canvas stretched over a light wooden frame. To turn the key in that cumbrous lock seemed to give her a feeling of security. If an officer suggested, teasingly, how quickly an entrance might be made with a penknife in the canvas, she took the sabre in her vigorous hand, and replied, " Whoever comes will not get very far." Often and often our soldier-servants pitched their shelter tents outside ours, or brought their blankets and slept under the fly to assure us that they were watching, if we happened to be alone.

One night Mrs. Smithy was by herself, as her husband was officer of the guard. She was awakened with a start by hearing muffled sounds of voices. An altercation was going on at the creek, which was so near her tent that every word could be heard through the canvas. The main camp was too far to be reached by the sound of her voice, she reasoned, and she asked herself what sort of showing she should have even if her soldier-servant came from his shelter tent at the rear of hers, as they would be but two against so many. All the voices were threatening but one, and that tremblingly appealing. She shivered with fright, and sat up in her camp-bed with her pistol in her hand. There was scuffling, and suppressed though angry and profane conversation. All this fracas, as these men crossed the stream, was unlike the conduct of soldiers; she felt sure that it was a party of desperadoes from the town, coming to the border of the camp to pillage and murder. It seemed ages before the threatening sounds ceased. Then there was a splashing and plunging in the water, and all was still.

Next morning brought a solution of the mystery. A cavalry horse, tied in front of one of the saloons in town, had been stolen. As soon as the theft was discovered the soldiers gave chase, and came up with the thief in a ravine beyond the town. The man knew perfectly that death was the recognized penalty for horse-stealing. Murder was considered a comparatively trivial crime by all the border people. The soldiers bound the man, put a rope around his neck, and started him towards camp. There were no trees on which to hang him, so he was brought on and on, with the expectation that his last hour had come. As he neared Big Creek, and the trees appeared, he was sure that he would soon dangle from a limb; but the soldiers,

12

having recovered their horse, had no idea of such vengeance. They considered that many a man would rather be shot down at once than live through such a period of fear as he had passed while travelling over miles of prairie to eternity, as he supposed. After some parting words of admonition, mingled with oaths and threats, he was set free; and it was to all this sermon from the soldiers, and to the entreaties for mercy from the criminal, that Mrs. Smithy had listened.

Civilians were not so lenient with offenders. I was set into terror of excitement by knowing that crime was going on so near us—and unpunished as it was, there was no manner of doubt that it would be repeated until some culprit should suffer. But there was nothing at hand to serve as a gallows. There was no lumber, and logs could not be dragged from the stream even had any one taken time from the gambling, the dickering, and the horse-racing to so much as fell them. Finally, a horse-thief was caught in the town, and the citizens, aflame with wrath which had no time to cool, dragged the culprit to the nearest railroad bridge— really not much more than a culvert—and here the thief hung as a warning to all. From that time forward the improvised gallows had many such a burden swaying in the Kansas wind. In our hunts and our pleasure rides I asked to shun the railroad track, for I never felt sure that we might not come upon a ghastly body swinging from the beams that supported the bridge.

Watering.

CHAPTER XII.

WILD BILL AS A MAGISTRATE.

SOMETIMES the fights took place in broad daylight, and the streets were soon cleared, for even those outlaws were not willing to encounter a stray bullet, if they were not personally engaged in the altercation. At one time General Miles and General Custer went to meet General Schofield and his staff, and while they waited at the station a terrific row began; the air was filled with flying bullets, and no one had any thought, seemingly, but of murder. The two officers in the station could not attempt to quell this maddening crowd, and their only course was to remain quietly in the building; but General Custer, being in some exposed position, was intensely amused to have his brave comrade, in looking out for his safety, say, " Lie low, Custer, lie low!"

Occasionally we went to the train to see excursionists who had telegraphed us to meet them. The officers were all of them more than strict in their injunctions to us to look neither to the right nor to the left in the town, and as they shut us in behind the closed curtains of the travelling-carriage they called out, laughingly, but nevertheless in earnest, " No peeking, now."

The driver had his loaded carbine beside him, and listened attentively to some whispered instructions as he took up his reins. He was told, in addition, to draw up at the depot on the side farthest from the town, where our escort, having ridden beside the wagon, lifted us down and hurried us out of what seemed like a "Black Maria," it was so dismal in the carriage, and we were taken into the station, where the crowd was kept away by the dignity and authority of the officers' manner. One of the guests did "peek" through, and seeing the tables in the saloons with heaps of money, guarded by knives and revolvers, she was frightened into never looking again.

In one of these excursion parties were some of our Eastern acquaintances, and they begged to see Wild Bill. They sent the brakeman into the little street to ask him to come in, and they gave flowers to any bystander whom they saw, requesting that they be given to the renowned scout. But the more he was pursued with messages the more he retired from sight, hiding in the little back room of one of the drinking-saloons opposite. He was really a very modest man and very free from swagger and bravado. Finally, General Custer, persuaded by pretty girls, whom no one ever can resist, returned with the hero of the hour, for Wild Bill and General Custer were fast friends, having faced danger together many times.

Bill's face was confused at the words of praise with which General Custer introduced him, and his fearless eyes were cast down in chagrin at the torture of being gazed at by the crowd. He went through the enforced introduction for General Custer's sake, but it was a relief when the engine whistle sounded that released him.

Physically, he was a delight to look upon. Tall, lithe, and free in every motion, he rode and walked as if every muscle was perfection, and the careless swing of his body as he moved seemed perfectly in keeping with the man, the country, the time in which he lived. I do not recall anything finer in the way of physical perfection than Wild Bill when he swung himself lightly from his saddle, and with graceful, swaying step, squarely set shoulders and well poised head, approached our tent for orders. He was rather fantastically clad, of course, but all that seemed perfectly in keeping with the time and place. He did not make an armory of his waist, but carried two pistols. He wore top-boots, riding breeches, and dark-blue flannel shirt, with scarlet set in the front. A loose neck-handkerchief left his fine firm throat free. I do not at all remember his features, but the frank, manly expression of his fearless eyes and his courteous manner gave one a feeling of confidence in his word and in his undaunted courage.

There was no question that in the affrays in which he was often engaged he dealt murderous blows and shot unerring bullets; and one of the stories others told of him, as he was not given to boasting of his prowess, was of the invasion of five men in his sleeping-room in one of the new towns, where no law was established,

These desperate characters locked the door, but though Wild Bill was in bed he did not lose his presence of mind. Some one hearing the noise of the contest burst open the door, and found four of the assailants dead on the floor, and Wild Bill stretched fainting on the bed across the dead body of the fifth assassin. His appearance bore no traces of this desperate side of his life. He was "the mildest manner'd man that ever scuttled ship or cut a throat." While on duty, carrying despatches, he let no temptation lure him into the company of the carousers who acknowledged him as their king. His word was law and gospel in that little town, for even where no laws are respected the word and the will of one man, who is chosen leader, is often absolute.

The impression left upon my mind by the scouts of which Wild Bill was the chief was of their extreme grace. Their muscles were like steel, but they might have been velvet, so smooth and flexible seemed every movement. Wild Bill reminded me of a thorough-bred horse. Uncertain as was his origin, he looked as if he had descended from a race who valued the body as a choice possession, and therefore gave it every care. He not only looked like a thorough-bred, but like a racer, for he seemed, even in repose, to give evidence of great capabilities of endurance—of fine "staying powers," in his own vernacular. The days of the Greeks are slowly returning to us, when the human form will be so cared for that no development it is capable of will be neglected. Among the white aborigines of the plains, the frontiersmen and scouts, there have long existed fine specimens of physical development that one seldom encounters among people who live an in-door life.

When not in camp, Wild Bill was off duty, and consequently ruling his realm, the turbulent town. Some of our men having received, as they considered, a deadly insult to their company, determined to right their wrongs, and planned to assassinate the renowned scout. In these feuds there was very little margin for the right on either side. In our ranks were just as lawless men as were found in Hays City, but the strict discipline of military life soon subdues the most violent spirits. In the town, however, with restraints removed, the bluff and the bully showed forth in his true colors. A little of the very bad liquor sold there turned an obedient soldier into a wrangling boor. Three desperate characters, planning to kill Wild Bill, decided that no one of them stood any chance if the scout was left the use of his arms; not only was his every shot sure, but he was so lithe and quick, and so constantly on the alert for attack, that it was next to impossible to do him any injury. It was planned that one soldier should leap upon his back, and hold down his head and chest, while another should pinion his arms. It is impossible in the crowded little dens, imperfectly lighted, and with air dense with smoke, always to face a foe. Wild Bill was attacked from behind, as had been planned. His broad back was borne down by a powerful soldier, and his arms seized, but only one was held in the clinching grasp of the assailant. With the free hand the scout drew his pistol from the belt, fired backward without seeing, and his shot, even under these circumstances, was a fatal one. The soldier dropped dead, the citizens rallied round Wild Bill, the troopers were driven out of the town, but not without loud threats of vengeance. There was no question among the citizens but that every threat would be carried out, and it was decided that if Wild Bill hoped for life at all he must flee. It was impossible for General Custer to interfere in such a contest. His jurisdiction did not extend to the brawls of the town; the soldiers off duty were not punished, unless the citizens found something so flagrant, and proof of the dereliction so positive, that the offence must be investigated by a court-martial.

So Wild Bill, the most daring and valuable scout in the West, had to leave. I have heard General Custer say that he did not believe the scout ever shot a man except in self-defence; but no one who mingled in such *mêlées*, where infuriated mobs of men followed every savage impulse of their nature, could possibly hope for justice. The regiment heard with regret of his being murdered afterwards in the Black Hills. A man whose brother had been shot in an affray in which Wild Bill had been a participant followed him into the Black Hills, and finding him sitting at table with his companions, the miners, shot him in the back. With his marvellous coolness, courage, and self-control, above all, with that rare gift which is given to few, compara-

THE SCOUT.

tively, of control over men—doubly, trebly remarkable when exercised over outlaws—with a nature that evidently was not devoid of refinement (for he was singularly free, the officers told me, from profanity or coarse ribald language), his seemed to all of us as conspicuous an instance of wasted life as we had ever known. A nature trained in such a career as his was, however, could never have submitted itself to civilization, and his death was the necessary ending of such a life. His grave, on a bleak hill-side, bore this inscription:

I. B. HICKOCK,

("WILD BILL,")

KILLED BY THE ASSASSIN JACK McCALL,

JULY 4TH, 1876.

Pard, we shall meet again in the happy hunting-ground, to part no more.

D. H. UTTER.

("COLORADO CHARLIE.")

It seems rather singular that two valued scouts like Wild Bill and California Joe should have lost their lives during the same summer that the man they so faithfully served offered up his life for his country. We had no letters from Wild Bill; but he sent friendly messages by many a roundabout route. California Joe wrote several letters, the last of which is given as characteristic of himself. The "counsil house," we inferred, alluded to the State legislature.

SIERE NEVADA MOUNTIANS CALIFORNIA *Mar.* 16 '74

Dear Geneal after my respets to you and Lady i thought that i tell you that i am still on top of land yet i have been in the rocky mountian the most of the time sence last i seen you but i got on the railroad and and started west and the first thing i knew i landed in san Francisco so i could not go any farther except going by water and salt water at that so i turned back and headed for the mountains once more resolved never to go railroading no more i drifted up with the tide to sacramento city and i landed my boat so i took up through town they say there is 20 thousand people living there but it look to me to be 100 thousand counting chinaman and all i cant discribe my wolfish feeling but i think that i look just like i did when we was chaseing Buffalo on the simarone so i struk up though town and i come to a large fine builing crouded with people so i bulged in to see what was going on and when i got in to the counsil house i took a look around at the croud and i seen the most of them had bald heads so i thaught to myself i struck it now that they are indian peace commissioners so i look to see if i would know any of them but not one, so after while the smartest look one got up and said gentlemen i introduce a bill to have speckle mountain trout and fish eggs imported to Cal. to be put in the american Bear and Yuba rivers (those rivers is so muddy that a tadpole could not live in them caused by minging) did any body ever hear of a speckle trout living in muddy water and the next thing was the game law and that was very near as bad as the Fish for they aint no game in the country as big as mawking bird i heard some fellow behind me ask now long is the legislature been in sesion then i dropt on myself so i slid out took acros to chinatown and they smelt like a Ciowa camp in August with plenty buffalo meat around it was getting late so no place to go not got a red cent so i hapen to thing of an old friend back of town that i knowed 25 years ago so i lit out and sure enough he was thar just as i left him 25 yr ago backing so i got a few seads i going to platte in a few day give my respects to the 7th Calvery and excipt the same yourself   CALIFORNIA JOE

A little journey we made that summer comes to me now, and as it does not seem at all like any travelling one would ever be likely to do in the States, an account of it is offered by way of contrast. A great event was about to happen to the Custers. The family idol, the petted mare, was to run a race at Leavenworth. There was incessant gabble in the tent, and it was all horse-talk. The past records of other famous animals were taken out for inspection ; the newspapers chronicling the feats of the mare's competitors were spread over chairs and tables ; the men who had seen races talked wisely and well, and every one was on tiptoe of anticipation. The mare I dearly loved. She had shared our hardships with us. Once, in a prolonged cold and penetrating storm, General Custer had brought her up from the picket line, loaded her with blankets, and placed her under our fly. I peered at her from the opening between the tapes that secured the front of the tent, handed out sugar, patted her sleek neck, and mourned over the shivering of the chilled and delicate creature. General Custer asked me if I minded her being there, and I promptly replied that it seemed only providential that horses rarely lie down, or I knew I should be wheedled into offering her the camp-bed.

After this bitter experience she was sent away to better quarters, and given into the care of some professional horseman, who, after a time, wrote that he had entered her for a race. The racing part I hated, especially on a public course, but it was our mare, and the curse seemed somehow to be taken off. Besides, we had nothing to do with it; we had no money at stake, and Government gave us too much to do to permit us to dissuade people who might put up money on our mare. We had but three or four days' leave of absence, and it would require great expedition to get back at its expiration. When I was put in the travelling-carriage the curtains were all strapped down, and the driver armed, as usual, in case of disturbance in the town. I went through the usual exhortations from the two men—for Colonel Tom was going with us. They made a rather general statement that women are forever trying to look where they ought not to. "Now mind, old lady, don't you try to look out if there is a crevice left open. The town is nothing but a medley of disreputable people, and we don't wish you to see or be seen." The vehement Custers poured these injunctions in on me like hot shot. I did not "look"; I was so glad to be taken along on this rare outing that no veteran soldier could have been more obedient.

They lifted me out at the station from my temporary prison, and, as the train approached, I was hurried into the car, and we found a seat among the usual collection of armed men, whose guns, leaning against the backs of the seats, made me as uncomfortable as possible, for I was very much afraid of fire-arms. If a fleeing antelope sped over the plains the window was shoved violently up, out went a rifle, and off went a bullet that was simply absurd in its aim, for even our best hunters found it difficult to bring down antelope under what were considered favorable circumstances. Peace being restored, the unsuccessful marksman was loudly laughed at and jeered for missing his aim. Suddenly all the windows on one side went up with a bang, heads were thrust out, most of the men on the other side of the car plunged over, and ran their rifles out through any window they could reach, and dangerously near to any head that might occupy the opening; and all this to attack a prairie-dog village.

These men were dressed in every sort of costume, from the tattered remains of what were once tailor-made clothes to buckskin fashioned by their own fingers. They were ragged and unkempt in most instances. Many of the plainsmen scorned water in any form, and even the Texan's definition, when offered a glass of water, "Oh yes, that's what you wash with," was lost upon the real Nimrod of the West. Still with all this ignoring of the "tub" there are alleviating circumstances. An exasperated writer speaks of "inhaling your fellow-creature"; and on entering a Pullman-car, lately, at night, I heard some one say, "Here are all breaths of our brother man, carefully preserved from Chicago to New York." All this we were spared, for in the West we seldom found ourselves packed in crowds, as happens every day in the city. In addition to the soiled clothing of the foreign laborer, next which you sniff and shudder in the horse-car, you have the additional odors of sewer gas, stale beer emptied into the gutters, a leaking gas-pipe, and hundreds of cabbage and onion dinners sending their domestic incense to heaven. All this one escapes on the plains. With the plainsman, Nature at least makes up for this ignoring of one element by blowing another through him, and sometimes taking him in a little encircling embrace, or touching him up with a small hurricane of wind which dances the delinquent on his feet and airs him well, *nolens volens.*

Our soldiers were often nearly desperate when water was scarce, for it is their duty first, and afterwards their habit, to be clean. If a good stream was reached, the whole command was sometimes halted for a day on the march to permit the enlisted men to have a wash-day. When water was scarce, I have seen a buffalo-wallow in the West look for all the world like a heathen deity. Around the circular edge knelt as many men as could crowd in, dipping their canteens, hollowing their horny hands into a cup, or holding their caps in the shallow pool of standing water that owed its storage-basin to the gambols of the buffalo. After tearing the turf, pawing the sod, and digging his horns in the ground, the buffalo rolls his huge body in the loosened soil, and rubs off the loose hair from his coat. When he is shedding he is a tattered old tramp, with flying bunches of faded hair sticking at intervals among the new. After the monster has rolled himself free from his last year's rags he leaves quite a hollow in the ground. The rain comes, is soon dried by the scorching sun, and the basin has a baked surface that holds water afterwards for many a parched throat.

As our journey advanced, blood-curdling stories were

strung out with no end of ghastly detail, with minute particulars of encounters with Indians, game, and desperadoes. I could not help but hear, and I saw the frontiersmen shyly eying me, as if I had been a curiosity from another world; but they smoked their pipes, and handed round the inevitable black bottle out on the platform, instead of in the car, for my sake; but the talking, the boasting, the shooting—those were their best manners, under any circumstances, and they never thought to suppress a detail. The bones of any brakeman who should have had the temerity to try to subdue these reckless characters would have bleached on the plains in those days. The mounds along the route of travel to the Rocky Mountains were not always raised over the mouldering bodies of exhausted pioneers; they marked the spot of many a deadly affray where some one of a party had paid the penalty which is usually attached to such encounters.

The Kansas Pacific trains did not run at night, and we were compelled to stop at the little town of Ellsworth, if possible, even worse than Hays City. There was but one hotel, and that not worthy of the name. The building, twenty by fifty feet, had a great loft, low and close, where cots were as thick as they could stand. One narrow room was boarded off, and to this we were assigned. As the house was unplastered, and built mostly of canvas and slabs, the Kansas wind waved it about at will. The one large room on the ground-floor had the bar and billiard-table at one end, and the tables for dining at the other. We were, of course, hungry, and the crowd of drinking, smoking brawlers was kept in some sort of subjection by the landlord, who mentioned the talismanic name of lady to quiet them. It was unusual for them to see any one save themselves on their ground. After a hasty dinner — and such a dinner! — only people savagely hungry, as we were, could have eaten it at all—I was hurried up to the little den of which the landlord was extremely proud. The noise below going on till dawn, the snoring heard through the thin partition that separated us from the lodgers, the ominous vibration of the rickety old building—all helped to murder sleep for us.

The frontiersman had then, as now, a great "despise," as they put it, for the tenderfoot, and a party of buffalo-hunters, who had stopped at this hotel a short time before, were the subjects of much derision and criticism. One of the men had insisted upon wearing a "stove-pipe" hat from the East—which, to say the least, was inappropriate, and attracted almost as much attention as if he had worn a French bonnet. The frontiersmen scoffed and jeered at this offending hat, discussed the "biled shirts," and viewed the whole party with lofty scorn.

The tourists did not look much like the active muscular hunter, without an ounce of superfluous flesh, who could ride fifty miles as easily as most people do five. Two of the party were over size, and had the contour which betokens good dinners and convivial life. One of the number was inclined to match a little Eastern swagger with Western bravado, by telling with pride where they were going, and what they expected to do, etc. A burly border ruffian raised his voice in the crowd that surrounded the would-be Nimrods, and said, "You uns is the folks General Custer is expectin'?" "Yes," promptly answered our friends, exultant, and sure no game would escape them. Emptying one cheek to transfer the quid of tobacco to the other, the latter jaw evidently not being the better talking side, the frontiersman looked at these huge men with half-closed, sarcastic eyes, and said, "Stranger, I was at Custer's camp on Saturday, and he was awful busy a-preparing." "What was he doing?" asked the eager tourists. "Why, stranger, he had men out all the week a-corrallin' buffaloes for you fellows to kill." The point of the retort is lost unless one knows that wild buffaloes are not the animals that submit tamely to corralling.

A family discussion took place, after we reached our room in the loft, about what to do with our brother Tom. All the cots outside were engaged, and had a roll of blankets been available everything would have gone well, for Tom could sleep anywhere. As it was, we decided to take him in, as there was an extra bed in our narrow room. We went in first, prepared for sleeping, put out the light, and called to Colonel Tom. He came for the place gratefully—for, with all our vicissitudes, we nearly always had a tent to ourselves, and whole families were not obliged to live in one room, as in a tenement. Tom praised me; thought I not only remembered when in "Rome to be a Roman," but, since I had been willing to take him in, it was his opinion I was the "noblest Roman of them all"; and then he dropped to sleep, soon to wake with a start, thinking the brawlers down-stairs had ascended to make an attack. It was only his affectionate brother, who, from time to time, threw over on his bed, with such accurate aim that each shot told, shoes, stockings, brushes, and any other available missile. It hardly seemed a breath before the voice of the landlord woke us, saying that some one had forgotten to call us; that it was late, and we must hurry, as the train was nearly ready. Tom rose first, and dressed partly in the dark, for the one train of the day started at dawn. The landlord came again, saying the conductor was holding the train. As the road depended upon the Seventh Cavalry to protect it, there was no lack of courtesy to the commanding officer. He did not wish to take advantage of any such favor, so Colonel Tom was hurried with half his clothes to dress in the dark passageway, and on me fell the whole responsibility of the day, for if I was late we would miss the coming sport. In moments of excitement the two men always talked as if I were not present. "What shall we do with the old lady?" (this name was given me by these youngsters when I first began to write myself Mrs.). "Can't we bundle her up and carry her?" "Will you go as you are?" General Custer said, turning to me at last. "If you say so, I can go," I replied. It would not take a paragraph to describe my toilet as far as I had advanced. I thrust my feet into my shoes, General Custer threw my large travelling-cloak about me, Tom seized the hand-bags and a heap of my clothing, and down the rickety steps we sprang, across the little space between the hotel and the cars, I not daring to look to the right or left among the usual crowd of idlers who surround all stations. I was lifted into the car, hurried into one corner, and the two began to plan about me again. This sounds as if I had no voice in the discussions, but that is giving too modest a representation, for I did my share; but I only refer to it as a droll way the two men had of going on talking and arranging regardless of my vote. They decided that the fast-approaching day necessitated my being clad more fully than I then was; so one said he would hold up the travelling-cloak while the other buttoned my shoes and helped put on the tumbled mass of apparel that was to make me presentable. Between the hurry, the laughter, and the embarrassment, no button would button, no hook would fasten, but the cloak was lowered at last, and I looked out of the window most of the time, preferring the monotonous scenery to any chance glance I might encounter from what I feared would be the amused eyes of the people.

At Leavenworth we had just time to make our toilet, get something to eat, and take a carriage for the race-course. We went, of course, to the stall of the family idol. The mare was sleeker, finer, more lovely than ever. She knew us, and vibrated her delicate ears, whinnied, and arched her glossy neck in pride and love.

Colonel Tom reminded her of some of his past encounters, and of his very first ride, when saddle, bridle, and
man were gracefully lifted over her head and dropped
at her feet.   It had been a family riddle ever since,
how even such an.agile creature as she could shed every trapping, and the rider as well, with one flourish
of her nimble heels.   Colonel Tom took occasion to remind me of the noble sacrifice I had been willing to
make of my husband's relatives.   It seems that when we
first had the mare, she reared and plunged with such
violence, gave such agile leaps from one side to the
other, that I, with tears of terror streaming down my
face, had called to General Custer, " Don't, don't mount
the dangerous creature, let the bachelor officers try her
first."   The men without wives heard me, and as they
valued their lives in spite of the fact that they were
single, I never heard the last of it.

The adulation which the slender, beautifully proportioned creature had from the whole regiment was delightful to us.   We frequently stood about her noting
her fine points, and assenting with responsive nods to
any new beauty discovered.   One of the pretty girls we
entertained was somewhat discomfited one day when a
group had gathered around the mare.   Her boy brother,
in rapt admiration, called out, " Why, sister, her ankles
are as small as yours."   The blushing girl sank down
into her petticoats, fearing the rude and daring Kansas
wind would try to indorse her brother's praise by lifting the concealed drapery.

I haven't the least idea how the race at Leavenworth

turned out; I only know that had the mare been beaten, her admiring owners would have been certain that it was due to every other cause than that there was in existence a faster, finer horse than our beloved property.

To the Color.

End.

D. C.

CHAPTER XIII.

HOME OF THE BUFFALO.

THE buffaloes were in such enormous herds all about us in Kansas that it seemed as if nothing could diminish their numbers. General Sherman told me, not long since, that from the time we were there until the date of their almost total annihilation nine millions had been killed. After the Pacific railroads were completed the Indian was partially subdued, and civilization spread along the routes of travel; the frontiersmen were more daring, and buffalo-hunting became a slaughter. The skin-hunters carried on a great traffic. Wherever the steamers stopped to wood along the Missouri the river was lined with heaps of hides, tied in bales ready for shipment. At the railroad stations in Kansas the same thing was true. Seven hundred and fifty thousand hides were shipped from one station on the Atchison, Topeka, and Santa Fé road about 1874. The skin-hunters used this plan: One of the number still-hunted, singling out his animal, and firing at long range so that the sound of the bullet did not disturb the herd. The smell of the blood drew perhaps twenty about the slain animal, and the hunter fired at them from behind the carcass, where he had hidden himself on coming up to his dead game. The rest of the party skinned the carcasses, and then proceeded to follow up the herd. One man, an expert, has thus shot over a hundred in a day. The bones were gathered and shipped East also. In this systematic killing it is no wonder that great numbers disappeared, and that now only a small herd in the Black Hills is reported in existence. While we were in Kansas the Indians were on the war-path, and no men were sufficiently daring in the pursuit of pelf to make hunting a business. The fearful destruction of buffaloes seems to cause national regret; and yet, on the other hand, according to the theory of Mr. Theodore Roosevelt, who is an authority on Western matters, nothing has done more to settle the Indian question. He does not detract from our army, and its patient service for so many years, but less than twenty-five thousand men to guard our immense frontier could do little more than protect the settlers, and guard the builders of the railroads. It was a grief to lay waste the beautiful valley of the Shenandoah and destroy that garden of the South, thus cutting off the source of fruitful supplies for General Lee's army, and yet, here again, it shortened our war and saved thousands of valiant men. General Miles differs from Mr. Roosevelt, and thinks that were not the Indians subdued by our army nothing would keep them from the war-path, as they would not hesitate to kill the cattle on the ranches which now replace the buffaloes. The Cheyennes, in a raid from the Indian Territory to Montana, did live on the cattle of the ranchmen for the entire distance.

All the wide plains about us for hundreds of miles— and thousands, for aught I know—were stamped with the presence of the American bison. Innumerable proofs that they had long been monarchs in that great desert were encountered on our long marches, no matter in what direction we moved. No other animal impressed itself so on the land as to have its trail become a feature of the vast country. The most noticeable of these evidences of their presence were the interminable trails to the streams. Many a desert mariner, guiding his canvas-covered wagon across the trackless Western sea of prairie to the El Dorado of America, has saved his life by following these unfailing guides. The ruts were sometimes in four parallel lines, and so deeply cut by the huge monsters that patiently plodded through them that we often had to check our horses to cross safely. The narrowness of these paths —for they were not much wider than the impression of a cart-wheel—was a surprise, until I saw how closely,

how evenly each hoof seemed to replace the other
as the steady march went on. We learned very soon
that we need not count on finding a stream near, by
following the trail, unless it was by some rare chance,
if in hunting it became necessary to give the horses
and dogs water. It might be a journey of hours—for
with a buffalo what was time? He lived but to eat
and drink. There was never the wild, exultant run of
deer or antelope, which flew over the plains apparently
from joy and excess of animal life. The solemn, practical existence of the lumbering buffalo seemed to have
begun before calfdom was fairly over.

It is true there was much fighting for supremacy
and leadership, and the heartless conduct towards the
old bachelors of the herd is well known. When they
showed signs of antiquity, the stronger, younger bulls
drove the enfeebled ones out into a dreary existence,
which, happily for them, was soon ended by the wolves
that pursued the solitary tramp until exhaustion gave
him up a prey to those persistent followers. Occasionally several of the outcasts from the different herds
evidently met, even in that vast extent of country,
and, exchanging their grievances, concluded to join
forces and defy their joint enemy, the wolves. With
us, unaccustomed that summer to the habits of the
buffalo, the sight of a single animal browsing, apparently contentedly, augured an approaching herd; and
great was our disappointment, when the antediluvian
was allowed to gallop off at sight of us and escape, to
find that he was not the forerunner of a herd, but only

an animal in disgrace because the gods did not love him enough to decree that he should die young.

Many combats occurred among the bulls of the herd because two selected the same cow for a wife, and the painter who could have fixed these monsters on his canvas while they were raging with the fierceness of rivalry would have made his mark. The heads bent forward to the ground in attempts to gore each other, the burning eyeballs, the desperate plunges which they made, apparently oblivious of their great weight, the turf torn with their maddened hoofs, the air thick with dust and bits of loosened sod, the temporary retreats of the contestants only to enable them to rush at one another with renewed force, afforded the most magnificent example of jealous fury. Meanwhile the cow over which this war was waged quietly browsed near by. When domestic life began, the winner of the hard-fought battle became a very good defender of his family. In the great herds the cows were always in the centre, and a cordon of bulls surrounded them and their young, while outside them all were the pickets, which kept watch, and whose warnings were heeded at once if danger threatened.

The circles, perhaps fifteen feet in circumference, that I saw for the first time, were one of the mysteries of that strange land. When the officers told me that the rut was made by the buffalo mother's walking round and round to protect her newly born and sleeping calf from the wolves at night, I listened only to smile incredulously, with the look peculiar to an innocent who desires to convince the narrator of fables that he has met one person of superior intuition who cannot be gulled. I had been so often "guyed" with ridiculous stories, of which this last seemed the crowning example, that I did not believe the tale. In time, however, I found that it was true, and I never came across these pathetic circles in our rides or in hunting without a sentiment of deepest sympathy for the anxious mother whose vigilance kept up the ceaseless tramp during the long night.

The calf is born with wonderful strength and vitality, and soon does remarkable feats in marching. He is quite a big fellow in a year, but keeps on growing until he is seven. We always waited quietly for developments, and could not resist the temptation to let the stranger try, when a guest said, " I shall begin on the first day's hunt with a calf, for practice." He never tried again, for a yearling will get over the ground so much faster than his elders, which weigh perhaps eight hundred pounds, that one chase after him is enough to decide the novice to keep to the larger animals if he hopes to bring down game. Before the war, when our officers were on the march to New Mexico, they used to pass a ranch kept by two men, Booth and Allison, at Walnut Creek, on the Santa Fé trail. The ranchmen had devised a plan to capture buffalo calves which seems inhuman, but is nevertheless true, as an old campaigner told me of it. When a herd of buffaloes passed near the ranch, the cows travelling slowly on account of their young, the buffalo bulls guarding their families, the hunters rode suddenly into the herd, caught a young calf by the tail, whirled it round two or three times until the little thing had not only lost its bearings but its mother also, and there never was the slightest difficulty in driving the calf back to the ranch, where it grew up with the domestic cattle.

The spring and activity of the largest buffaloes are marvellous. One day General Custer, returning from a hunt, called me to the tent-fly to see his favorite horse Dandy. He was so quick, strong, and intelligent that he was accounted as good a buffalo-horse as there was in the regiment. General Custer said that he was so ambitious that as soon as he saw which animal was singled out for pursuit he bent every nerve to the work. When the game became angry Dandy grew more wary, and, leaping to the right and left to escape the butting horns, he carried his master so near that the side of the buffalo was almost rubbed in passing. Dandy knew that the only way to bring an animal down was by sending the fatal shot behind the shoulder, so he darted for the side, plunged off at a tangent when the animal wheeled, gathered and sprang for the unguarded quarter, and his master had to exercise vigilance lest through the animal's ambition both he and Dandy should be impaled on the wicked horns of the adversary. The bridle did not need to be touched, so clever was the horse in getting into favorable position for firing.

One day, however—there always comes a " one day " in all stories of adventure—Dandy pursued a buffalo down the side of a ravine, where the footing was inse-

SHOOTING BUFFALO FROM CAR-WINDOWS.

cure and narrow. The furious beast, raging because he
was followed into what he considered a fastness, suddenly wheeled, and before horse or rider could escape
or even turn General Custer felt himself poised in air.
The huge animal had actually lifted both man and beast
on his strong vicious horns. It was only by Dandy's
sudden leap to one side, and the coolness of both, that
General Custer and his favorite gained a place of safety, for an enraged buffalo is not a safe animal to encounter, especially with all odds on his side. When I
came out to the fly, on their return that day, Dandy
had a hole in his side, where one horn had gored him,
while the thick felt saddle-cloth was cut through by the
other. This very narrow escape had no effect on Dandy's nerves. The very next hunt he recognized the
animal selected for game, and did not draw breath till
he had darted up to its side, when he slackened to enable the bullet to be sent home to the vulnerable spot.

In certain places the cactus-beds were almost continuous for miles, and it required great patience to pick
our way through the thorny route. Dandy could be as
patient as any horse, if it was necessary, but when solitary clumps were encountered he made short work and
leaped them. His master, knowing this little playful-
ness, was rarely unprepared ; but woe be to the guest
to whom Dandy was lent as a great favor. He made
so sudden and unexpected a spring that the rider was
apt to be quickly seated either on the crupper or astride
Dandy's neck; or, worse still, impaled in the very cactus-bed that Dandy had cleared.

The servant of one of our surgeons, a negro of about fifteen, bought himself a bucking pony, as he was too ambitious to ride any steady-going animal. He delighted in racing his animal in front of the command, to show his horsemanship, and being a negro, and droll, he was not restrained as much as he perhaps deserved. Suddenly he came upon one of the cactus-beds that continue for miles, not in masses but in clumps, through which a horse can pick his way slowly if left to himself. The darky's pony knew this sort of ground well, and was not going to be sent galloping into such a snare, so he refused to go, suddenly settled himself on his haunches, and sent John over his head, landing him squarely on his back in the cactus-bed. The thorns fairly pinned the poor fellow's clothes to his flesh. He slowly picked himself up, even the hand that he used to raise himself being stuck full of thorns, and struggled to pull off his coat, exclaiming, " Holy Moses, but ain't them jaggers !" The doctor thought so, after spending two hours extracting the thorns from John's lacerated back ; but the pointed lesson made the youth wary of racing in future.

At first the bleaching bones of thousands of buffaloes were rather a melancholy sight to me, but I soon became as much accustomed to the ghastly sockets of an upturned skull as the field-mouse which ran in and out either orifice with food for her nest of little ones inside. All evidences of death are sad to a woman. The bones were often very old, for the bone collectors did not dare carry on their traffic at that dangerous time ;

and it seemed to me that the sadness of thinking of the death of these naturally peaceful creatures was softened, as it is when one goes into a very old burying-ground, and the crumbling stones, covered with lichen, prove that the hearts that once bled for those under the sod are themselves at rest beneath some grass-covered spot elsewhere. There would be few hunters if women had to be the Nimrods. I suppose in a world where woman reigned there would be little question that, unwilling to kill anything, in time she would be crowded out by the animal kingdom. But the buffaloes were singularly pitiful prey to me. They fought terribly when brought to bay, but when simply startled by the enemy, they ambled off as if saying, "See here, this place is surely big enough for all of us; we'll get out of the way." Then when they were pursued, and the herd broke into a frightened stampede, my heart was wrung with sympathy, especially if I chanced to spy calves. I hardly need say how careful the officers were not to shoot the cows. The reverence for motherhood is an instinct that is seldom absent from educated men. Besides, I know too many instances in proof of the poet's words, "the bravest are the tenderest." Our officers taught the coarsest soldier, in time, to regard maternity as something sacred.

It was only by the merest chance that I heard something of the gentleness of one of our officers, whose brave heart ceased to beat on the battle-field of the Little Big Horn. In marching on a scouting expedition one day he went in advance a short distance with his sergeant, and when his ten men caught up with him he found that they had shot the mothers of some young antelopes they had chased. Captain Yates, in righteous indignation at this desecration of sacred rights, ordered the men to return to, the young, and each take a baby antelope in his arms and care for it until they reached the post. For two days the men marched on, bearing the tender little things, cushioning them as best they could in their folded blouses. One man had twins to look out for, and as a baby antelope is all legs and head, this squirming collection of tiny hoofs and legs stuck out from all sides as the soldier guided his horse as best he could with one hand, the arm of which encircled the bleating little orphans.

I also heard, only a year or so since, of an incident that happened perhaps fifteen years ago. A representative of the press, Mr. Barrows of Boston, was sent for scientific purposes with our regiment during the summer campaign. He told me that General Custer, riding at the head of the column, seeing the nest of a meadow-lark, with birdlings in it, in the grass, guided his horse around it, and resumed the straight course again without saying a word or giving a direction. The whole command of many hundred cavalrymen made the same detour, each detachment coming up to the place where the preceding horsemen had turned out, and looking down into the nest to find the reason for the unusual departure from the straight line of march.

Our officers' tenderness to children was unceasing. One of them, going to the steamer which made its rare stops at Fort Lincoln, to meet an aunt he had not seen for a long time, found among the crowd that swarmed over the narrow guards a frontiersman who was attending a child with croup. The mother of the child had died a few days before. The little one was dying, apparently, but, thinking there was time to save its life, our Seventh Cavalryman put spurs to his horse, went to the post, sought out the doctor, secured medicine, wrote a letter to the surgeon at the next post, asking him to go to the steamer while it was wooding, and prescribe for the child; he then returned to the boat, giving the distressed father the medicine, and not even explaining to his aunt why he had left her so summarily.

But how shall I ever hope to paint the surroundings? How can any one imagine a country where there were no apothecaries, no physicians, no nurses outside a military post, and where an act of kindness so common in the States means the saving of life that otherwise would have perished on the isolated frontier? I cannot name the instances where officers, unused to children, have taught themselves to be helpful when the overtaxed mother, the wife of his comrade, needed help with an ill child. Those gallant men, walking the floor with a peevish baby, had not one moment's thought of whether they presented a ridiculous appearance or not.

And when they tamed their fiery charger to a walk, and took the little boy of a friend in front of them on the saddle, suiting the gait of the animal to the soft wabbling of the fat little body and legs, there was no

14

turning in fear to notice a smile of derision in the corner of any scoffer's mouth. On one of the through trains I knew an officer to offer, soon after he left Chicago, to get warm milk at the stations for a fellow-traveller whom he did not know, a poor woman with two little children, and until they reached the Pacific coast he kept this up three times a day. The Pacific road was then new, and the journey was not made in the few days that it occupies at present. No amount of comic speeches from his brother officers at the figure he cut as milkman with his tin cups moved him to forsake his mission.

When we were first in Kansas women had never, to any one's knowledge, been taken on buffalo-hunts, and our officers determined to begin. General Miles, who commanded Fort Hays, and General Custer, who were most congenial friends, loving hunting next to their profession, determined to take their wives. It was an extraordinary privilege, for we were undoubtedly in the way, and it required a good deal of planning to arrange for us, and see that we were protected with an escort while the officers made the charge into the herd. As I remember what an amount of bother it was for them, I do not think, in common parlance, it "paid" to take us along, but it was a very great pleasure to us. From the very first I was not permitted to ride on horseback. The country was so full of prairie-dog and gopher holes that the best and surest-footed horse was apt to stumble, and sometimes even break a leg when the honeycombed earth gave way suddenly, and let him into the subterranean homes of the little burrowing animals. It was difficult to ride full tilt over the trails the buffaloes made to the streams, for the earth was baked hard by the water that had gathered and dried in these narrow trenches. The buffalo-wallow was another serious obstacle to rapid riding. There again the hard surface of the sun-baked rim to this basin did not give under the flying hoofs of a running horse. Unless they were seen in time to go round them—for they were from ten to fifteen feet in circumference—it was a sudden and dangerous slackening of speed to leap into the depression and spring out again. All the muscles of the officers' lithe bodies were free to resist such sudden plunges, while one half of us was as useless as if paralyzed as we clung to the side of the horse. There were no limits to what we contended we could have done if it had been the custom for us to ride as they did. Fortunately for us, our boasts were never put to the test, and thus our reputations as horsewomen were not imperilled.

The officers considered all these dangers, and dissuaded us from riding. Our coachman drove so well, and entered so into the spirit of the hour, that I was often in at the death, though living a lifetime of fear in getting there. He had strong horses, and he especially prepared the stout Government harness, which was always of the best material, before a hunt, and examined the wagon-springs carefully. General Custer rode by the carriage until they struck the herd, and then, giving Henry orders to follow slowly, off went the gay riders. Henry, true to his orders, drove slowly for a time over divide after divide until the chase began to be spirited, and then, forgetting the wagon-break, forgetting his orders, oblivious of everything except the vanishing herd, he urged his steeds on and on until they broke into a gallop. Henry rose to his feet to urge them forward, and flourishing his whip, we tore over the country at a real breakneck speed. I cowered on the back seat with fear, and of course I remonstrated. Henry argued, his eyes eagerly watching the horsemen. Finally I implored, and said, " Oh, don't, *don't,* Henry ; we'll go to pieces, I'm sure !" With his kindly voice, talking to me as he would to a scared child, he would reply, " There ain't no kind of danger, Miss Libbie ; I'll take keer of you ; you jest wait till I get to see 'em from the top of that next divide, and I'll stop."

With all our experience, we, officers and all, lived day after day with the delusion that " the top of the next divide" would reveal us some sight, and wave after wave of land swept on without discovering anything but the ever-deluding knoll beyond the gentle undulation into which we descended. So Henry followed with all the speed he could get out of his horses, telling me, " The next divide, Miss Libbie, we's sho' to see 'em."

How he managed to guide his excited horses without accident around the wallows, through the prairie-dog villages, and to twist through the cactus-beds, to descend the gullies, and to jerk the wagon up the ascending knoll, was of course an unsolved mystery. The wagon creaked out an occasional protest, the harness snapped threateningly, but on we flew in safety. Everything rattled and clattered and banged as we tore over the prairie, but the ambitious Jehu, with every faith in his horses and harness, chuckled with delight.

Finally we would begin to overtake the hunters, and at last, as the successful sportsmen were dismounting to cut up the game, Henry, triumphant and beaming, drove his galloping, panting, foam-flecked horses into the circle, and a shout of laughter went up from the hunters at the very idea of chasing buffaloes in a carriage.

Sick.

Go get your pills, go get your pills, Go
get your pills, go get your pills, Go get your pills, go get your
pills, Go get your pills,........ go... get your pills.

CHAPTER XIV.

FIRST WOMEN TO HUNT BUFFALOES.

HENRY did not drive us on the hunt when we women were taken for the first time. We had an ambulance fitted up as a travelling-wagon, with the seats across instead of lengthwise, as in the regulation ambulance. Under the rear axle hung the keg of water, and under the front was suspended the bucket for the animals. There were four mules, and the whole establishment, from the rack for luncheon-hampers, at the rear, to the farthermost tip of the lead-mules' ears, was a long-drawn-out affair, and as we halted in front of the commanding officer's quarters at Fort Hays we cast a lengthened shadow on the burning sand of the almost bare parade-ground.

The driver, a faithful soldier, had his carbine by his side and his cartridge-belt buckled around his waist.

These ominous preparations for a pleasure-party made me shudder a little, while the detachment of cavalry waiting outside the post, with jingling spurs, rattling arms, and impatient, stamping horses, suggested further precaution, and added still more to my fears. The escort was unusually large, as the unfortunate shooting of the Indian chiefs in the corral was too recent an event not to make the officers realize the necessity for caution. It was impossible to communicate with the hostiles and explain this catastrophe, and no one knew at what moment a band of warriors, intent on revenge, would start out from a ravine and attack any one venturing outside the post.

I was not the only one of the four women who were so honored as to be taken along who trembled at these warlike preparations, for Mrs. Miles, then a bride, and having her first experience of the plains, watched her husband anxiously as he rode about giving final directions, and would gladly have urged him to drive with us, thus striving to secure his safety, had she hoped to dislodge a born cavalryman from his seat in the saddle that he so loved, and that he filled so well. General Miles had been a cavalry officer during the war, and though at that time an infantry colonel, he took to this mounted pleasuring as naturally as if leading a charge. When the officers declared that all was ready the bugle sounded, the impatient horses started, and the little cavalcade was, after many delays, set in motion. There was an ambulance at the rear, and that was another rather gloomy accompani-

ment of a laughing, singing, rollicking hunting party.
It was considered necessary, however; for, though the
accidents were never serious, there was rarely a hunt
in which some one was not hurt.

Our progress to the part of the plains where the buffaloes grazed was slow, as all the officers tried to save
their horses until the actual chase began. The only
variety for some miles was the sudden darting off of
the dogs in pursuit of the jack-rabbits that lifted their
fawn-like heads above the tufts of grass where they had
been nibbling, and then shot over the plain in terrified
haste. We were so much in sympathy with the little
creatures that we did not share the sportsman's disappointment when they succeeded in getting so great a
start of the dogs that they were soon too dim a speck
on the prairie to be discernible. The officers occasionally came riding back from the advance to chat with
us; but through all the day the doctor, who had constituted himself our escort, never left us. He rode a
cumbersome gray, and he himself, having started out
in his military career with over six feet of person one
way, was busy with good dinners getting himself into
condition to measure that much the other, and the circumference he had acquired made him anything but a
light weight or a typical cavalryman.

All the novelty of the occasion, the soft air of the
plains, deliciously pure and exhilarating, the rare sensation when we looked about us and saw the entire
horizon with "the sky fitting close down all around,"
as our officers expressed it, did not banish from my

mind the dread of the Indian. Every tuft of grass, or sage-bush, or clump of cactus, silhouetted against the sky seemed to sway slowly as if a human being were hiding behind the low barricade. As one rides or drives with cavalry the least diversion seems to tremble along through the column and reach you in a dozen mute ways. The sudden rattle of steel or accoutrements as the rider turns slightly in the saddle, the short, low ejaculation of the troopers, the horses' ears starting from a listless droop into alert erectness, the click of the hoof evidencing a change in gait—all these simple signals reached me, and before a word was spoken my heart pounded a wild tattoo on my ribs, and to solve the mystery my eyes quickly scanned the great circle bounding the sky. Perhaps a herd of antelopes stood transfixed by curiosity as we were discovered approaching; possibly a deer, taking fright for himself and the pretty doe and fawn, sprang off with marvellous bounds to lead the way to securer haunts. The ever-vigilant eyes of a terrified woman soon have a whole collection of small signs that telegraph to her quick sensibilities the possibility of danger. If in description of the trifles that produce this tremor of almost imperceptible excitement through a cavalry column Longfellow had framed a line such as he wrote for the ship—" She feels a thrill of life along her keel "—it would have saved much prose which cannot even clumsily portray the momentary precursor of disturbance that pervades a body of horsemen. When the disturbing object presents itself, then the voices are outspoken, and after the mystery is solved the column resumes its even gait of four miles an hour.

After several of these slight interruptions, which gave me, nevertheless, a start of agitation, finally there came something that even the troopers watched with suspense. Human beings, whether white or red men, were seen far away to our left. The command was instantly halted, and the officers consulted together. We were too far at the rear to hear a word of the discussion. All eyes were turned to the left. Our lead-mules' ears began to express excitement as their eyes descried the distant figures. The driver, trying not to let us see him, quietly freed his carbine from the reins and litter that had been tossed on the front seat. The doctor instinctively put his hand to his belt and tugged at his pistol, which, uncomfortable at being jostled about his broad proportions, had settled itself in the small of his back. The officers rode back to us in a few moments, and St. Peter recorded another of those fibs of which he has such a list laid up against officers who tell women "there is not the slightest danger." I had then been married several years, and this assertion, that I had heard so often, had no effect in calming me.

General Miles and General Custer determined to ride on and investigate, and an Irish officer, a reckless rider, begged to accompany them. Both officers had field-glasses, but the distance was too great to discover anything definite. The Irishman's horse was like himself, and plunged on in advance at headlong speed; General Miles and General Custer were mounted on animals that combined other traits even more desirable in buffalo-hunting — tenacity of will and strength. As the horseman in advance dashed on precipitately, the figures we were watching so closely began to ride in a circle. Still, though this, all over the plains, was the established signal for a parley, we knew that Indians had sometimes used it as a ruse to decoy the white man into their power. When the daring captain was near enough to speak to them, we saw him turn and ride back; and as we gazed through our opera-glasses, which we found aided us even then, it was with intense relief that we saw the circle-riding given up, and the captain's own pace become more moderate. The horsemen proved to be herders looking for their mules, and seeing our little cavalcade, they were as much frightened as we were, and only too glad to be relieved of their terrors.

Finally, after the beautiful cool morning merged into the warmth of noon, and the quivering heat over the scorching ground made us feel thirsty, and sigh for a murmuring stream, it was decided that our pursuit of game could go on more actively if the inner man were fortified. We might look in vain for a tree, or for a brook, or even a pool: there was no shade except a very narrow strip beside the wagon, for the sun was still almost above us. The water in the kegs was not improved by the constant swinging that had been kept up with the motion of the wagon; the "cold" tea and coffee were lukewarm, but what did we care? I wish that I could see such sparkling eyes, such devouring appetites, such enthusiastic diners at Delmonico's, as were gathered about the luncheon-baskets on that glorious summer day. Every one had contributed something, and the jumble was amusing; but when we had finished there was scarcely enough left to give the driver a taste of each of the viands to add to his hard-tack, pork, and the tepid water in his canteen. The dogs sat around the outside of the circle, disputing, as usual, with their hungry eyes every mouthful we took, and jumping for the bones that were tossed them. Then the two generals poured from the keg containing the only water we might see during the entire day, a little for each hound, and in return got an affectionate lick from the rough but loving tongues, and a gambol of grateful delight as they sprang off for the march.

Coming to a stream, we found the column suddenly halted, and our heads were instantly out of the side of the wagon to see what could be the matter. The doctor soon came hurrying back to say that the passage was disputed by a small but well-armed foe, and added that " as soon as that essence-peddler saw fit to move on, the major-general commanding would issue his order to march." It was rather laughable to have a whole command held at bay by one small animal.

Not long after we had started again there was a shout from the head of the column, and on came to us the word " Buffaloes!" It conveyed to me another tremor of agitation. I am ashamed to confess that I was even afraid of buffaloes. I had not then seen them, for, though in previous chapters reference may have been made to them, the allusions were to the events of the summer. These great black blotches against the fault-less sky were my introduction to the American buffalo. They loomed up like elephants to my scared vision. I thought at that time that they combined the ferocity of the tiger with the strength of the lion. I had no idea how peaceful they really were if let alone. The soldiers who had gone in advance, and who had inform-ed us by riding in a circle (a preconcerted signal) that buffaloes were ahead, now joined the column, and a halt was called to prepare for the chase. The doctor and a few men were to remain as our escort, while we fol-lowed slowly.

There was no particular care as to the dress of the hunters, and officers and enlisted men took every lati-tude in the matter of costume. The legs of a cavalry-man are usually well cared for ; his corduroy or buck-skin breeches are an excellent fit, and his troop-boots, coming to the knee, set off a shapely thigh. A flannel shirt, with the loose collar confined by a soft tie, was especially becoming to those bronzed men. The sol-diers were nondescript in their dress. There was a pre-vailing tint of army blue throughout ; but there were picturesque patches, and the gaudy shirts bought from the army sutler seemed an appropriate costume for their fine muscular forms. Every sort of close cap and hat appeared, for nothing broad in the brim could with-stand the furious speed with which they rode against the wind. It was impossible for women to make toilets on such an occasion. We simply looked up the strongest garments we had, for the rough riding, the constant clambering in and out of the carriage, the absence of any protection to our clothes when we halted and sat on the ground for luncheon or to rest, made havoc with anything good.

Our opera-glasses looked just a little "frilly" in such a place, but they were really useful. It struck us as rather odd, when taking them from their velvet cases on the barren desert of a plain, to contrast our surroundings with the last place where they were used. The brilliantly lighted opera-house, the air scented with hot-house flowers, the rich costumes of the women, the faultlessly dressed men, the studied conventionality of the calmly listening audience, hearing ravishing music unmoved — all these recollections presented a scene about as different from that on the plains as can be imagined. Here we were, after all that glimpse of luxurious life, rolling over the arid desert, breathing with joy the intoxicating air, and going into ecstasies over everything, even over the one flower the hot summer had spared—the soapwort with its scentless blossom, its dagger-like leaves, and its prosaic root, which was really used as a substitute for soap.

As soon as the men dismounted every soldier began to examine his girth, bit, bridle, stirrups, and fire-arms, to buckle his carbine-belt, and fasten on his hat. The little company of troopers was told off into detachments, and directed to approach the herd to leeward, so that the quick nostrils of the buffalo picket might

not sniff danger. There were only murmuring voices—
no loud talking was allowed—and the merriment which
rarely leaves the happy-go-lucky trooper was momentarily suppressed. Some took off their caps, and tied
them, with their blouses, to the saddle; other superfluous articles were strapped down so as not to make a
sound. Then, with a low signal, they all gave rein to
their already excited horses, and dashed up from the
little divide in which these preparations had gone on,
and were off like a flash. The buffaloes, finally startled
by the noise of the hoofs of the advancing steeds,
awakened from their lazy, stupid browsing, started
their cumbrous gait, and made over the country far
more rapidly than any one would imagine possible
in view of their enormous size. Soon our men were
among the herd, singling out the especial buffalo they
wished to kill; and with our glasses we saw them for
some time, but at last a divide hid pursuers and pursued.

After a time Colonel Tom was discovered riding towards us. He brought the news that his brother had
wounded a buffalo, and waited for us before he put
in the death-shot. We were guided to the spot, and
found a huge beast pawing the ground, his short tail
waving defiance and rage, his bloodshot eyes glittering
from beneath the thick mat of bushy hair on his fore-
head, his horns ripping up the sod. As the officers
darted up to him he plunged forward to gore their
horses, and failing, dug his hoofs in the soil and tore
up the earth, throwing the dust about him in his fury.

It was a repetition of the Spanish bull-fight with the matadore for a few brief moments; but the telling shot was soon sent, and the great animal's tongue hung out helplessly, his nostrils bled as he rolled over, shook his huge frame, and struggled no more. We left the carriage in order to view him on all sides; and while we used up adjectives in the most reckless manner trying to find language fitting to describe our surprise at the size of the monster, we suddenly heard a scream, and found that General Custer had caught up the young lady of the party and set her down on the huge carcass of the dead game. She cried out in terror, but was firmly held there, and told to take the knife and cut a tuft from the buffalo's head as a trophy. Her hands trembled so much that Colonel Tom had to do the work, and then his brother laughingly handed the tuft to the temporarily enthroned queen of the hunt, telling her, with a droll twinkle of the eye, to take it to her sister with his compliments, and say that it was snatched from the head of a certain woman whom we knew that she despised. The brush was given to another one of us, and locks of hair secured for others; then we returned to the carriage while the buffalo was being cut up. It required much dexterity to take out the tongue. I know that our officers did some awkward hacking before they learned from a scout that it is skill and experience that are necessary. The rump-steaks were easily removed, and then the soldiers cut where they chose, and strung the meat to their saddles. It was a great privilege to the enlisted man to get this salutary change from his ration* of salt pork to fresh meat.

We were placed again in the carriage, the horsemen mounted, and the hunt was resumed. Finally we came to the edge of a cliff, and our carriage halted to find a safe descent. The officers and soldiers descended carefully, while the buffaloes seemed to go down head-first, but gathered themselves quickly, and started off so rapidly that they gained considerably on the riders, who had to take more time in getting again to the comparatively level ground. From our rather elevated position we had a fine view of the chase, and began to enjoy it all as we found what daring and splendid horsemanship was exhibited without accident. The manner in which the soldiers and officers rode was alone worth our trouble in coming as spectators. On our ordinary daily rides, or on the hunts after jack-rabbits or wolves, or even antelopes, there was not

---

* THE RATION (Par. 1367, Army Regulations).—A ration is the established daily allowance of food for one person. As now fixed, its components are as follows:

Twelve ounces of pork or bacon or canned beef (fresh or corned), or one pound and four ounces of fresh beef, or twenty-two ounces of salt beef; eighteen ounces of soft bread or flour, or sixteen ounces of hard bread, or one pound and four ounces of cornmeal; and to have, every one hundred rations, fifteen pounds of pease or beans, or ten pounds of rice or hominy; ten pounds of green coffee, or eight of roasted (or roasted and ground) coffee, or two pounds of tea; fifteen pounds of sugar, four quarts of vinegar; four pounds of soap, four pounds of salt; four ounces of pepper; one pound and eight ounces of adamantine or star candles; and to troops in the field, when necessary, four pounds of yeast-powder to one hundred rations of flour.

15

much opportunity for us to see the remarkable intelligence of some of the best horses, or have an exhibition of the superb equestrianship of a wild charge into a herd of buffaloes. Horse and rider were keyed up to such a pitch that not a word, and hardly a touch of the bridle, much less of a spur, was necessary. Without any guiding, the intelligent beast swung one moment into a graceful semicircle as he avoided the buffalo-wallow, hardly slackening his speed, or sprang with a powerful leap over a bunch of cactus, or made his tortuous way through the prairie-dog village, planting his hoofs with such unerring precision, it seemed incredible in view of the speed kept up. Then, when the one animal singled out as game was reached, the speed of the steed slackened, and a series of tactics worthy of a trained circus-horse began. The sudden rearing, and the quick backing in retreat to avoid the threatening horns, the dash forward beside the beast, the leaping to one side on all fours when the buffalo made a charge, were movements repeated with wonderful agility.

All amateurs fired at a buffalo's head, but the largest bullets made no impression on the thick skull. The animal shook his huge head as if dislodging a fly when a shot struck him in the face, or perhaps he paid no attention at all to the leaden hail as the bullets glanced off him as from an iron-clad.

With all the quick veering from side to side, the rapid wheeling to get out of the way, the rider, with body swaying at every movement of the horse, met

BUFFALO BROUGHT TO BAY.

each new change of gait, each fresh impulse of the vigilant animal, as if man and beast were one. In all these evolutions, so quickly and skilfully effected, the rider was able to load the poor hunted beast with lead in aiming for the telling spot, giving scarcely a thought to his horse. It goes without saying that our officers were good shots; but it was no easy affair to get a bullet just outside the edge of the great mass of tangled woolly hair that was packed so densely around the huge head. I remember one buffalo into which forty shots had been fired, and yet, with his hide thus perforated with bullets, he fought with desperation, even with his tongue hanging out, the unerring signal of fast-coming death.

One of the sights of the day, and one to remember for many a long day afterwards, was a contest with a buffalo which General Miles and General Custer had singled out of the herd and driven to bay. The exasperated animal made a furious fight, his great eyeballs red and glittering with rage, his huge head thrust downward as he hurled himself first at one officer who rode at him on one side, and then suddenly wheeling, he made desperate lunges towards the other when the hunter's temerity brought him too near. These lithe young men, without an ounce of superfluous flesh, with their bright eyes dancing with excitement, their fair hair flying, their throats bared and throbbing with the hot blood that rushed through their veins, their muscles steeled to the absorbing work before them, made such pictures of vigorous manhood that are not soon effaced from the camera of the mind. They thrust their feet out of the stirrups, and held themselves in place by their powerful and pliable legs ; and as neither weighed over one hundred and sixty pounds, they knew how to sit their horses lightly, and so favor the nervous, active animals under them.

It was something to occupy every energy, and keep even young and agile men vigilant, when the colossal animal suddenly wakened out of the usual dull lethargy of his humdrum life into the ferocity of rage. Had not the horses been so attuned to their riders, and so one with them in the excitement of the chase, one of the wildly tossing horns of the beast would have been thrust into the side from which such persistent aim was taken. The hunters trusted to their faithful steeds, and believed that they would take care of themselves as well as of their riders. The bridle was scarcely touched, and as the horses whirled first to one side and then to the other, the swaying supple forms of the athletic riders followed instinctively every motion of their steeds. Sometimes one of the horses sprang back almost upon his haunches in his struggle to retreat from the threatening head of the foe. Then, had not the skilful horseman, poised so lightly in the saddle as he was, been quick to dig his muscular legs into the horse's sides, and had not the bridle been loosely held so that there was not the least pull on the animal's mouth, there would surely have been a heap of tumbled-up and prostrate humanity floundering in the soil, and sending up a cloud equal to that which the hoofs of the great fierce monster threw into the air at every lunge of his enormous body. No one can conceive what marvellous activity was exhibited by these great creatures weighing eight hundred pounds, and cumbered as they were with a thick matted coat of hair about the head and shoulders, which alone seemed enough to retard their celerity.

As this battle was being waged by these two determined men with an equally resolute foe, they firing the pistols held constantly cocked and aimed at the foreshoulder of the buffalo, there was still a fourth assailant in the fray. A large and courageous dog had separated himself from the pack and followed the hunters. He began a series of attacks on the buffalo's hind-legs, his instinct pointing out, if not the vulnerable point, still one that was likely to prove a telling one on the animal's nerves and temper.

At last the frantic beast, coming just short of goring the horses that darted before him, condescended to bend his huge head lower, and while the dog leaped to secure another hold on the flying legs, the ponderous creature wheeled, and was for once too quick for the poor canine. He tossed him thirty feet in the air, and when the daring dog descended to the upturned turf it seemed as if his last yelp of pain was sounding.

But whatever crunching of bones went on in his terrible tumble, those of his legs were still intact, for he rose to his feet, dragged his tail between his legs, and started with a limp and a howl for home, possibly twenty miles away over a country without landmarks.

Still the buffalo fought on, his short, tufted tail, that

usually hangs so limp, raised in air and waving defiance. The blood at last trickled from his nostrils, one front-leg went under, and with a mighty crash down came the conquered foe, floundering and wallowing in the loosened soil, yielding reluctantly to the bullet that had pierced his side.

As we women watched this panorama spread at our feet we were filled with alarm, and trembling with anxiety one moment, triumphant and delighted with the horsemanship the next. Several buffaloes in different parts of the field were down, and we began to hope that the set of instruments one of the younger surgeons had carelessly exposed, and which had given us shudders when we started, would lie in their case undisturbed. This hope was suddenly dissipated when we saw one of the riders plunge over his horse's head, and lie motionless on the ground. There were three women who could not breathe except in gasps for a few moments, and the unmarried woman, in deep sympathy, strained her eyes to see if the wounded man could not be identified. Our gallant escort, the doctor, pitying the suspense of those who feared the prostrate man was the one of all the world to them, rode forward and soon brought us news. A sergeant's horse, getting his foot into a prairie-dog hole, had thrown him. The officers and soldiers gathered about the prostrate man, who almost instantly sprang to his feet, and declared himself "all right" with only his arm sprained, he thought. The young surgeon was only too proud to produce the instrument-case, so odious to us in the

morning; but it was no sprain. The arm of the fine
fellow was broken, and the surgeon had work to do.

However, with all his courage, the officers feared the
man would faint, and there was wild riding about to
see if among the hunters there was any whiskey. The
young follower of Esculapius, familiarly called "Little
Pills," had all the apparatus to cut up his patients, but
nothing to resuscitate them afterwards. Finally, after
a fruitless search among the officers, the orderly rode
on to our carriage to give the doctor's compliments,
and ask if the ladies had any whiskey. There was just
a momentary smile awakened, but a real round laugh
came from three throats when one of us asked to look
under the carriage seat, where the wraps and extra
necessaries were kept, and from a bag a little flask was
quietly brought forth. By this time some officers had
joined us, and deep and long was the peal of laughter
that they gave, for the woman who produced the whiskey was the one of the four who never tasted it, nor
even had so much as a gill in her house. In a twinkling this little joke spread among the hunters, with
the following questions : " Who produced the 'need-
ful?'"   "Why, who do you suppose?—Mrs. So-and-
So!"   At sound of the name another shout, and such
ejaculations as, "Well, I should just as soon have expected old Gough himself to have handed out a flask
from his pocket!" and it was in vain that the woman
protested that she had "feared accidents." When merry people want to get a joke out of anything it is difficult to turn the tide into another channel.

The sergeant, thanks to his pluck and to his splendid physical condition, was able to ride back to garrison, and as no one had much heart for further hunting, we all turned our faces in the direction in which the compass told us our home lay. There was not a distinguishing mark in the landscape to guide us. The utter monotony of the plains prevents any one from attempting to be a path-finder; and sometimes a boastful one among us, proud of his bump of locality, attempted to find his way, but travelled in a circle invariably as the lost traveller has always done. Soon the stars came out to light and guide us onward, and at ten o'clock we entered the camp, chaffing, singing, and chattering in spite of fatigue.

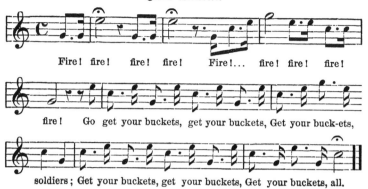

Fire Alarm.

Fire! fire! fire! fire! Fire!... fire! fire! fire!

fire! Go get your buckets, get your buckets, Get your buck-ets,

soldiers; Get your buckets, get your buckets, Get your buckets, all.

CHAPTER XV.

HUNTING RECORDS.

THE summer on Big Creek was not an idle one for our regiment, though the village of white canvas seemed to nestle so peacefully in the bend of the sinuous stream. The tents represented many hundred men, and always gave that impression to marauding Indians, who hover near booty in the shape of horses, even if they do not take regularly to the war-path. They estimate numbers among themselves by the tepees, allowing so many warriors to a lodge. But two-thirds of our tents were often empty, as two or three scouting parties might be out at one time.

There were several young graduates, who came from West Point that summer, who sighed to make a record, hearing every day with envious ears the constant reference to the glorious success of the Washita. These youths were called "tads" and "plebes," and treated in a half-contemptuous manner by officers of their own age possibly, but whose one successful winter's campaign lifted them a generation beyond. The exultant way in which these youngsters strutted about afterwards, when they had been in a fight, and the vaunting tone they assumed when they told me no one could call them "tads" or "plebes" now, was amusing to one who believed that the most delightful paths were those of peace. Still there was so much teasing that I was inclined always to side with the minority, for in the general tormenting I often felt the need of a champion myself. No one but these embryo warriors sighed for war. It is a mistaken impression that our army hailed the anticipation of a fighting campaign with delight. The change from their dull life to one of variety made our people rejoice at the prospect of active duty, but to fight Indians was not their desire. The outrages that brought on the winter's campaign had fired all hearts with the determination that punishment should be inflicted; but now that peace had been established, the whole command believed in doing everything to preserve it. I lately came across a telegram that General Custer sent to General Sheridan that summer, which has been preserved only by accident, but which bears upon this subject:

(Confidential.)

HAYS CITY, KANSAS.

Lieutenant-general Sheridan, Chicago, Ill. :

Without delicate handling of the Indian question by persons of experience in Indian affairs, we are liable to lose all benefit of our last winter's campaign, and be plunged into another general war with the southern tribes. I think this can be avoided.   G. A. CUSTER,

Brevet Major-General.

There were parties of northern hostiles in our vicinity often, and sometimes, had they known how many of the tents were empty, it would have been an easy affair to have overcome us. The coming or going of the scouting parties was a fresh occasion of interest every time. It was General Custer's policy to keep troops travelling all the summer. Though he did not hope to engage the wily red men in open combat while their ponies were in sufficiently good condition to enable them to run, still he did not mean to permit them to think that our people were not ready for them.

Sometimes on these scouts the officers and men killed enough game to give us all a treat on their return. Of all the scouting parties that summer, our brother Tom and another officer had the best shooting score. On the return to camp they harrowed the rest by describing their success. They had had deer, antelope, elk, and wild turkey every day; while we had been blessed with little besides buffalo-meat, as the cars had frightened away the more timid game. They saw two different herds of elks which numbered about a hundred each. They brought in the splendid antlers of one, which were six feet in height, and so wide that we seemed to have no place large enough to put them. Tom said, prosaically, when we were hunting for words grand enough to describe them, "Oh, the ani-

mal looked as if he had a chair-factory on his head!"
Tom was alone when he saw the owner of those branching horns. Three elks were approaching him. Jumping from his horse, he tied him to a bush, and shot
the leader of the three, a noble buck; the other two
stopped to look at him, and without changing his position he shot the second. The elks, like the deer and
antelopes, occasionally make themselves easy prey for
the hunter, because of their curiosity. I know that
Colonel Tom let the elks he shot approach, gazing at
him, till within seventy yards before he took aim.

In one of General Custer's letters to a friend, whom
he was trying to persuade to join him in camp, he describes some of his own successes:

I wish that you could have been with me on some of my
elk-hunts. I killed three in one run of four miles. A party
of us killed sixteen in one day. At another time, without
even stirring out of my tracks, I shot, off-hand, three antelopes the nearest of which was three hundred and twenty
yards. I aimed each time at a single animal and not at a herd.
Day before yesterday I saw a fine buck antelope standing
full front towards me; I could see only his head and part of
his neck above the grass. I fired, and dropped him; the distance was two hundred and sixty-seven yards, and the ball
entered his neck as accurately as if I had been close enough
to touch it with the muzzle of the gun. You should have
been with me the day I shot the big buck elsewhere referred
to in my letter to you.

After wounding him badly, and having a fine chase after
him mounted and with the stag-hounds, he took to the river,
and the dogs after him. Talk about Landseer's engraving!
I would not give the sight I witnessed that day for all the

engravings ever framed. The buck could stand on the bottom, but the dogs had to swim. One seized him by the ear, another by the nose, others were catching at his sides and neck, while he was striking right and left, sometimes catching a dog and keeping him in the water until I lost all hope of ever seeing him alive again. The marks of the dogs' teeth are in the buck's ears and along his sides, where they endeavored to jump up and seize him as he ran. All this time I was on the river-bank, within twenty yards of the conflict, rifle in hand, and vainly watching an opportunity to put a ball in and end the battle and save the lives of my dogs; but so active and mixed up were elk and dogs that for a long time I was unable to aim at the elk without at the same time covering a dog, until finally all the dogs concentrated at and about his head, when I quickly sent a rifle-ball through his loins, and thus terminated one of the most exciting hunting scenes I ever witnessed. I sent back for a wagon, and had him carried to camp entire. His photograph was taken as he lay in front of my tent, I, in my buckskins, seated on the ground near his head. He was about fifteen hands high, and his estimated weight, dressed, was eight hundred pounds. Fortunately I have learned the principles of taxidermy, and I have preserved in splendid order not only the antlers, head, and neck, but the skin and hoofs of the entire animal, so that it can be mounted as "natural as life." The zoologists accompanying us think it is the finest specimen of the elk anywhere in the United States.

On many of General Custer's hunts he took an Indian scout—one of those who came from a friendly tribe —to accompany the expeditions, and run a trail, or carry despatches back to the posts, or from one officer in the field to another commanding an expedition. These Indians were sometimes very faithful, and every kindness was shown them. They were like children, full of humors, often sulking for days over imaginary injuries; but, with patience, much valuable service could be had from them. They knew the country so well, and were so acquainted with its topography, that they could take a pointed stick and draw an intelligible map in the sand when they tried to explain the route our troops wished to take, or the encampment of the hostile Indians. In the picture in the frontispiece, a copy of a photograph, General Custer is represented holding a map which his celebrated scout Bloody Knife is studying, while another scout and the half-breed interpreter stand near. It was stupid work for Bloody Knife to remain about garrison when there was no expedition in progress, and he became as nearly animated as he ever allowed himself to be if word were sent for him to go on the hunt, if he wished to do so. The good shots of our officers did not go unnoticed; and I remember that Bloody Knife entreated General Custer to be cautious when he shot his first grizzly bear in the Yellowstone.

The elks were so much larger than other game that the officers often lost their first shots from buck-fever. I could readily understand it, for the first one I ever saw so startled me that it seemed as if some old fossil of the Megatherium period had sprung out of the petrified earth and taken up life again. The huge animal was lying down very near the place selected for our camp; and hearing our voices as we sat on the ground waiting for our tents to be pitched, he leaped into the air, and bounded off like a gazelle instead of a beast of such proportions. His antlers rose, seemingly, as far above his head as his head was from the ground. Colonel Tom said it was as large as a large-sized mule. With almost as quick a leap as the game, General Custer sprang for his rifle, flung himself on an unsaddled horse, and sped over the ground after the splendid game, but it had too much the start of him, and we lost the elk-steak that, in his brief absence, our men had begun to count on for their dinner. Elks were rare along any route that was travelled; so that it was an immense privilege if, when the officers went off for a distance on a scout, or a hunt was planned that took us away twenty miles or so, we had the good-fortune to include that animal in the game killed.

It was not an every-day affair to go hunting, however; for, to find buffaloes in abundance, we were obliged to travel some miles, and the knowledge that the northern Indians were hovering near much of the time made it a risk to ride without an escort. Our dogs sometimes hunted by themselves when tired of waiting to be taken out. In one of General Custer's letters to the same friend mentioned before, he speaks with pride of the ambition which took the hounds off by themselves:

My dogs hunt up and down the creek every day. Last night a man living eight miles below here came to camp and told me that four of my dogs—Lufra, Juno, Blucher, and Maida—had driven a large buffalo near his ranch, and that he had gone to them when he found the buffalo about used up and unable to get away, and that they would have killed it alone but he finished it with his rifle. They had probably been running it for several miles. I call that pretty good work for green dogs. I took them with me the other day, and it was sport. Juno sprang right at the nose the first time she ever saw a buffalo. Lufra took the ear, and Blucher got hold of the side. Juno is as savage as a tiger, and so is Lufra.

I do not know that I remember a man with more temerity than the ranchman to whom General Custer refers. He lived alone, and seemed perfectly insensible to fear. His place was a sort of a Mecca to us. The nearest ranch besides his was eighty miles distant, adjoining the town of Ellsworth. To see growing things that had been planted and were allowed to advance without either being compelled to move and leave them, as we usually were, or to hear of their destruction by the Indians while the first shoots were starting, as in the case of hundreds of ranchmen at that time, was an event in life ; and I remember how "homey" the rows of potatoes, the hills of corn, and the climbing beans seemed after years without the sight of a garden. The man had made himself very comfortable in his dug-out in the side of a bank; and even that I envied, for the wind could not toy with his habitation and blow it away as it did our "rag houses." I confess to great curiosity as to what circumstances in the States had been so disastrous as to make him willing to leave every one and risk his life down on that lonely creek. Our men, with one voice, attributed it to some woman's work. "Depend upon it," they said, "he prefers the wilderness to being nagged to death in the States." If I suggested that he might be a fugitive from justice I was silenced by a laughing, teasing retort to the effect that some men were more fortunate than others: a desert like ours would frighten most women, but there were others who could penetrate any wilderness and pursue a man into the extremest solitude.

One night we were trying to entertain an officer from another station, and a ride was our only resource, as it was impossible to get up a hunt for some reason, I have forgotten what. We started off, a gay, rollicking party, three women, with perhaps twenty officers, and a few orderlies. All the dogs of the regiment were with us, apparently—from the lofty and highborn stag-hounds down to the little "feist," or mongrel, of the trooper, whose plebeian tail, that usually curled over his back, was now drooping, and his sides panting with the speed he had to keep up. We laughed and sang as we let our horses out, and the college choruses or West Point songs rang on the air as clearly and joyously as if we had been riding down a safe country glade at home. Of course, with the unusual spectacle of a garden within eight miles of the camp to show, we followed the creek, and enjoyed the surprise of our guest's face when the domestic turnip and the thrifty beet of civilization greeted his sight. This was our last ride so far without an escort, for the next day news came that the Indians had crossed the stream the

16

night before, burned the first stage-station, and killed the men in charge.

The red man has exhibited great awe of telegraph lines, believing that there was something supernatural in their workings, and for this fortunate reason, in our worst border troubles, many a warning was flashed along the wires when an attack was even so much as anticipated; but in this instance the lawless band, setting at defiance superstitious fears, had cut the wire, and in torturing the men bits of it had been stuck in their flesh beside the arrow that every Indian leaves in a dead body, whether it be sent from the bow before or after the fatal shot.

There was one caution that the officers dinned in our ears day after day—namely, that we women should never leave camp alone even for a stroll. We were usually obedient about this, for we felt always that we had been brought out on sufferance, as it were. Great trouble had been taken to prepare for us, and all had been done with the understanding that we should not allow ourselves to be in the way. These warnings about the Indians were "line upon line" with General Custer, and he had only to refer to the captives I had seen soon after their release to elicit promises of caution from me. It was due to events like the capture of the Box family that the winter's campaign in the Washita country had been undertaken. While we were at Fort Riley the mother and three daughters were brought to the post. Their release had been effected by the tact of our officers, and by the payment of a large ransom.

At the time of their capture a year previous, the father and one babe were killed at once. The mother and her daughters—one a girl of eighteen, another ten, and the third three years old—were bound on ponies and started on the march. The mother was allowed to carry the child still younger, but the infant's crying angered the savages, and they dashed its little brains out against a tree before the anguished mother's eyes. When the division of spoils and prisoners was made, the three children and the mother were separated, and assigned to different bands of the same tribe. I could not find any language to repeat what the poor mother and eldest daughter told me of their horrible sufferings during the year of their captivity. Their melancholy was most heart-rending, for even their release from captivity would not bring them back to the husband and father so dear to them, or put in the maternal arms the two little innocent infants that had been murdered.

The little girl of ten, when separated from her mother, grieved and mourned so that, to stifle her sobs and prevent her repeating them, the Indians had burned the soles of her feet. She turned them up to show me the scars as I sat in the midst of this pitiful group. The girl, then nineteen years old, in the captivity which was worse than death, had lost all trace of girlhood. Had she been retained as the property of one chief her fate would have been more deplorable than any that a woman ever endures, but even this misery was intensified, for she was traded from one chief to another in the everlasting dickering that the Indians keep up. The suffering of these poor captives made a lasting impression on me. I had not been long away from a home where my parents not only shielded me from all sorrow and trouble, but guarded me from even tales of misery which would have made a spot on the sun of a most radiant girlhood.

Still, this story of suffering was not considered enough by General Custer to warn me against taking any risks where Indians roamed. He came to me after that, while we were stopping a day or two at the hotel in Leavenworth, to ask me to see a distracted man with whom he had been talking. When I found that the man was almost wild with grief over the capture of his wife by Indians, and the murder of his children, I begged to be spared witnessing such a painful sight when I could do no good. The reply was that sympathy was something every one needed, and I made no further resistance. The man was as nearly a madman as can be. His eyes wild, frenzied, and sunken with grief, his voice weak with suffering, his tear-stained, haggard face—all told a terrible tale of what he had been and was enduring. He wildly waved his arms as he paced the floor like some caged thing, and implored General Custer to use his influence to organize an expedition to secure the release of his wife. He turned to me with trembling tones, describing the return to his desolated cabin. As he came from the field where he was at work, full of pleasure at approaching the rude hut where he had left his little ones playing about the door, he saw no sign of life, no movement of any kind; no little feet ran out to meet him, no piping voice called a welcome to him. With the darkest forebodings—for those were troublous days to the early settler—he began to run, and, near some logs, he almost fell upon the dead and mutilated body of one child. Not far off was a little shoe, and some light hair, evidently torn from the downy head of another child, and a few steps from the door the two younger children lay in pools of blood, their little heads scalped, their soft flesh still pierced with arrows. Worse by far was the further discovery that awaited him. The silence in the cabin told its awful tale, and he knew, without entering, that the mother of the little ones had met with the horrible fate which every woman in those days considered worse than death. General Custer was so moved by this story that he could not speak, and I became so unnerved that it was many a night before I could shut my eyes without seeing the little yellow heads of those innocent children clotted with blood, and their sightless blue eyes turned to heaven as if for redress. The lesson was effectual for a time, for not only was I moved to deepest pity for the bereaved man, but I became so terrified that I could not even ride out of camp with an escort without inward quakings, and every strange or unaccountable speck on the horizon meant to me a lurking foe.

Soup - y, soup - y, soup - y, not a.... sin - gle bean;

Cof - fee, cof - fee, cof - fee, not a.... bit of cream;

Pork - y, pork - y, pork - y, not a.... streak of lean.

CHAPTER XVI.

ARMY HOUSE-KEEPING.

I HAVE often been asked questions about house-keeping on the frontier—how we furnished our quarters, what occupations we had, and other similar matters. There were no conveniences for house-keeping; we had little furniture, and we women occupied ourselves mostly in finding amusement for the men, who looked to us for diversion in their leisure hours. In the summer, while the regiment was absent on a campaign, our lives were occupied with reading and domestic detail in order to fill up the time and make it go faster. In the winter we tried to vary the monotony of the table with all the ingenuity we were capable of, in order to make up to our men for the deprivations of the summer, when they were on the march.

Government wastes no money in ornamenting army

quarters. They are severely plain, with plastered walls, wood-work that was once painted, perhaps, but bears little trace of the brush now. On the plains they were usually disfigured by huge stoves, unless one fought, as we did, for one room with an open fire. It was very hard to give a cosey, home-like look to a sitting-room without blinds, with plastered walls, and without an open fire.

The kitchen was the exasperating place. It often lacked the simplest contrivances to make work easy. I remember an army friend who began her frontier life during the Mexican war. She was fearless in stating her opinions, and was dreaded by the quartermaster because of the determined manner in which she went at him when it was necessary to have her house repaired or painted. People used to say that he habitually went round by the rear of the quarters, trying to avoid her, as she often came out on the piazza to intercept him. Once, however, I heard him receiving a very pronounced expression of her views, and the last word sent after him, as he pleaded " pressing business," was, "Next time you build army quarters do, in pity's name, ask your wife how a kitchen ought to be built."

It really did seem as if whoever planned our kitchens had never considered for a moment that the " women who work from sun to sun, and whose work is never done," would be blessed by even the smallest effort to lighten their labors. Fortunately our cooks were colored women. Army people like the negroes, and find a quality of devotion in them that is most grateful when one is so dependent on servants, as every one is in military life. As the Southern cook is taught to live in kitchens built outside, and to cook by a fire-place with few modern utensils, we were not distressed by "warnings," as we should undoubtedly have been had a servant accustomed to an Eastern kitchen been consigned to ours.

The quartermaster's own house was something to turn us all green with envy, for he had all the work-men at his disposal. It was painted, had closets, with little shelves here and there, that women dote on, and many trifles that seemed to us the sum and substance of domestic elegance, for everything was comparative there in those days of deprivation. We women called on his pretty, fascinating wife, and loved her in spite of her superior environments; but our roaming eyes took in every improvement, and we went out to say, at a safe distance, "I don't blame *her;* but I would like to read him a lesson on equal distribution."

There was joy in garrison one morning when a little tale of what we considered a case of justice meted out came travelling along from one woman to another. It was Christmas morning, and though there were no chimes to ring us up, no carols to delight our ears, we felt convivial even over the extra nap with which we celebrated the day. The quartermaster, sleeping in his comfortable bed, was called out in the gray of early dawn, that coldest chill, just before daybreak, striking him as he went barefooted through his hall, while his heart was beating with alarm for fear of disaster or fire, as he answered the bell. "Glad he was punished for having a bell when we had none," we said, savagely, when we heard this. On opening the door a dishevelled tipsy Jezebel of a camp-woman, bracing herself against the wood-work as best she could, said to him, "It's cold, and my nose bleeds," and with this information she departed. The woman who clamored for paint, another who appealed in vain for necessary repairs, had no compunctions in laughing at this case of woman's inhumanity to man, and if we suffered for anything after that, we summed up every misery with the words, "It's cold, and my nose bleeds."

There was no sink in the kitchen or outside. The cook opened the door and flung the contents of the dishpan or garbage bucket as far to one side as the vigorous force of her arms would send it. This always left an unsightly spot, to which we were compelled to shut our eyes, as there was no remedy. The prisoners of a post have as their punishment the duty of cutting wood and policing the garrison, which means an attempt to keep it clean. If they lingered in our yard longer than in another, a careful study of the scene revealed the fact that the sergeant who guarded them was being regaled with coffee, with the unusual luxury to them of condensed milk; and after the ranking officer (for rank tells even that far down in the scale) had feasted, came the appeal of the soldiers under him turning hungry eyes towards the kitchen, and saying, in a voice that was so modulated as to "carry" no farther than was necessary, "Say, you wouldn't see a fellow starve?" or

"You hain't got none of those fine white biscuit, have you?"

Generally after these healthful, able-bodied men had cut a few sticks they wearily sat down and eyed the house, waiting for the door to open. They resorted to any subterfuge to prolong their stay out of the guard-house. There was nothing like it except the crescent of dogs that replaced them about the kitchen door, whining, and uttering short suggestive barks until our Eliza, exasperated beyond control, burst open the door and hurled any convenient missile at them, always accompanied by invectives anything but flattering to their character.

I ought not to leave the impression that Uncle Sam neglected his wards. The prisoners were abundantly fed at the guard-house. The army ration is so large that few instances have been known where one man was able to consume it. Our dogs also were especially provided for by us. A huge kettle of mush was boiled with meat, bones, and grease; but they, like the soldiers, preferred what they considered dainties from the family table. As for water, it was kept in barrels outside the door. Over the one especially for drinking and culinary purposes there was an effort made to keep a cover securely fastened down with a convenient stone, and this was emptied every day; but the others were open to the winds of heaven, as a board to cover anything was hardly to be had at all. We had enough cotton-wood timber sawed at the Government mill near the river; but should that be used it would warp into

a curve almost in a day, and the dogs tilting and jog-
gling it could dislodge such a cover easily. As the
plains winds are never lulled, all the floating grass,
leaves, and dust found a resting-place in the water.
These foreign substances soon offered a home for "wig-
glers," which in an incredible time were transformed
into mosquitoes.

The water was very hard, and it was difficult to make
a successful Monday without a labor of preparation,
for there were straining, settling, and softening with
alum to be done. White of eggs is advised by the
cook-books; but, considering that we were not likely
to get either the yolk or white of an egg to eat for
months at a time, we were not very likely to waste
them (when we had them) on the water-barrels. When
the clothes were finally on the line, then came the
struggles to keep them there. The wind blew them
over the prairie if they were not most securely fastened,
and rarely did Eliza return from the line without talking to herself in an ominous way, as the corners of the
strong table-covers and sheets were whipped into fringe,
while articles that were becoming tender with age were
frequently in ribbons.

On the awful Mondays that we called "black Fri-
days" we took turns in giving our cook an order, if it
was absolutely necessary to give her any. It was very
odd to hear a grown person, the head of the house, perhaps, say, "You tackle Eliza this time, I did the last
time."

Once we were stationed in the States for a short

time, and had great difficulty in getting a house, as there were none to rent in the small town, and naturally the citizens were averse to moving out in order to lease us theirs. Finally an officer on General Custer's staff found a place, and as our cook was absent at the time, we decided to try co-operative house-keeping, I taking charge one week, and the wife of the officer the next. We tried to have every dainty of the market on our table. After our long season of enforced frugality on the plains, we felt ourselves entitled to all the season afforded. We sat round the open fire at night and planned new dishes for the next day. We revelled in a house fully furnished, for so we had rented it, and drew comparisons between it and our army quarters, where there were often vacant spaces and yawning gaps in place of furniture, to which we never could attain. The closets bewildered us, so long had we suffered for such conveniences. We lost our things, having so much space, and the men said that they owed a debt of gratitude to their government for the privilege of quickly finding their coats and pantaloons, which heretofore had been hidden under a mass of dresses and petticoats.

Our friend's cook had lived long on the frontier, for she was a soldier's wife, and being out at service with the officers, she was accustomed to husband all supplies most carefully, not knowing when they would be replaced; there was in consequence a distressing meagreness about her dishes, and hardly a suspicion of butter in anything she prepared. We requested her to use more material, adding that while we had the opportu-

nity we desired to live well, as we never knew at what
hour we might be ordered out to the frontier, where
deprivations were the order of the day. The cook,
quite devoted to our interests, was inclined to protest.
She replied, "But oh, ma'am, iggs is twenty cints a
dozen," forgetting that when we did have them in the
West they cost us seventy-five cents or a dollar. She
began the new week the same way with both of us,
and with a doleful countenance exclaimed, after receiving her orders, "And have you any *idee*, ma'am, what
your *mate* bill will be this month?"

The question of cake and pastry was a momentous
one. Here we were in a land that seemed to run over
with milk and honey, or better still for us, where butter, eggs, and cream were in abundance for delicacies,
and yet we were very stupid in their use. Living for
years without these luxuries had either dulled our
memories as to the method of concocting nice dishes,
or, beginning our married life so young as we did on
the plains, we had never known how. Armed with a
cook-book, we tried experiments, and the men courage-
ously partook of the results. Being in perfect health,
they survived the experiments, and, as is usual with
officers, overrated all we did. At the time of the
church festivals of the different denominations we
fared well, and our table was supplied with delicious
cake made by zealous churchwomen. We all bought
so much that I remember one occasion when the wom-
en who were getting up a festival postponed it until
General Custer returned from duty out of town.

There never seemed to be any way of preparing for unexpected guests on the frontier, and yet it was a land of surprises. If we were near the railroad we could usually count on six trains out of seven bringing us company, and if our visitors were thoughtful enough to telegraph, some sort of preparation could be made; but were we stationed at a post or encamped in the field where the only access to us was by overland travel, there could be no warning note. People rode in on horseback or drove by wagon at all hours of the day and night. Should they prove to be officers who came on duty, or *en route* to some other station, we felt little solicitude, for they knew the usages so far away from a base of supplies, and could joke about a meagre larder with us as merrily as if they were not hungry— could even quote the old story of an officer who was out of supplies but not deficient in hospitality, and who invited a friend to a dinner of two dishes; when one, the rice, was declined, he was asked to help himself to the mustard.

The commissary was nearly always accessible when we halted at night on the march, or daily in camp; but there was but one issue of meat for the day, and having eaten the steak for breakfast, it was somewhat embarrassing to have guests arrive, perhaps an hour afterwards, and the awful fact pressed upon us that if we gave them meat from the roast there would be nothing left for their dinner. Even the commanding officer had sometimes to be called into the kitchen tent for consultation in emergencies, and he fortunately never felt embarrassed over what was a serious question to both Eliza and me. He offered to take the people off to see the horses, the camp, the stream on which we lived, the bluff beyond, to view the vastness of the plains. Then, left to ourselves, we sent round at once to the other messes to find if any one had meat, game, eggs, or anything cookable. If they failed us, as they generally did, for no one had any better facilities for keeping food than we had, then the commissary ham or bacon, often inexpressibly salty and dry, became the *pièce de résistance* for the hurried breakfast-table. But the undaunted head of the house came back with his people in fine humor, and managed to whisper to me, in a roguish manner, " I've got them good and hungry; they won't mind what they eat now."

Occasionally, when we were alone, all the breakfast was not eaten, and enough meat went off on the platter for croquettes or hash, or a savory stew, but it was never Eliza's plan to attempt to save anything for the unexpected guest. If I expostulated with her, and said I wondered if everybody's cupboard was always as bare as ours, she protested in reply, " Miss Libbie, you don't spect to keep anything, do you, without no 'frigerator, no cellah ?—why, things would spile." If I went out to the kitchen tent hungry, between meals, it was a very different affair ; she instantly said, " Miss Libbie, there ain't no bread, but it won't take me no time at all to beat you up some biscuit or poach you an egg."

If we were in a permanent camp—that is, if our tents

were pitched for a stay of some weeks or months—we often had all the canvas we needed. Sometimes the kitchen and dining tent were put opposite each other, with a fly covering the space between. If we had the good-fortune to have a table at all, it was usually of rough boards spread on two carpenter's horses; those sitting at one end could not lean on the table or emphasize an after-dinner story by coming down with their fists on the boards. If they did, the table came too. The time appointed for other people's "walnuts and wine" was to us the hour for the officers' pipe and cup of coffee, and at many merrymakings the sudden coming down of expressively gesturing hands on the unreliable table set the dishes joining in the concert. We sometimes had stout camp-stools made of oak, for which we sent into the States, and the soldier who made them knew all that would be expected of them; but even oak, leather, or the strongest canvas used would get rickety after being tumbled round in the baggage-wagon in its descents into a cañon, or in its plunges and jerks through heavy mud. There was a degree of uncertainty and insecurity about the legs of tables, stools, and camp-beds in those days that made us all sit down at first very gently.

In the kitchen tent we found it well to leave the field completely to Eliza when dinner was in course of preparation. If we rejoiced in a cook-stove, it was battered and broken after our journeys; the utensils were pretty well wrecked also, while often a vicious change in the ever-varying wind drove the smoke into poor Eliza's eyes. The wood was frequently damp, and usually soft cotton-wood, which would not burn at all if it was wet, and burned out quickly if it was dry. There was no kitchen-table. The mess chest was large, but its lid could not be utilized with safety. Filled as it was with dozens of slides for plates, saucers, platters, vegetable dishes, with holes cut for bowls and cups, compartments for sugar, flour, tea, coffee, rice, etc., it could not be used conveniently for a table, as, once its lid was down and in use, there was sure to be a little baking powder or a pinch of salt needed, and they were usually in the very depths of its centre. Eliza, knowing this, put her pans, skillets, and kettles on the ground, mixed her baking-powder biscuit on a board on the grass, peeled her potatoes kneeling, and ground her coffee sitting *a la Turque*.

If the wind did not blow her tent quite down, she had to fight its continual bursts through the insecure fastenings at the front. Mingled with everything was the fine dust which the gusts of wind blew in, or which the continual flapping of the tent-wall on the ground sifted into every dish or cooking utensil. The tea blew away while being put into the teapot, the flour rose in little puffs while being moulded. No one ever gets quite used to the wind of the plains. We studied in vain to outwit its persistent intermeddling. I have seen poor Eliza ironing on the ground, the garment over which she worked held down by stones for weights, while she swiftly and vigorously plied her iron, holding down the other part with her free hand.

17

Under all these vexatious circumstances it was a marvel how she kept her temper at all. At times when it was raining, the wind opening the entrance, or blowing up from underneath the tent-walls, or sending puffs of smoke out of the damper, or around the hole cut in the canvas for the pipe, no one approached the poor woman. If we heard the things rattle ominously, or wood being pitched about recklessly among the tins and kettles, or sounds of a voice deep and emphatic, or, more significant still, if the soldier who was our striker, and usually waited on the cook assiduously, slid quietly out into the rain and wandered about aimlessly, we knew that it was the better part of valor to let Eliza work out her own salvation. She certainly had a right to be in a fury, and why she did not set the tent on fire, or take a skillet and brain those who brought her out there, was, and is, an unsolved problem.

I have quoted one of her sayings before, but must beg the liberty of repeating it here. When the day was over, and twilight came, there was nothing to do. She sometimes grew lonely, and if I went to sit beside her, seeing that she had gone off by herself, and needed consoling, there was no answer to be made when she said, "Miss Libbie, you's always got the ginnel, but I hain't got nobody, and there ain't no picnics nor church sociables nor no buryings out here." Her whole heart was wrapped up in our interests, and many a device she resorted to in concocting some new dish with which to surprise us. I remember, when we were very far out in the wilderness, having tomato catsup to add to the flavor of the ever-recurring beef, Eliza's face shone with pleasure when we called her in and found that she had used canned tomatoes, which the commissary always has, to get up this treat for us.

Once I had what seemed to me old-fashioned peach preserves, carrying me back in memory from the very heart of the great American desert to my mother's table in the East when I was a child. Again it was one of Eliza's surprises with canned peaches—which, like tomatoes, are always good at the commissary. If our butter melted on the march, and we prepared to eat dry bread all summer, she would say, "Don't none of you fret, it ain't spoiled, it's biled, and now it won't get rancid no matter what comes."

Sometimes we saw no eggs all summer long, after the supply that we had brought from the last town we had passed through on our way to camp was exhausted. The cook-books were maddening to us, for a casual glance at any of them proves how necessary eggs, butter, and cream are to every recipe. In those days, when the army lived beyond the railroad, it would have been a boon if some clever army woman could have prepared a little manual for the use of house-keepers stranded on the frontier, and if she had also realized that we had no mothers to ask, and consequently had omitted the tormenting advice to "use your own judgment."

Eliza knew that her master was extremely fond of apples, and when the supply sent out began to decay, she took the utmost pains to put them up in glass jars;

and when spring came, and there was dearth of every-thing in our snow-bound home, and we were aggra-vated by reading of strawberries, etc., in the States, Eliza brought the jars out from their concealment, and setting the apples before the head of the house, she said, " Ginnel, these is your strawberries."

Infantry Dinner-call.

[Called "Pease upon a Trencher."]

CHAPTER XVII.

NECESSITY THE MOTHER OF INVENTION.

SOMETIMES I have been asked, when speaking of the monotony of our fare, why we did not rely on game to vary the inevitable beef that Uncle Sam allowed us to buy. The Indians were about us a great deal of the time, and though perhaps unseen — for they are very wary—we had proof that they lurked in our vicinity. In Dakota we were never able to go on hunting parties without an escort, unless in the depths of winter. The danger of men getting so excited with the pursuit of game as to separate themselves from the others made the commanding officer dread sending hunting parties out to any distance. In the dead of winter, when the Indian was buried in his tepee, our officers and soldiers went often, and were able to bring back enough deer for many tables.

It was a charming sight, the return of the hunters.

If Eliza ran to the door, her frugal eye took in the game before anything picturesque made an impression; and she used to say: " Lord-a-massey's sake, Miss Libbie, ain't I glad that the ginnel's got a deer! I've eat so much beef since I come to live with you that I spects to bellow and grow horns foh' I get back to God's land."

The deer was taken into the wood-house, where the hunters cut it up, and sent, with their compliments, portions to the different families. If any one had been fortunate enough to have bull or buffalo berries, gathered in the autumn, the jar of jelly added the tart flavor that game needs. These berries were red, and grew along the stem very thickly, so that gathering consisted in shaking the bush, under which a soldier's poncho was spread, to save the ripe fruit from being lost in the close buffalo-grass. Naturally there were not so many berries gathered as might have been, had not our foe been watching to steal stray horses in the cañons or bottom-land, where the fruit grew. The commanding officer was somewhat embarrassed one day when he sat visiting in the quarters of our neighbor, to whom he had sent a quarter of venison a few moments before. There was a tremendous scuffle and growling heard in the half-story (or attic) above, where the meat had been hung; and the host going up to see the meaning of the fracas, found nine of our dogs, that had followed their master in, and chased up-stairs when no one was looking, busy eating the venison as fast as their powerful jaws could tear it apart. Of course the hunters could do nothing else than go out next day for another deer to replace the stolen meat.

In Kansas we had buffalo most of the time, and that was a great change for us. The rump-steak is juicy, and requires little basting, while buffalo tongues, which were such a rare treat in the market of the Eastern cities, were then to be had in abundance with us. It is remarkable how luxuries that are unheeded in the midst of plenty will impress themselves on our minds for years and years if they come to us in the midst of deprivations. We rarely had small game, except the few ducks that came to the pools formed by heavy rains on the prairie in the autumn; but I remember those, and the prairie-chickens of Kansas, and the plover of Dakota, that were shot on the march up the Missouri River, as if I had never tasted birds before or since. I also recollect a little butter I once made, as seemingly the first and last occasion of my ever eating any, so good did it seem.. An officer made me a miniature churn with a bottle, and a little wooden dasher put through a cork. We were at the time marching each day farther and farther into the wilderness, but occasionally came to a ranch where some venturesome frontiersman had established himself, and located his claim to Government land. Of course our people galloped on in advance, and soon bought out the madam. There was a little cream among other things, and as I sat under the tent-fly after we made camp, it was soon transformed into butter in the toy churn.

In garrison the head of our household was almost inconsolable without soup. On the march he could do without almost everything; but once in a house, there were certain articles on the bill of fare he made every effort to obtain. Ox-tail soup was, of course, easy to have when the beef was killed daily at a post; but if it failed, the following dialogue between the master and cook took place: " Where's my soup?" like some small boy demanding his supper. Eliza, with maternal look, and protesting: "Ginnel, what you s'pose I'se gwine to make soup of? I ain't got nothing." He: "Go out and get some stones, and boil them up with something; only I want soup." Exit Eliza, perplexed, but set to thinking how to concoct something out of nothing.

Eliza really needed few suggestions, for her mind was intent on inventions, and ready to improve every opportunity that presented itself. While we were encamped near Fort Hays, General Miles offered us many civilities, and among other kindnesses we received ice occasionally from the post ice-house. Eliza, in order to celebrate the arrival of some Eastern guest whom she wished to impress with our resources, served as a surprise one day peach ice-cream. Investigation revealed that it was made of condensed milk, with canned peaches, and frozen in a bucket which her willing "Man Friday" manipulated, no one knows for how long a time, during the freezing process.

One day the cook of one of my friends offered to make her some vinegar-pies, and declared, in appetiz-

ing description, that "lemon-pies was nothing to them."
So, carefully following the direction of her soldier-
lover, she made the pastry, and for the pie part prepared a paste more like that used by the paper-hang-
er than anything else, and flavored this with vinegar.
The poor mistress, divided between the desire to thank
the cook for trying to do something for her, and her
repugnance to the odious pie, was in a state of extreme
perplexity, but was able to decline with thanks when
soldier pies were suggested again.

One officer, coming from Bismarck one day, brought
butter, and as the commissary had been out of that
article for some time, all the messes sent over to the
town to get some. Shortly after we learned that the
commissary butter, at seventy-five cents, which had
been condemned and sold to the grocer in town, had
been put by him through some process that temporarily helped it, placed in jars, and resold to us for one
dollar a pound.

Sometimes the tiresome bill of fare to which we had
to submit when far from the railroad, or in a country
where it was dangerous to hunt, was a sore trial if a
woman chanced to be ailing and craved dainty food.
Nearly every one was well, and our plain dishes were
flavored by that inexhaustible "sauce," good appetite;
but when any one was ill, and the appetite had to
be tempted, it was hard. One of my friends had listened with eager pleasure to the bill of fare that another friend had described as having been served at a
luncheon she had attended in the States; and if the

less fortunate woman, who had not been on leave of absence, and who could not eat the food healthful people enjoyed, became desperate, she used to say, "Come, M——, let us go to Mrs. So-and-So's to luncheon;" and her eyes brightened at the recapitulation of every dainty, as she let her powerful imagination deceive her into thinking she was actually a participant.

It was constantly a wonder to me that officers who were leading a rough existence on the campaigns so much of the year, could take up all the amenities of life so readily when living in garrison again. We could rarely find any subject for criticism in their conduct. Once General Custer forgot himself when he came home to his mother, after a long summer in the field. He took up his plate as he talked, and brushed it off with his napkin, as on the march it was almost a necessity to do, on account of the wind blowing the dust over everything. His sensitive old mother, always hovering around him, slipped to his place and critically examined the plate, saying, "My son, is there anything wrong with it?" He blushed furiously, as blond people are apt to do if they redden at all, tossed back his hair, as he was wont to do in embarrassment, apologized, and at once turned to tell me that I must break him of that habit, or he would do so at Judge S——'s, or the Honorable Mr. M——'s, where we were accustomed to dine sumptuously while on leave in New York.

Every one in camp or garrison pounced upon the slightest chance for a joke, and a certain officer would blush now if reminded of the time we all let him, in an absent-minded way, sit down to our table in garrison, on the day he returned from a march, with his hat on, just on purpose to laugh at him afterwards. Of course, with the persistent fatality of things, he was the most punctilious of us all, which made his slip all the funnier. Our officers ate out-of-doors six and eight months of the year, and necessarily dined with their heads covered; consequently, it was little wonder that it took a day or two to get accustomed to in-door life. On a similar occasion, after months in the field, General Custer found Eliza transfixed with surprise, her face full of reproof, saying, as if he had been a spoiled boy, while she pointed to the floor, "What you s'pose your mother goin' to think of you if you do them careless tricks when you get home?" Accustomed in camp to toss the remnant of water in his tumbler on the grass before having it refilled, he had forgotten that he was not on a campaign until the splash on the bare floor of our dining-room was pointed out to him. Two or three trifles like these, occurring directly after their return from an expedition, were all that I ever saw of the *gaucheries* that many expected from men who lived almost constantly in the open air.

If company came, there was recourse to borrowing. Our friends deprived themselves of everything, except, perhaps, a spoon or knife and fork and plate apiece, to supply our table. We had only six of everything in the mess chest, and it was no unusual thing to have a dozen people come unexpectedly; then there was scurrying about to the different messes to borrow everything that could be spared. The term mess is applied either to a family or a number of officers who for convenience live together, engaging one cook, and each of the mess taking his turn in the domestic details and providing the supplies. At the end of the month the expenses are equally divided. I find that it is the impression among civilians that officers have their food provided as the soldiers do their rations. Officers buy everything for themselves, but Government makes no extra charge for the transportation. The commissary sells in Arizona, or any equally remote place, at the same rate at which the articles were bought in the East. There are commissioners who examine everything submitted to the Commissary Department, so that what we bought was, as a rule, of the best quality. There was always this drawback, however, that the supplies might have been on hand so long as to have lost freshness, and sometimes the Government warehouses were far from suitable for the storing of groceries and provisions.

We thought no more of borrowing for any company or unusual festivity that we had, than if all had been making these demands on our mothers or sisters living near. We lent our houses and everything in them for months at a time. It was surprising how little was lost living in that careless way. We had no locks on our doors, nor was ever a key turned in a trunk or on a closet, if we happened ever to have the latter luxury. I never remember losing anything except some valuable lace, and that was taken by a woman to whom we gave a home while she was trying to get a place as cook. We slept always with unlocked doors. The sentinel was at some distance from us, but we did not look to him for the protection of our property. It was to the honor and kindly feeling towards us that we trusted. As I have said, our soldiers sometimes took things to replace our worn-out outfit, but made what they thought very trifling exchanges, and they were in turn so zealous in guarding our effects that we never lost anything. We were careless enough—so much so that if any trifling addition was made to our equipments we did not know enough about our belongings to notice it. Once I remember seeing a chest of carpenter's tools in the stable. That did surprise me, but the story told was plausible, and it was impossible to get at the exact truth. Soon afterwards we suddenly moved, on imperative orders, and the chest could not be transported, so I always hoped that it finally reached its rightful owner. The servants knew that every one was welcome to our things, so they did not even ask us; and if I recognized anything at a friend's house when the refreshments were served in the evening, there was a significant smile from the hostess as I ate with my own spoon and used a napkin with a big C in the corner.

There was in the family a mania for auctions. A red flag out of a house in a city through which we were rushing to catch a train set us in a perfect flutter, and was a sad disquieter of the domestic peace, so hard did

it seem to pass it by. While stationed at Leavenworth
there was wide scope for the exercise of this family
predilection. Sometimes the queerest imaginable articles came home, and if one of the family of two had
not had a hand in the excitement of bidding and pur-
chasing, there was very apt to follow an inquiry common in domestic circles—"What on earth do you
suppose one can ever do with *that?*"—some scorn
underlying the emphasized "that" Once a huge bowl
—too big for any ordinary occasion—made its *entrée*
with just such a welcome. But a great "find" it
proved eventually; there came to be no festive occasion complete without it. My dish was a belle; it was
invited to more dinners than any one in garrison, and
it was too hard that it could not have caught and retained in its deep bowl some of the wit and *bonho-
mie* that surrounded it, for officers are the best of
diners. In the short half-hour allowed for dressing, a
business man must shake off the cares and perplexities
that have consumed him all day, and put himself into
visiting trim. Our officers have not that to do. They
have hard duty in the day, but much of it is routine
work, and is not accompanied with carking care, consequently it can be thrown off the moment it no longer
requires attention. But then it is their nature, and
the life encourages them to work very hard when work
is before them to do, but to set aside the burdens
quickly. Indeed, take out of every man's life the necessity for anxiety about food and clothes, give him a
house to live in and for those he loves, secure these

permanently, and the wrinkles would be smoothed out of many a fast-furrowing face. The Government gives one a house free of rent—ofttimes not much more than a barrack, but still a shelter—wood to warm you, forage for two horses; and the pay, small as it is, enables at least two people to have what they need to eat and to wear. There was very little competition in the way of living out on our border. Take that out of life and see what a difference it makes. It was no wonder, then, that men came to dinner full to the brim of capacity for enjoyment.

When there is an invalid wife to send into the States for treatment, or there are children to educate, the perplexities begin, for the pay account soon evaporates; but there is no life from which care can be entirely excluded, and even under these circumstances I have rarely known men and women inflict their anxieties upon others on any social occasion. I knew a major-general whom New York's choicest people often dined. He was something superb to look at physically, and, besides his wide experience in life and his splendid military record, he was full of the delicate niceties of a courteous gentleman, apparently free from anxieties, in perfect health, faultlessly dressed, and his smooth and handsome face bore no trace of care; still his pockets were often nearly empty if it happened to be the latter part of the month, and once, I know, when he was visiting some of our friends, he had but forty-five cents and no bank account. His pay was not small, but he was generous and hospitable, and if a major-general is expected to live as he ought to live, the pay is hardly adequate.

If in the autumn we left camp and came into garrison for a few winter months, we seemed to have nothing. The rooms of our quarters, only of ordinary size, made the few pieces of furniture look isolated, with such awful distances between them. A woman's ingenuity came then into play. The companies had all sorts of artisans as enlisted men, and we first borrowed a carpenter. With rough boards he made us inexpensive lounge-frames that we felt no hesitancy in throwing away when we left again in the spring. For these we bought single mattresses, and then made covers of cretonne or common calico. As the covers were boxed, the frill fully pleated on, and the pillows also boxed, it looked like a lounge, and did not have a " beddy " look, as we used to say. The pillows were stuffed with hay, perhaps, for it was a long time before we attained to all the feather-pillows we needed. We could have several of these lounges, and after we had learned to accumulate bright Mexican or gay striped blankets, and things that fold up, we could soon make ourselves comfortable.

A roll of anything can almost always be stuffed in a closely packed wagon, while actual furniture is a problem. So we became very expert in choosing stuffs that would cover furniture and curtain windows. Some of the old curtain-covers of those far-away days are still in use. With a lounge in every room and curtains at the windows, there was a great step made towards furnishing. We had low boxes with lids to fit in the windows, and these we covered and stuffed for seats. Sometimes two of our packing-chests were made just the right height and size, so that when put side by side they would make a good foundation for a lounge. Our camp-chairs were freshly covered, and stools made of boxes again covered. The few books we were able to take with us the carpenter arranged shelves for, or by good-fortune the little parlor had a wide cupboard beside the fireplace, with shelves above.

We tried to keep one carpet intact; but in our own chamber four gray Government blankets, bought at a sale of condemned goods, were darned, sewed together, and spread in the centre of the room. Our bureaus were always called bureaus; but they were in part packing boxes, shelved inside, and covered with the calico which did much to hide angularities and ugliness. The wash-stands were similarly constructed. How often we Bedouins, who came in so late in the autumn and left so early in the spring, wished that Uncle Sam would put in the quarters the roughest sort of furniture as a permanency! These makeshifts were resorted to only when we were to stay a short time. If we were able to remain long enough in one place to call a post our regimental headquarters, we could accumulate a few really good articles, and leave them stored in garrison in our absence in the field.

There are not many quarters that do not have a few pictures. Even in those days if we had chromos we were glad, for the walls of army quarters were not papered and a poor picture even took away a little of

18

the bare look. Occasionally some one who painted in oils or water colors would triumph over the obstacles of our life, and their walls were our envy. The soldier carpenter made clumsy frames, which were painted or ebonized at home, and such a relief to the eye were these pictures that the artist bade fair to have his or her head so effectually turned that he would consider further artistic effort unnecessary.

We rarely had flowers to brighten our houses. Sometimes in the underbrush, where the sole trees we had—the cotton-woods—grew, we found clematis, and the joy of draping our pictures or mantles with this graceful vine, covered with its soft tufts of fluffy gray, was something to be remembered. For a brief time in the early summer the plains were aflame with wild flowers of the most brilliant dyes; but the hot summer scorched them, as well as the grass, out of existence. As ferns only grew in rather damp and shady places, it can be imagined that we never saw them. I had given me some pressed ferns in the States once, and pasted them on one of our windows when we reached the arid sunbaked plains. They seemed like a bit of fairy-land, and looking at them while they lasted transported us to cool nooks on a pretty brook overhung with thick foliage. Flowers are in such common use nowadays that few tables are without them. Perhaps only a cheap little basket of ferns and foliage plants, or a bowl of wild daisies, but that flowerless land seems like the desert of Sahara as I look back at it as it was after early summer was past.

During our stay at a post when the hot sun had dried all vegetation, and we were surrounded with prairies burned with the heat, one of our number planted some Madeira bulbs in boxes on each side of the mantle, and we laughed at her credulity when she looked for results.   But one day she was able to laugh back, as tiny shoots appeared.   When her soldier husband came home from the campaign, the vines had stretched on up to the chimney, and were following a lattice of scarlet strings that were stretched across above the mantel, making a verdant side to the bare room.   This same friend left us to go with her husband on detached duty, and they found that they must spend the winter in huts in an isolated part of unsettled Kansas.   To keep the cold from coming through the unplastered walls, she papered them with *Army and Navy Journals*, and ornamented them with illustrations from *Harper's Weekly*, finishing with a few poems as a dado.   The soldiers sometimes gave us " pointers " as we rode by their quarters.   One had a box for a dressing-table, and covering it a gunny sack, such as the grain came in, fringed all around as a cover.   For his wash-stand he had driven a pole into the ground of the proper height, and nailed to this a board to hold his tin basin.   Sometimes the soldiers made mats similar to those the sailors fashion, and it is difficult to realize how effective rags hooked through burlaps can be made when so few colors are available.   Old blue army cloth, both light and dark, bits of white muslin and red flannel, were everything the men had, and their home-made hooks, made of a bit of wire, seemed to do just as good work as the loom. People are mistaken if they imagine for a moment that happiness arises from their accessaries or surroundings. These certainly add, but the most contented people I ever knew lived in the very heart of the great American desert.

Those women who cared for fancy-work would beautify their quarters, and there was much leisure for needle-work. Military people are very social. They sat on the gallery a great deal, and officers going about the garrison on duty stopped for a chat coming from the stables, or spent an hour waiting for drill call, or in helmet and spurs smoked a cigarette while the orderly brought their horses for parade. Each woman coming from leave of absence was prepared to teach a new stitch, lend her fresh designs, or send back to have those she had brought reproduced.

During the long summers, when we women were left alone, and had nothing to fill up our time except work that we purposely made to occupy the lonely hours, there came to be great improvement in our stitchery. We sat on the galleries at work while one read, and the delicate fingers of some fashioned the bullion shoulder-straps, or ripped a military cap to copy it, or even had the courage to attempt shirt-making. Others painted, or drew, or learned new guitar accompaniments. One of our number was so industrious that she could not sit with idle hands in camp, but resorted to knitting, and was soon dubbed "the little grandmother."

Harper's Bazar was as thoroughly read out there as at any point in its wide wanderings. The question of clothes was not a serious one, for we dared, when so far beyond the railroad, to wear things out of date. It was rather difficult to teach ourselves to be dress-makers, and things looked pretty botchy and home-made for a long time after we had begun to do such work; but there was much goodness in helping and teaching, and sometimes, if one of us was plunged into difficulties— for instance, coming from a long march literally in tatters—the rest came in for a " bee," and made light work about the sewing-machine. We could get cotton gowns at the sutler's (the one store allowed in a garrison) or in the little town that is often located on the edge of a reservation. We sent into the States by every available opportunity for anything so serious as a stuff gown or outer garment. We all carried lists into the States to fill for others. It was amusing to see a bachelor officer go into a shop in the East with his lists, where the superciliousness of the smart young woman who waited on him almost made him beat a hasty retreat. The shop-girl is often a superior order of being even with experienced shoppers, and sometimes loftily undertakes to prove that she knows what you want much better than you do yourself; but take a blushing youth, with all sorts of articles that he has talked calmly over with the women in garrison, where all are like one family, these very articles seem very formidable when he attempts to utter them in the presence of a city saleswoman. The girl does not help him in his embarrassment, you may be sure, and a red and uncomfortable time is perhaps his while selecting even stockings. The officers' devotion to women was so great that they did not hesitate to make exhibitions of themselves in front of many a counter. I remember a bridegroom sent out on his wedding journey to buy a neck ruche. Before starting he was well drilled, and said his lesson quite fluently; but he was no sooner on the crowded street than the "ruche of illusion footing" became so jumbled in his mind that he could not straighten out the words in the order in which they should go. He described himself on his return as passing shop after shop in trying to get courage to enter and utter the strange jumble of sounds into which the commission had got itself tangled. It was wartime, and officers wore their uniforms in the cities, so that a very youthful and violently red brigadier-general presented himself before the surprised shop-girl, and excitedly blurted out his request for a " foot of Russian illusion." The smile of the shop-girl seemed sardonic to him; but he bravely stood his ground, and after many labored explanations he succeeded in returning to the hotel, triumphantly carrying a brown-paper parcel.

Sometimes boots or shoes were ordered by mail and sent separately, on account of bulk or postage. Any one anxiously looking for his second shoe in two or three successive mails was told, in a teasing and foreboding way, that the other shoe would never come, and that there was nothing left for him but to " put his best foot forward " from that time on.

If we went on leave of absence we borrowed each other's clothes—or, rather, they were offered before we could ask. Our neighbors stepped in with a mysterious bundle, which meant the one choice article in their wardrobe. It used to seem to me that if I was once complete, it would be a gala-day. If I had a gown, there was no appropriate outer garment; if I possessed a charming bonnet, it made my gown look as if it had belonged to a *Mayflower* ancestor. This was all because we stayed so short a time in the States that we considered it foolish to make any permanent preparations; besides, there were so many useful things for our quarters on which we wished to expend our money. I recall our once starting suddenly for a large city for a few days' pleasure. I had a lovely gown that was a surprise to me, having been sent for by General Custer perhaps fifteen hundred miles. My bonnet was admissible, but I had no wrap of any sort except a winter cloak. I had no idea of having my pleasure destroyed by such a need, so I inwardly prayed that no early autumn cold snap would visit us and necessitate a warm outer garment. As I left the house, a generous friend ran up the steps with an heirloom—a camel's-hair shawl. I protested, the carriage was waiting, impatient feet beat a tattoo; I laid the beautiful shawl back on my friend's arm reluctantly, I confess, but as we rushed down the steps she flung it on my shoulder. I wonder if a borrowed baby makes any more anxiety than an heirloom loaned? In the many mirrors of a hotel I surveyed myself with serenity; but oh, what inward consciousness of responsibility! If I took the shawl with me when driving, I feared that it would be lost, if I left it at the hotel, I was wild about thieves. To crown all this I met a friend from my girlhood's home whose eyes fastened on this bit of elegance I was wearing, and who, I knew, would report me as parading in purple and fine linen, whereupon our towns-people, knowing that we were too poor to buy India shawls, would extract a confession that my "fine feathers" belonged to another bird. This little tale I leave without a moral; I have only told it to prove that people in that life had nothing so choice that it could not be shared with others.

I rather think our "get up" for a garrison hop was our greatest failure in the way of dress, for we tried to do something then, and it sometimes ended in a lamentable failure. We fished out from the little finery in the bottom of our trunks some frivolities in the way of ribbons or flowers or trimmings that had served their time, and were ready for retirement even before coming West. But in our efforts to emphasize the occasion, a white or a black gown was decorated with trimmings, perhaps crushed, wrinkled, or out of date. Fortunately we had no city toilets to compete with, and it took a good deal to disfigure fresh, healthful, happy women in the eyes of men who always gave them their meed of praise. I tremble to make the statement, but there is a familiar look in the windows of second-hand establishments in the cities as I pass them, and the flounces and plaits out of date, the ribbons and trimmings quite *passé*, do remind me a little of evenings when we all tried to look smart out there beyond the pale of civilization. I do remember a French gown, the box containing which we saw on its way to a post hundreds of miles beyond us. The officer dared not crush it into his small trunk, so he had carried it in the cars on his lap, in a stage, in an ambulance, and still had another stage ride before him when we entertained him; but our men were not often put to such a test of good-nature, for there were few women who did not try to make the wardrobe they brought out last two or three years with simple additions, easily obtained.

At one time we all came in from the plains when our regiment was ordered South on duty. The women hurriedly retreated to their rooms at the hotel to escape curious eyes, for it was written all over us that we were, in Western terms, "waybacks from wayback." The retreat was not so quickly made that one pair of observing eyes did not take in a few women on the way, and discover that basques were worn instead of round waists. The scissors were soon snipping, the needle flying, and the result was a basque ready for dinner. Meanwhile a charge of our brave men was made through the town hunting for back hair to remodel the antique coiffures of their better halves. It was no easy task, for the sun fades and streaks the glossiest locks out there, and the wind breaks and dries the silkiest mane. Fashion had dictated a chignon of heavy braids and curls during our long absence on the plains, and the poor martyred men made many a sally before a perfect match could be obtained. At last we made our appearance, revelling in all the glory of a protuberance of regulation size, and the little company of blue-coats marshalled their forces and advanced on the dinner-table, and then had the heartlessness to laugh at the unusual dignity with which the overburdened heads were carried.

CHAPTER XVIII.

"GARRYOWEN" LEADS THE HUNT.

GENERAL CUSTER was delighted to hear at last that his friend, the Hon. K. C. Barker, was about to accept one of the many invitations we had sent him, and come to our camp for a hunt. Several other Detroiters, eager sportsmen, also, were to accompany him. They had hardly been our guests in camp long enough to dispose of luncheon before all were asked to don the hunting-garb and prepare for the setting out; as the good buffalo ground was twelve miles distant, it was necessary to reach it before dark. Already had the troopers who were to go as escort received their orders, and saddles, girths, bridles, and lariats were put in order, carbines and pistols cleaned and loaded, horses fed and groomed to the last degree of shine. The band also put their instruments into a brighter condition, to add to the general glitter of the column.

Nearly all of the officers of the regiment engaged in the hunt were mounted on their second-best horses, having their trusty chargers led, in order that they might be fresh next day for the run. There were all the wagons necessary for supplies, and mess chests for the various groups of officers who lived together; tents were carried, and there was also a certain amount of forage, for it was necessary to prepare for several days' absence of the cavalcade of seventy. A brave sight it was as they started out, a column half a mile long, and the eyes of our delighted guests shone with excitement as they noted the dashing cavalry officers sitting their mettlesome steeds with such ease, the troopers riding equally well and brilliant in touches, as the sun caught the polished steel of their fire-arms or sent radiating lines of light from the shining bit or burnished spur— the band playing the regimental tune " Garryowen," as their wise and steady gray horses paced their way without guiding. The stag-hounds bounded along on their cushioned feet, spurning the soft turf in their active leaps. One of the guests, enthusiastically happy, and fearless in expression of his joy, kept turning to take in the rare sight, declaring that nothing in our prosaic nineteenth century was so like the days of chivalry, when some feudal lord went out to war or to the chase, followed by his retainers.

There were two heavy weights in the party, and they had taken the precaution to start in the ambulances, knowing that the saddle would exact some terrible penance from them next day, when, unaccustomed to riding, they pounded up and down over the rough country. The gay scene was too much for them, however; the merry voices of the officers, story telling, singing, laughing, the more subdued but none the less jubilant tones of the troopers who rejoiced at this unusual holiday, the quick happy bark of the dogs, the neigh of the horses, delighting in the fresh, exhilarating air of the plains, made them feel themselves prisoners inside a vehicle, so a halt was made, and the men of solid flesh began at once to play cavalrymen. At the end of the twelve miles, unvaried except by some jack-rabbit chases, when by their speed the dogs enchanted Mr. Barker, who had given them to us, a camping-ground was selected and the fire for supper soon sent its cheerful gleam into the twilight shadows. The soldiers, with the ease of practice, had put up two rows of wall-tents facing each other, and near them another line of their own A tents. The wagons and ambulances were so placed at the rear of each line of tents that they formed a temporary barricade, for, even on such a pleasuring as that was, none of the usual precautions for safety were neglected.

The camp named for Mr. Barker was a noisy one for a time. The twelve-mile march had not tired the guests sufficiently to produce quiet, while to the officers and troopers it was a mere bagatelle. They smoked and told frontier tales, while the guests brought out their choicest collection of after-dinner stories from the States; it was only the consideration of the early reveille that induced them to turn in on their blankets and buffalo-robes for sleep. Reveille at dawn brought the party out again, fresh and enthusiastic for the day's sport.

After breakfast the distribution of horses began. By that time all the best buffalo-horses in the regiment were well known, and as this was an occasion when it was the desire of all of us to make the hunt a success, the trustworthy, experienced animals had been brought along. The only problem was the mounting of Mr. Barker and Judge Beckwith, weighing, as they did, nearly two hundred and thirty pounds each. It was always difficult for the heavier men of our regiment to get good mounts, and even if they found horses strong enough to carry them on the march, on drill, or ordinary garrison duty, it always remained a query whether these powerful animals had enough speed to join in the chase. This question was studied pretty thoroughly, and the strongest horse in the regiment with any speed had been selected for Mr. Barker, but by one of those unfortunate accidents that thwart the best laid plans, the scout sent out at daybreak to look up a buffalo herd had taken the strong horse held in reserve, and blown him so that there was no good work to be expected of him for the next twenty-four hours.

Fifty horsemen were soon in line of march, followed by wagons to bring back the meat ; and, much to the guests' distress, two ambulances brought up the rear to carry the wounded should any one be hurt. These vehicles seemed like birds of evil omen following slowly along after a thoughtless, jubilant company, and no one wanted to look backward if he hoped to keep the gloomy side of life out of his mind. When the gay cavalcade had gone a few miles the scouts sent out returned, to report the direction of the buffalo they had found. When the black specks appeared against the horizon the enthusiasm of the Eastern men knew no bounds; each burned with a desire to take back a record to those unfortunate Detroiters who had not had the good-luck to come. The officers experienced in the chase made each guest their special care, so that there was no lack of hints regarding the preparations for the charge. The usual halt took place to dismount, examine bits, surcingles, spurs and fire-arms, and to discard coats, and secure hats with handkerchiefs or strings; for the thought was not of appearances at such a moment.

Finally, at the signal the fifty horsemen vaulted into saddles and were off. To the tourists the buffalo seemed huge. One of the party, describing them, after their return, said they had the grace of an elephant and the beauty of a hippopotamus. The monsters were not long in discovering the enemy coming towards them; they promptly started their cumbrous bodies into a lumbering run, and, as usual, got over the country at such a surprising rate that it took all the best riding of the old hunters, and the very best skill of the "tenderfeet" to keep their poise in the saddle, and let the experienced horse take them down divides, up the constantly recurring slopes, through the softened soil where the gopher and prairie-dog had undermined the earth.

The buffalo pitches down any descent in a headlong, reckless manner. He never spares himself. The Indians often drove them to a bluff, knowing that if stampeded they would leap down the steepest declivity, and plunging below on their huge heads, it became an easy affair to finish them with the knife if they were not killed outright. This inhumanity was not a practice with the white man. In any descent, therefore, the buffalo gained on his pursuer, but in the ascent of the divide the horse was superior, and often caught up with the groaning, puffing, laboring buffalo.

The herd of thirty first seen that day was soon scattered, the hunters starting out in all directions in pursuit of the isolated animals. After a sharp run of a few miles the riders began to return, dusty, heated, all talking at once—gesticulating, explaining why such-and-such a shot was missed, narrating narrow escapes, chronicling successes. The count was good, for twenty-four buffaloes lay scattered on all sides within a radius of three miles. The accidents were told over next. One of the guests had had his horse pushed into a creek by a buffalo, but being an old soldier, he knew how to extricate himself. The horse of a soldier had been gored, another trooper's horse showed the long trail of a buffalo-horn where the hair had been scraped off on the side. A hole in the sleeve of one of the novices in buffalo-hunting revealed the fact that the aim of his pistol had not been quite what he intended it to be; another had evidently been equally unfortunate in his aim, for the palm of his hand was black, and smarting with powder, and he could not explain where the ball went. The party, satisfied with their success, turned back to camp, but with much anxiety regarding the missing ones. Before they reached there the lost came up, and General Custer's description gives some idea of what a dangerous pastime buffalo-hunting was:

Mr. Barker, mounted upon an animal that had justly excited his suspicions from the first (for he had discovered an ugly cut on the knee, and a tendency to stumble), singled out his buffalo on the first charge, and after separating him from the main herd, began emptying his revolver into the sides of the buffalo—horse, rider, and buffalo going at breakneck pace. He must be a bold rider who, mounted upon a strange horse, is willing to strike out at full speed over a country known to be infested with prairie-dog holes, wolf dens, and quicksands. The risk of a fall is always great, but to a man of K. C. B.'s weight it is fearful. The horse proved unsteady under fire. Barker concluded to go from the right to the left side of the buffalo; in doing so he passed close to the haunches of the latter. The buffalo at this moment concluded to give battle, and turned to intercept the horse. "Look out for him, Barker!" was the warning cry of a friend; but Barker's eyes were directed to the front. Again is the warning repeated. This time it is heard, and Barker glances towards the buffalo, but too late. Already the horns are partly concealed by the long flowing tail of the horse, while the latter, feeling the points of the enraged animal's horns pressing his flanks, leaps with affrighted vigor to elude the coming blow, but in doing so unsettles the rider's seat. For a moment Barker is seen attempting to recover himself; but the horse, now unmanageable from fear, plunges madly forward, the rider loses his balance, and the next instant goes headlong to the ground. What I did, or what any of the half-dozen friends following closely did at the time, cannot be clearly stated. That we all realized the full extent of the danger that surrounded our comrade was certain, but how to relieve him?

As if by intuition, and without uttering a word, all headed their horses towards the buffalo, who, finding himself the object of so much undivided attention, allowed himself to be diverted from continuing his attack on Barker, now lying perfectly helpless and insensible within three bounds of the buffalo. The latter again chose to confide in the swiftness of his legs rather than in the strength of his horns—a decision which spared to Detroit one of its most estimable citizens, and to the sporting world one of its brightest ornaments.

Seeing the buffalo well under way, our attention was next directed to ascertaining the extent of the injuries received by our friend. He was still lying insensible, breathing as if partly suffocated. By means of restoratives and fresh air—of the latter there being an abundance—we soon had him on his feet; and upon " time being called," in the course of a quarter of an hour he announced himself ready to mount his horse. This time a change was effected by which, although placed astride a lighter animal, it was with the assurance that he was " sure-footed, and not afraid of buffaloes." If timidity had been one of Mr. Barker's characteristics, he would have been content to call it " quits " with the buffalo; but no, his " dander" was up, and he surprised his hearers by announcing that his late narrow escape from a possible death was " just the thing." To use his own expressions: " I know now just how to take them and how to ride;" and as for the blackened eye and bruised cheek, he declared that " no money could buy them."

It would not do to leave a renowned hunter thus worsted on the field, so I omit portions of the letter and continue General Custer's account of his final success:

Turning our faces towards camp, we had not proceeded far before we discovered a fine herd off to our right. Approaching as near as possible without giving the alarm, a very good start was effected. K. C. B. singled out his buffalo, which proved to be a fine bull about five years old, and very fleet. It required a good run to bring pursuer and pursued within pistol range of each other; but once accomplished, Mr. B. began to make his presence known by deliberately emptying his large Colt's revolver, directing his shots immediately in rear of the fore-shoulder and below the middle of the body. Barrel after barrel was discharged until the revolver was empty, and still the speed seemed unslackened. Replacing this revolver in its holster and drawing another, the firing was continued. The last shot of the second revolver had been fired, making twelve in all, and still the race went on without signs of distress. An attendant handed Barker a third revolver. This in turn was emptied into the buffalo, and all, apparently, to no purpose. A fourth revolver is supplied, from which four shots are fired, when the buffalo's never-failing signal of defeat, bleeding at the nose, is perceptible. Slowly decreasing his speed the buffalo soon comes to a halt, the next instant he is down on his side, and before his heart ceases to beat, or he to struggle, Barker is out of the saddle, and with hat in hand leaps upon the buffalo and gives three hearty cheers, in which he is joined by all of the party who are within hearing. The head of the animal is soon removed from the carcass, and conveyed with the party to camp, from which point it was expressed the same day to Detroit, there to be placed in the hands of the taxidermist for preservation.

After all had gathered about the camp-fire at night there was the usual vehement exchange of experiences, and the customary recounting of ludicrous situations, or occasions when danger was looked in the face. Of course the tourists were much spent and very hungry, and the camp supper, with their own game for the principal dish, was " food fit for the gods," they said. The story-telling and merriment was somewhat subdued on account of fatigue, and our guests were not aware, in a few moments after touching the blankets, that they were not sleeping on the soft beds of civilization.

General Custer continues:

The following day was the Sabbath, and although hundreds of miles from church or chapel, it was nevertheless determined to "Remember the Sabbath-day to keep it holy," a resolution which gave no little pleasure. At sunset the band played "Old Hundred," the effect of which on our little party was more powerful than if sung by a well-organized choir with all the accompaniments of church and congregation.

The merriest man of all these guests was a rollicking Irishman, who, though living quietly in Canada at that time, had been an extensive traveller, and in many adventures by sea and by land. His stories, his songs, his repartee were some things not to be forgotten. Without pretension or the least self-consciousness he took the lead in everything, and the moment he opened his mouth the others became silent, knowing that it was "not best to miss anything that Morgan said, if a fellow cared a rap for fun." As I remember him and his bright comrade of a wife, a vivacious Frenchwoman, my lips involuntarily form themselves into a smile, and a dozen instances of their clever wit come trooping back to amuse me. The one picture I best recall is of an occasion when Mr. Morgan was nearly drowned in the Detroit River. I was visiting at the Barkers' on Grosse Isle, and at evening we rowed over to the Morgans', where we first heard of the narrow escape. With the merriest twinkle in his eye he gave us so amusing an account of himself while he clung to the boat, in peril of drowning, that we shouted over it exactly as if it had been the best joke in the world, instead of the story of a hair-breadth escape from a watery grave. His cries for help were heard first by his wife, who ran for the boatman, and while he was getting his oars Mrs. Morgan tore up to the house, bringing back with her a brandy-flask and waved it to the struggling man, who clung rather feebly to the upturned boat, for Mr. Morgan was not strong. Even weak and chilled as he was, the pluck of his wife, when she was so frightened, and the fun of the whole affair, took possession of him, and he shouted, " Thank you, Tillie, I'll be there, directly !"

The brogue added to every story he told, and we all, long after he had left us, repeated and laughed over his quick sallies and his fresh, unhackneyed dinner and camp-fire tales. Out of the fifty-three buffaloes killed on the two days' hunt, Mr. Morgan had the best score, for, unaided, he had despatched seven. He allows me to use an extract or so from letters to his wife at that time :

The fatigue of yesterday's hunt was too much for most of the visitors, many of whom were unfamiliar with equestrianism, and they were slow to respond to the reveille; when they did come forth from their tents it was with that peculiar gait which a pair of compasses must adopt if compelled to walk across a table. We were all willing to rest our laurels of yesterday's running for one day, and the morning was devoted to recounting our deeds of valor and hair-breadth escapes. I had a bullet-hole though the sleeve of my coat. Mr. L——'s horse shied at a polecat, his plug hat fell of, and came in for the full phials of the beast's wrath; the tile was subsequently recovered and made a target of.

After one of the hunts we satisfied our appetites with a glorious dinner, thanks to General Custer's bountiful larder and our own hunting successes, not to forget a good-sized locker which we brought from the East, and which was known as the "medicine-chest." One of the general's guests, who seemed to enjoy the good things with a gusto that only a hunter can feel, after getting up from dinner hastened to take possession of a large crate which was about half full of straw, and which was used for packing our earthen and glass ware. Here he stretched his aching limbs, and was soon in a deep sleep, notwithstanding that the band was playing but a short distance from him. I and one or two others asked the general to aid us in getting up a funeral, as evidently our friend had gone (in dreams) to the happy hunting-ground, or the land of Nod. The general, with rollicking glee worthy of a school-boy, entered into our plans, a procession was formed, six stalwart troopers carried the bier, the guests acted as chief mourners, the band played the "Dead March in Saul," and the cortege advanced across the prairie. The motion, the music, and the ringing laughter, that might almost be taken for wailing, seemed to cause our sleeping friend to dream; he then awakened, and stared around in bewilderment; it would seem that he failed to immediately take in the situation, for he asked, in the most serious tone: "What is the matter? What has happened?" The general and his friends congratulated him on his marvellous recovery and his escape from a lonely grave.

This same crockery-crate was still to be the central object in a joke, after the return of the party to the

main camp. Our guests had found out by some shrewd
questioning that our mess chest held only six of a kind
for setting our camp table, so they had decided to bring
with them a supply of dishes. The crate had served
as their packing-case. One day I remember seeing the
empty crate the centre of a group of softly moving
figures, stealthily lifting and carefully carrying it a little distance nearer the tents. Soon it was revealed
that our guests had enlisted General Custer in another
practical joke. One of the citizens having dined and
wined well, had thrown himself down on the ground to
take a nap. His sleep was either that of one who has
a light conscience, or whose senses were steeped in that
oblivious dream that comes from too frequent tips of
the flowing bowl. I haven't the faintest remembrance
who it was, so that if I account for his lethargy in this
way I hope that I may be forgiven. A number of
picket-pins were sharpened, and while the good diner
slumbered the crockery-crate was carefully placed over
him and tacked down to the baked earth. Then the
perpetrators of this joke came under our fly to watch
for the awakening. It was very funny, and quite worth
the long vigil kept up while waiting the end of his
sleep. The manner in which the imprisoned man partially arose and gazed at the twisted and knotted roof
above him was simply convulsing to us. Then he
kicked wildly in impatience, and endeavored to throw
the light crate off him; still it resisted. Finally, the
figure of this reputable and highly respected citizen
on his knees, scrambling and pushing and struggling

to lift the crate by his bowed back, like a bucking horse, sent us into screams of laughter, and it was no longer possible to refuse to go to his assistance.

When an expedition reaches the bed of a stream which has no water, the place is marked on the map as a dry camp. There is still another application of the term, and our guests in anticipation of this had brought good cheer in the locker which they called the "medicine-chest," but after that day there was pretty good care taken not to visit it any oftener than would leave a man in condition to leap from sound sleep into vigilant wakefulness. This caution was necessary by way of avoiding the too marked attention of those who pined ever for a practical joke.

With all this merrymaking there was mingled in General Custer's heart a pang of sorrow for almost an irreparable loss; but his own words will better convey his feelings:

To give our visitors an opportunity to witness the great speed of the antelope and American hare, or as it is best known on the plains, the jack-rabbit, I took with me from camp about half a dozen fine stag-hounds. Foremost among all these was Maida, my favorite dog, the companion of all my long and terrible marches of last winter; she who by day trotted by my side, and at night shared my camp-couch. In the first run after buffaloes the dogs, contrary to their usual custom, became separated from me and accompanied others of the party. They soon singled out a buffalo, and readily brought it to bay. With little forethought or prudence, several of the hunters opened fire upon the buffalo while the latter was contending with the dogs. Maida had seized hold of the buffalo, and while clinging to its throat was instantly killed by a carbine-ball fired by some one of the awkward soldiers who accompanied the party. Words fail to express the grief occasioned by the untimely death of so faithful a companion.

> "Poor Maida, in life the firmest friend;
> The first to welcome, foremost to defend;
> Whose honest heart is still your master's own,
> Who labors, fights, lives, breathes for him alone.
> But who with me shall hold thy former place,
> Thy image what new friendship can efface?
>   Best of they kind, adieu!
>   The frantic deed which laid thee low
>   This heart shall ever rue."

Infantry Call "To the Color."

CHAPTER XIX.

ARMY PROMOTIONS.

One of the pleasurable excitements of garrison or camp life was promotion. The lucky man who had long lingered and anxiously balanced himself at the head of the list, when he at last made the final file was instantly surrounded by his comrades, who, after congratulating him, immediately proceeded to besiege him for a "spread!" They daringly suggested how he should celebrate, and news went flying about as if they were a parcel of school-boys, one calling to another, "Come on up; —— is going to have a 'lay out,' his promotion's come."

At these celebrations we all made merry till the host despaired of getting rid of us. A messenger returned from the sutler wagons loaded with a heterogeneous display, and though there was so little in that meagre life to celebrate with, that made little difference; it was only one more occasion of the many we rejoiced in for all to come together; and if by chance no one had a pair of shoulder-straps to emphasize the accession to greatness, it was a chance if the host was not decorated with the insignia of rank cut out of white cotton and sewed on his fatigue jacket.

In an army of twenty-five thousand soldiers on paper, and a much smaller number in reality, it was not strange that the wail that was loudest was the conspicuous line in the old West Point song:

"Promotion's very slow."

The lieutenants referred almost everything, including the millennium, to the time "when I'm a captain." General Custer thought that the position of a captain was the most enjoyable and independent of all. The daily association with the company brings an officer into cordial communication with his men, and a personal attachment is the result if the officer be just, and his men the better sort of soldiers. By constant exchanging, or by court-martial, the company can be weeded of the absolutely worthless men, and by watchfulness there can be all sorts of craftsmen brought into the troop, so that the company barracks, and the captain's and subalterns' quarters, can be made habitable, no matter how dilapidated they may be, by the carpenter, blacksmith, painter, saddler, etc. After a higher grade is reached there is very little personal communication with the enlisted man, and that hearty sympathy which is so prized is almost entirely lost. When a man becomes a general he is removed so far that nearly all his intercourse with the ranks is at an end; besides, he really belongs then to no one body of men. The *esprit de corps* of the regiment is at an end; he really has around him only his staff and a few soldiers detailed from their companies for headquarters duty.

Our military women, who have been proud of the regiment, and who have shared its marches, dangers, deprivations, etc., as if it were a privilege, entering into the domestic life of its officers and enlisted men as if they were all akin, are completely at sea when removed, after years, from such association. I saw Mrs. Miles soon after her husband's promotion to be a brigadier-general. She was in Southern California, surrounded with the vineyards, rose trellises, the bloom and verdure of that American Italy; but her heart was still longing for the women with whom she had kept vigil when the men were on a campaign on the bleak wastes of Dakota. She could not forget those men and women with whom she had suffered in the blizzards, siroccos, hurricanes, and above all the unceasing fear and anxiety about hostile Indians. At their last station in Dakota the post was built on a dreary flat plain, with no trees, no anything to look at but one of those curious buttes rising directly out of the ground, the result of the cracking of the earth's heated surface during the upheavals of the far-away ages. Nothing could be more hideous than this bare, uninteresting, sharp elevation; it was a blot upon the face of the earth; but Mrs. Miles told me that instead of luxuriating among the flowers surrounding her, her eyes were turning back to those she loved, and to the spot where, though she had been so anxious, she still had been so happy, and she added, "Bear Butte seems now the most beautiful thing I ever saw."

Another woman, torn (as is the army's cruel fate) from those associates she valued, was asked if, after all those years of dearth, she did not enjoy the wonderful climbing roses that cover the quarters at the Presidio in San Francisco. Petulantly, and almost tearfully, she replied, " I *hate* roses." And so it goes. I believe that military people come as near getting happiness independent of surroundings as any class of people I know; but then domestic happiness is the rule in army life, and if there are no storms inside the quarters, what boisterous wind or rain outside is going to make much difference?

A bright woman whom I know, born in the purple, was courageous enough to marry out of a fashionable New York life into the simplicity and poverty of the army. It was a decade since, when Indians roamed at will where now a web of five Pacific Railroads, with their collateral branches, spreads over the rapidly filling plains. It took months of marching to reach the Rocky Mountains. Hardships could not be avoided; scarcely anything but the barest necessities could be taken along, with the limited transportation. Still this belle in Gotham looked all this life in the face, and set over against her sheltered, luxurious existence the privilege of marrying the man of her choice, and taking up a career full of sacrifices. After she had experimented for a time in this new life, and knew its trials as well as its compensations, she heard some one say that a certain woman whom she knew had married into the army, and married for love. "Good heavens!" she exclaimed in her excitement, "what else *could* she marry for?"

One of the edicts which this woman could not quietly accept was the manner in which the Government saw fit to arrange promotion. Until after a colonelcy is reached everything advances by grade. Death, dismissal, resignation, and retiring from illness or from age are the causes that make vacancies. The bride tenderly reared could not reconcile herself to the calm calculation of officers who sat down to go over the list of those who ranked them, and to estimate how many years it would take for those in the way to be removed, either by Divine Providence or by dismissal. With finger on the *Army Register* they disposed of one after another in something after this fashion: Such a one "will 'hand in his chips' soon if he don't leave John Barleycorn alone." Such and such a one "is going under from disease contracted during the war, or from an old wound." A third "has had a fortune left him, and he will 'light out' for civil life soon." Still another "begins to totter with age and imbecility, and can't sit a horse any longer; he will be re-

tired shortly." Of another who was constantly being
tried it was said, "Some court-martial will get him yet
and send him flying."

The new-comer listened to all this calculating of
chances as to vacancies and promotions with outraged
feelings; but her horror culminated when her own husband, a lieutenant, rushed into the quarters one day per-
forming a can-can, swinging his cap, and calling out to
her in glee, "Fan, such and such a ship has gone down
at sea, so and so is lost, and I'm a captain." I laughed
till the tears came, to see her face as she told me of this
shock to her sensibilities, and of her astonishment to
think that her own husband could manifest such apparent heartlessness; and even though all this occurred
years ago, she became rigid with indignation at the rec-
ollection.

I felt with her most keenly, and could not become
accustomed to the manner in which news of the death
of an officer at some other post was met. The officers
said, if they liked him, "Poor fellow! I'm sorry he's
gone"; but the inevitable question that followed was,
"Whom will it promote?" The *Army Register* was at
once in requisition, and the file looked up. Still I think
that apparent momentary want of feeling is no worse
than the manner in which civilians receive the news of
a man's demise by asking, "Did he leave any money?"

A law that has gone into effect within the last few
years, retiring an officer at sixty-two years of age, does
away with the somewhat unseemly haste with which
the rank of an officer dying was looked up, for the

reckoning is all made out lông before the period of retirement approaches; and a very good estimate in many
instances can be obtained by a man waiting for his promotion, by summing up the length of service or age of
officers who are near or at the head of the list. Even
now there occurs a calculation that verges on cruelty,
for one of my friends, who was recovering from the
lingering fever that invaded our ranks at the South,
nearly went into a relapse at sight of the pencil-marks
of a brother officer—fortunately a man of a type that
is not common among our warm-hearted military men.
The doors of the quarters of most military posts stand
invitingly open, and an entrance, if closed, is rarely
locked, so the invalid feebly made his way into adjoining quarters, and sat down by the table to rest and
await the return of the occupant. The open *Army
Register*, always more fascinating to an officer than a
novel, attracted him. Name after name was either
marked out or had annotations explaining causes why
there was uncertainty about the person remaining in
service; but, to his anger and disgust, there was no
query-mark opposite his; the neighbor, calculating on
his death, had already drawn a line through the entire
name. Slamming the book shut, he left with far more
vigor than he had entered, and from that time on he
determined to get well.

During our war officers were often overslaughed,
and this setting aside of the old rule of promotion by
file rankled in the heart of an officer whom we knew.
He was irreproachable on duty, but once inside his quar-

ters he brooded over his wrongs until he was almost frenzied with anger, and wild sounds of an upraised voice, and the clatter and thumps of disturbed furniture, slamming doors, etc., penetrated the walls ; in garrison, where the houses are so near each other, it was impossible to ignore the turmoil. An officer entering to inform himself regarding the disturbance found a farce going on, that he quietly witnessed, and afterwards as quietly withdrew from, for the subject that brought on the fracas was one that produced too lively sympathy in a brother officer to induce him to interfere. The overslaughed man had called a number of chairs by the name of each of the officers who had jumped him in promotion. Addressing them individually by their old title, and calling himself by the rank he should have had if promotion had gone on regularly, he said : " You will rank Colonel So-and-so " (calling his own name), " will you ? Well, I'll see," and immediately kicked the chair out of the room. Each chair suffered the same fate, and when the room was empty the incensed man banged the door, and sat down, with a sigh of satisfaction, to get back his breath and to cool off.

I still think, as I have said before, that there is no profession with such drawbacks to ambition as the army. No amount of merit, not even years of constant successful achievement, can give an officer the slightest promotion. In other professions the winner leaps over the heads of his contestants. In military life the way of an ambitious man is often clogged by an officer just

20

above him who has ciphered out the problem of doing only the barest necessary duties, and he frequently gets himself into such a beaten path that he goes
through the form loaded with liquor, which leaves his
knees a little uncertain and wobbly, but he preserves
sufficient intellect, befogged as it is, to pass muster.   I
believe in belonging to a profession where every one
knows that in striving for mastery there is no impedi-
ment to gaining the reward of success, and where, if
one is gifted or persevering, he can leap over the dull
or indifferent to a higher rung in the ladder.

Another excitement besides the promotion of an officer was the advent of the paymaster.   If the country
over which he had to travel would admit of it, he came
every two months; and money, even out there in that
desert, where there was little chance to use it except
for the prosaic necessities of life, had much the same
effect on every one as it has in the States.   The officers
often found roll-call a farce for a day or two, as the
soldiers drew their pay and slid off around the quarters
to the sutler's store, or waited till nightfall and went in
groups to the little collection of gin-shops usually just
outside the confines of the reservation, and invariably
called a city, even if there were but six huts.   If their
comrades brought the drunkest of them home they hid
them until the next day, and a sorrier sight than those
bruised, pallid, broken-up men after a tipsy brawl cannot be imagined.   I know that citizens will ask why
is not drunkenness abolished in the service, but they
must go out to our posts, and see the material of which

PAYMASTER'S ESCORT.

our army is composed, before they judge the question. Certainly the best efforts of the most earnest and honorable men I have ever known were brought to bear on this question, and it is still an unsolved problem.

I should be the last to say our ranks were filled up with failures—I who am so indebted to the enlisted men for protection and a hundred kindnesses; and besides, do I not know well what superb soldiers they were in time of battle or in the hour of peril and emergency—even these very ones who celebrated payday with a brawl? If there could be a country where no whiskey was ever imported, and to which the paymaster never came, there would not be the difficulty that exists; but fortunately all the money in the possession of the easily tempted men changed hands soon, and peace reigned until the two months were up.

The paymasters of our army get little honorable mention of their service, which, in the Territories, is often very perilous. They have for many years travelled with comparatively small escorts through the most hotly contested of the Indian country, and as the railroads were being built and the towns laid out, a class of outlaws were the first to populate them. These desperadoes followed and robbed the paymaster unless the utmost vigilance was observed. On the open plain the escort could guard against an attack, but where a mountain defile was entered, or a cañon was being crossed, or the way lay through the Bad Lands, behind whose columnar buttes many Indians might hide or desperadoes lie in wait, the danger was often very great. Part of the escort dismounted and were deployed in advance of the ambulances containing the paymaster and his travelling outfit, and the drivers and officer himself rode over these dangerous routes with rifles in hand.

We often entertained the paymaster, and on one occasion I remember that he was going to luncheon with General Custer and me. Suddenly the innocent little valise that he carried attracted our attention, and General Custer asked me if I would mind staying in our room with it until the paymaster was through with his luncheon. Certainly I did not mind, but I was curious, of course. What daughter of Eve would not be? However, I shut myself in, and after a little I divined what this mysterious seclusion meant. One woman out of all those hundreds of men was sitting up there on guard over from fifty to seventy thousand dollars in bills, for it took fully that to pay officers, soldiers, and quartermaster's employés.

Retreat.

So goes the day, far, far a-way, So goes the day, So goes the day, far a - way with its light, And the night now comes a - long, comes a - long, comes a - long, and the night like a song comes a - long.

CHAPTER XX.

A FLOOD ON BIG CREEK.

BRIGHT and joyous as were those summer days on Big Creek, it was not all sunshine as to weather. The rainy season in the spring and early summer kept us in a damp, moist, unpleasant state, but after that was ended we had few showers. Whatever Kansas did was with a rush; the lightning was more terrific than lightning elsewhere, the rain poured down in floods, and the wind blew hurricanes. In the years that have since elapsed, the breaking of the soil into farms, and the planting of crops and trees, have materially changed the order of things. Our experience was in the tempestuous times, and we were always expecting some sudden announcement of Mother Nature, who did not propose to treat us to anything like a gentle shower, or a soft south wind that might be trying to "blow up rain." Everything came with a mighty "whew!" and we knew enough to rush our property into the tents, and begin to fortify, when that ominous vibrating of the upper branches of the cotton-wood trees began. The soldiers in charge of headquarters came with axes to drive down the picket-pins; the ropes were tightened, and the straps that secured the opening all tightly buckled.

I remember being thus strapped in one day, and thanking the sergeant, telling him that he need not stay as I was "all right"; but I was, in fact, anything but all right, for I was speechless with fear when the storm began. I would not call to Eliza, for she would get wet coming to me; General Custer was in another part of the camp, and I saw my fate was to brave the hurricane alone. I concluded to take up as secure a place as I could, and await the catastrophe which seemed inevitable. The lightning on the plains is omnipresent; it is such a continuous glare that the whole heavens seem a vast sheet of flame. I could not accustom myself to it, and as long as we lived out there each storm was a new terror to me. In a tent it is impossible to hide one's eyes from the flashes. To add to my terrors, immense hailstones pelted down on the cotton roof with such savage force that I believed no canvas could withstand their fury. My last look through the opening was at a deserted camp, the whole command having gone out of sight into their tents. When I believed myself condemned to meet fate alone, a quick tugging at the straps began, and General Custer leaped into the aperture, drenched with the storm. I came out from under the bed, where I had taken up what I thought a safe position, and began, woman-like, to question why he had ventured into such danger. He had remembered my terror of lightning, and had made a rush over the unprotected parade-ground, with the hailstones pounding down on him like a shower of lead. Such hail no one out there had ever seen before. The Smithies measured many of the hailstones that day, and the average was from an inch to an inch and a half through. Captain Smith made a dash for home from the grazing-ground, his horse running at a fearful pace, with a little dog yelping with pain from the pelting he got following at his heels. Lumps which were tender to the touch for days afterwards were raised on the captain's head.

The pitiful part of it was the unprotected condition of the horses; they had to endure all the violence of the elements, with no shelter. It was strange how wonderfully sleek, fat, and well they kept if there were no hard marches to wear them down. The prolonged storms of the rainy season did not appear to reduce them. They seemed to think their home, the picket rope, gave them every luxury. We were often amused to see the whole number out grazing voluntarily start home when a few drops of rain fell. They either ran up to the picket rope, or made those teetering and awkward leaps that a hobbled animal makes; and when the rope was reached they seemed to feel themselves as secure as if within the driest of stables.

There was one especial storm that I have cause to remember, for it came near being as serious as the one described in *Tenting on the Plains* the summer before, when lives were lost. One lovely day, with an azure sky and soft velvety wind that seemed to blow from the Arcady of the poets, I sat under the fly of our tent, reading, or living that *dolce far niente* existence which camp-life induces, when the air suddenly chilled, and I felt sure the change was some sort of a weather precursor. It was one of the vagaries of the Kansas climate that delighted in sudden alternations from summer to winter. After I had put on a wrap I sat down to await the next change. It was not long before the sky dulled, and an ominous roar came rumbling over the plains—"a voice of the noise of rain." Then I ran off to find Henry, and tell him that I feared a freshet. He confirmed my fears by telling me the water had "been on the rise right smart of time already." I left him to go to the headquarters sergeant, and ask him quietly to prepare for what I believed would be a terrible storm, and come to me if it began to rain. He was so accustomed to these frightened confidences of mine when terror overtook me that he was willing to come even if he himself thought it was only a "woman's notion." If in the military recommendation that General Custer wrote out for him I had been permitted to add a line, it would not have been official; it would only have been my testimony to his capability of making a good husband, he was such a patient man with a woman's fears.

When I came back to the fly General Custer looked up from his absorption in his book, and asked me where I had been. I temporized, for I did not like to admit that I was already scared before a drop of rain had fallen. He persisted, and finding out my agitation, assured me that I was foolish, that we were a good distance from the creek, that I need not be disturbed yet. I argued that our camp being on such a loop of land, the stream might cut a channel across the narrow part, and leave us on an island exactly as the little knot of men were cut off the summer before. Time enough to prepare for that, he replied; and not realizing the genuineness of my trepidation, he strolled off across the parade-ground to practise shots on the billiard-table that the sutler had put in the hall the soldiers built for their amusement. With the remembrance of what Big Creek could do in the way of a rise—for measurements the summer before proved that it went up an inch a minute—I prepared for what might come, and threw our few camp garments into the trunk, heaped the chairs, etc., on the table, tied down the window-flap at the rear, and sat down to watch the clouds. It seemed but a few moments before the sky darkened, and the shriek and whistle of the keen wind came over the prairie, and twisted the leaves and branches of our few protecting trees, cracking the dry twigs and breaking the exposed branches. Meanwhile the stream was beginning to tear along, carrying with it underbrush, logs, and saplings attached to great clumps of earth still held together by the net-work of roots. The sergeant and his men were soon all activity, and Henry ran hither and thither, intent on the horses' safety.

With the roar of the storm coming over the trackless waste beyond us at sixty miles an hour came big drops of rain and great clouds of dust. How I wished that we had a "dugout" in the side of the bank! Finally a wall of rain advanced towards us, cutting as clear a swath as it came as if it had marked out the path in advance. Whether it was due to water-spouts or to cloud-bursts we did not know; but there was some mighty power behind all that sudden change from sunshine to storm. No ordinary progress of nature's laws produced the startling transformation.

Not long since Eliza, the dear, faithful friend of those days, came to pay me a visit from her Ohio home, and in talking over the happy past she recalled the storm; the description was so characteristic that I shall give it: "The first notion that I had of the creek risin' was a crash, and things come tumblin' and knockin' against my tent. It had a wood floor, and it began to ride up and down, and out floated the things, and I dragged my trunk and all the cookin' utensils I could get hold of up on the hill-side. Then my tent cut loose from the moorin's. Big trees and roots and parts of cabins and a wash-stand and a bed-tick from a settler's place up near the fort came a-tearin' down by. It was all in a minute. My shoes and stockin's was off,'and I was a-wadin' around catchin' hold of my cookin' things and holdin' in a long pole to gather in the half-drowned chickens. I was a heap more concerned about my kitchen things than I was about my clothes. Those wind-storms come so sudden! They would just tear up everything, and while we was a-strivin' to save the beddin' and tins from the water the wind was twistin' the tent and whirlin' all sorts of things around our head. Well, the ginnel he come a-flyin' home then, and I says to him, 'There is goin' to be a big storm;' and he says 'Yes,' and sent right off for the men to drive the picket-pins in and tighten the ropes. My tent was so nice; but dear me! I heard the tins and the iron things a-rattlin', and the ginnel said, 'You needn't be afraid; there's no danger of your tent a-goin'.' It was down under the hill a bit, and I tell you it did go, though. Tin pans, buckets, fryin'-pans, all tumbled and pitched about in a heap, and the tent was lifted on high and blown away off on the parade-ground for good. Such a gatherin'! — such a gatherin' as I had of the things; and then the ginnel would stand and holler to me while I was a-pickin' them up and say, 'How long before dinner?' when I hadn't one thing to get dinner with, nor even a sliver of dry wood. I jest raised my head while I was a-clutchin' for the things knee-deep in water, and said, 'Ginnel, don't you say dinner to me!'"

Meanwhile Henry was not idle; his horses were his anxiety. He told me when I saw him last that the night succeeding the storm which I have described, after the tempest had subsided a little and we had gathered our scattered belongings together and set Eliza up in another tent on dry land, he was awakened by a great rumbling in the brush and trees. His tent was only fifty feet from the water: "I sprang from my bed, which was on four-foot stakes, right out into three feet of water. The night was very dark, and I raised the alarm; the general was as quick as a flash out of his tent and had the whole regiment standing ready for duty to remove camp in case the water broke over the banks. When I got to my horses they were almost ready to strike a swim, as the water only had to rise six inches more to break all over the camp. All the plunder was loaded on the wagons, and it had to stay loaded for over twelve hours before the water began to fall, and after it did fall the bridge at the fort fell, and there was no way to get supplies." Henry, after all this excitement, was completely disgusted with the Kansas climate. When I talked with him as he stayed by the water taking measurements on a stick to watch the rising of the stream, he acknowledged that he was tired of roughing it. "You see, Miss Libbie," he said, "Manda—that's the yellow girl that used to take care of Mrs. Card's baby—and me is going to be married, and she couldn't no more stand what you does than anything, so I must go; and I think as you have relatives in Topeka, like as not you and the general would be a-coming there and I should see you, so I am thinking of living there. Why, Miss Libbie, the times I've been washed out here this summer I can't count, but if you and the general can manage to pitch my tent on a boat I can stay."

Our tent had three feet of water in it during the

next day, and I sat a long time in the travelling wagon, in the midst of a collection of household possessions that almost buried me. The horses were harnessed, ready to be put to the wagon at the first intimation that the water had risen above the danger line. The hens, becoming almost human from intimate association and sharing hardships, were roosting on the tongue, or pecked at the grass under the wagon, while the dogs leaped in and out over me, and over the traps, all day. It was an unending day, for we could do nothing but wait and watch, but fortunately the rain had ceased. In the afternoon, fearing another cloud-burst, tents were sent out of camp to the divide that sloped gradually from the stream, and we slept there. Eliza had found a little wood, and putting it under her blankets at night to keep it dry, was able to make our breakfast for us.

The Smithies meanwhile were in equal dilemma, for their tent was also near the stream, though not so close to it as ours. They rose in the morning and found the water was rising very fast, but thought they might get breakfast before it rose higher. The stream had then reached to within a foot of the tent. When they came out from breakfast they were obliged to jump across a stream that had flowed over the grass during breakfast. Then they began to pack their traps. A detail from the company went down to the dining-tent, and lifted the table, just as it stood, with all the dishes onto the higher ground. The water increased so rapidly that the tent was in danger of being swept away, and Tuttle, their man, swam out to loosen the ropes. After this the luggage was bundled into the wagon, and the Smithies went to higher ground.

When the water subsided we were all anxious to get back to our tents and begin home life again. Everything in our place was soaked. My trunk had stood almost entirely under water during the storm, and the bedding was musty and moist. A bright sun helped us, and soon all we had was flying in the Kansas breeze. The whole camp became a perfect sea of floating pennants, while horse-blankets waved from the picket line like a brown cloud. The same wind that had blown itself into a hurricane now turned about and atoned for its rage by drying our clothes. In my eagerness to possess our home again I went back to the damp tent too soon, and soon fell ill with a fever, which continued long enough to prove that the oldest veteran, who may be proof against the active drenching of a storm, is likely to succumb if careless enough to sleep in a thoroughly soaked bed.

Tattoo.

CHAPTER XXI.

RATTLESNAKES AS NEIGHBORS.

BEFORE I close the story of our summer I would like to write of some of the neighbors about us whom we thought altogether too neighborly. The rattle-

snakes of the plains have been much written about by
Western editors, but they can scarcely have too elaborate English expended on them; they were everywhere, and it was almost impossible to exaggerate the
numbers of them that surrounded us. Our camp soon
became too much of a thoroughfare to make it safe for
a snake to dispute the territory, and the soldiers going
back and forth on duty, the dogs constantly racing over
every inch of the ground, the servants perpetually travelling to and fro from the cook tent to ours, protected
us in the immediate vicinity of our habitation; but
the moment we rode out of camp over the plains
the reptiles appeared, sometimes gliding away, often
coiled for a spring, occasionally torpid, and gorged
with a toad or a bird which they had swallowed whole,
and which went down slowly, distending and distorting
their sides. There was no trouble with our horses in
the matter of ceding to the snakes the right of way,
but it was surprising that they showed so little fear of
them.

It seems to need the support of the commanding
general of all the United States forces to fortify any
one who begins to talk about this subject. Snake
stories, like the tales of fishermen, must always, on the
part of the listener, be heard with a spirit of combative-
ness. People square themselves for a fight, and are
ready to dispute step by step the progress of a story.
It was, therefore, with genuine pleasure at the privilege of listening to so good a talker, but with an atom
of exultation, that I heard General Sherman hold forth

on our plains rattlesnakes. To begin with, the wildest spinner of yarns can scarcely say too much on the subject. The snakes swarmed over the route of our march; they lined the way when we went for a hunt or a pleasure ride. General Sherman, replying to a woman's question, "And were not the soldiers often bitten?" replied that they were seldom fatally injured, as they were instructed as recruits by their officers, the surgeons, and the veteran soldiers how to protect themselves in case of the fatal sting. It is found that the snake throws itself about three times its own length from where it is coiled for a spring. Not being able, therefore, to strike its fangs in higher than the calf of the leg, the trousers often absorb a portion of the poison. If the surgeon is near, he applies ammonia to the wound, and stupefies the injured man with liquor. The whiskey is poured down as fast as the man can swallow; this, retarding the circulation, prevents the blood-vessels from carrying the poison to the vitals.

The part of General Sherman's conversation that touched me was his tribute to the affection and devotion of the private soldier. If the surgeon is too far away to be reached, the soldier resorts to his homely devices to save his comrade's life. A bit of buffalo bone is used to scrape and irritate the flesh about the wound, and cause a flow of blood outwardly. One of the men, if he happens not to have an abrasion on the lips, stoops instantly to draw the poison from the places where the fangs have entered. There is never a lack of offers among those fearless devoted men to suck

21

into their own mouths the deadly fluid. If ammonia is not to be had, they seek the black mud which forms the baked surface of a sun-dried buffalo wallow. Wetting it, and applying this to the wound, enough ammonia is extracted to aid the cure. Then—ah! I know all this myself, because I have been among our self-sacrificing soldiers out there, and have been taught many a lesson of generosity and devotion; they either watch over their wounded comrade till he is restored, or if he be sunk into drunken lethargy, they lift him into an army wagon as carefully as the experienced surgeon and hospital nurse remove an injured man from our city pavement to the ambulance.

This reminds me of one of our surgeons, Dr. B. J. D. Irwin, of our army, General Custer's warm personal friend. I remember the pleasure with which he discovered, at our first post at Fort Riley, a weed that he had not supposed grew there, which was an antidote for a snake bite. He held this little ugly scrap of vegetation in his hand as if he had in his possession a rare work of art, and breaking the stem, from which exuded the thick white sap, he gave me so animated a description of what cures it would effect, and of what benefit this discovery was to suffering humanity, that I was as pervaded with his spirit as if I knew the blessed art of the healer. It was to him that I was indebted for my first insight into the fervor and enthusiasm of his profession, and the generous manner in which their discoveries are given to the world. He had written a paper, after making this successful investigation on a tour of duty in New Mexico, that there might be no delay in the use of this life-saving weed.

Our army surgeons have contributed a good deal to the learning of their profession, and yet how quietly! When the civilian doctor makes his successful experiments, he rarely is without rewards, often of a financial character, and he always receives the tribute of admiration from his professional brethren, from whom he hears personal acknowledgments on the street, at conventions, clubs, and the city hospitals. Our army surgeons experiment, study, practice in their distant hospitals, or in the field, and when they give some valuable discovery in science to their fellow-workers over the world they add nothing to their limited incomes, and the voice of applause is very faint when it reaches the isolated post where they live out their valuable lives.

My admiration of them—working as they must without the reward of wealth or the sound, sweet to every one, of deserved praise—must be my apology for leaving General Sherman and the snakes. His sense of humor made him stop in his descriptions, which are the result of his many years' experience, to tell one of his Eastern hearers that the Seventh Cavalry had to move out of a dugout on account of the snakes. The dugout, he explained, is a hole in the side of a gulch or slough; around the four sides the men lay a low wall of turf, leaving an entrance framed by a hardtack box; over the piled-up sods the boughs of trees are laid as a roof, and on this dirt is heaped until it can hardly be distinguished from the ground around it. In this fortress made of such materials as are supplied by mother-earth (barring the cracker-box door) he had known four men defend themselves against hundreds of Indians, as they stood on the dirt floor, only lifting themselves to the loop-hole in order to fire. But, he continued, when the Indians failed to dislodge them, and rode away discouraged, the rattlesnake succeeded. It was easy for them to crawl into the loop-holes, which were on a level with the surface of the plain, and short work to go on down into the blankets of the troopers. The general says they dearly love warmth. Finally, he added, the Seventh Cavalry grew discouraged, and made a bargain with the snakes, giving them the original dugout, while they went to work, patiently, to burrow themselves into another, and it was no easy thing, with few and poor tools, to get a hole excavated large enough to give shelter and safety to even a handful of soldiers.

When General Sherman began to speak of the soldiers utilizing the rattlesnake as food, his semicircle of women-listeners raised their hands in protest. I rejoiced to hear him speak of it, feeling sure he would fortify me in what I have already said, or intend to, about General Custer's experiments in that gastronomic feat. He says that when the rattlesnake pokes his head out of the prairie-dog hole, where he has invited himself to live, without giving the architect of his home a voice in the matter, the watching, hungry soldier clips the snake's head off with his sabre, and, skinning him, gets as good a dinner by broiling him over the coals of a camp-fire as if he had an eel. I know that they often did this; and, after all, what difference does it make to that devil-may-care trooper how he possesses himself of that which will vary his salt pork and hardtack? Besides, do we not remember our child-stories of the giants and hobgoblins, and how, when they encountered any one they hated, they were made to say, "I'll eat you?" Surely it is a most effectual way of disposing of an enemy, especially a reptile that retains life in portions of his wriggling body when one part is cleft entirely from the other.

General Custer was the first among our officers to experiment on the rattlesnake as an entrée. A scout told him how fine, juicy, and white the meat was, and straightway he tried it. The first difficulty was with the soldier cook. He was absolutely devoted to General Custer, and not only obedient to orders, but studied or anticipated what he might wish; but when his chief took a fine fat rattlesnake to his cook-tent, and gave directions to serve it, the man, really believing some mistake had been made, ventured to reply, "But it's a rattlesnake!" When answered in the affirmative, the obedient soldier accepted the situation, but was sure that the light of reason had fled forever from his chief. Still, sure that it was his duty to serve a crazy master as he would a sane one, he prepared the dish that had been ordered. While General Custer was eating the meat, which, he said, separated from the bones readily, and was as white and delicate as that of a young quail, he saw the distended eyes of the alarmed cook cautiously peering in through a crack of the tent, doubtless expecting that he would drop down in a fit.

Once, when General Custer was dining in New York with that epicure Mr. Sam Ward, the conversation turned on rare dishes, and Mr. Ward, having dined in all countries, and being able probably to give an expert opinion on a greater variety of food than is known to any other gourmet of our day, offered it as his belief that our natures partake of the characteristics of whatever fish, flesh, or fowl we eat. General Custer's eyes twinkled when he told me that he thought he gave a poser when he asked him, " What effect would the rattlesnake have on a fellow ?" Strange to say, Mr. Ward had never known that these reptiles were eaten either by Christian or savage.

One of our officers, to whom I have before referred, was terribly afraid of snakes. When a child one had wrapped itself about his body, and so unnerved him that he never regained his courage. Every one laughed at him, no one lost an opportunity to tease him; but, being a fearless rider, hunter, and fighter, he could afford to endure the taunts of his comrades. He had the advantage of a record for dauntless courage to back him.

Among our collection of pets was a strange little owl that had been dug out of a hole, where it and the rattlesnake and prairie-dog lived in a kind of co-operative house-keeping. Naturalists insist that there is no " happy-family " arrangement in this; that the rattlesnake is an intruder, and that he returns hospitality by eating a young prairie-dog for breakfast occasionally. But the fact of their living together our soldiers proved over and over again. The soldier who gave the owl to General Custer showed him this family group, after he had dug down to the hole the prairie-dog had prepared. It was a wonder to me how the strange partnership came about. The prairie-dog always made the home; but whether the snake came in and possessed the land, or why the owl was rash enough to creep into this deep excavation, were questions that no one had been able to answer satisfactorily. The owl which we had made a sound so like the noise of the rattlesnake that no one could distinguish between them. The water-bucket, as a protection against the obtrusiveness of the dogs, had a cover fitted upon it. But for this precaution not a drop of water would have been left for the toilet. As there was no box convenient, the owl was placed in the empty bucket. A favorite trick was purposely to occupy every seat, the bed and chairs, etc., as the officer who so hated snakes approached the tent. Then he was welcomed effusively, which alone ought to have warned him of mischief. The bucket being the only seat vacant, and he not knowing of this trick of the owl, of course took it; but the way in which he bounded into space when the disturbed little bird began to make the sound of the snake called forth shrieks of laughter. He was one of the athletes of the regiment, and the involuntary leap into the air was far better jumping than he did when he tried to accomplish some competitive feat at our famous trials of agility, strength, and speed at Fourth-of-July and other holiday celebrations, in which most of the officers joined.

But all this continual joking was drawing to a close; for though in winter-quarters the merriment continues, there is a degree of privacy attainable when one has walls to one's house, while in camp there is none. Through the thin cotton walls of a camp habitation men called out to each other very pointed remarks about snoring, or too much "chinning," as they said, when they wanted to sleep. From the intimate companionship there was no escape, and so the smallest fragment of a joke was apt to be worked up into something really amusing.

We could not but regret, when October came, that our happy summer was coming to an end; it had been such a peaceful time for our tired-out regiment. It is true the Indians had hovered round us to threaten, but they belonged to another department north; the southern tribes were only too glad to stay at home that year after their severe whipping the winter before. The plains were dear to us because of the happy hours spent there. Sometimes we sighed for hills, and occasionally for rocks, but our next thought was one of gratitude that the monotonous surface prevented us from being reminded by quack advertisements that we had livers. Indeed, out there, with the pure air and active life, we might be obliged to admit that we had the organ for the cure of which a nostrum was recommended, but it was a silent partner. Every one was well,

except when ill in consequence of some actual trifling
with splendid health. The orioles that sang in the trees
above our tents were not more contented than we. It
was absolutely a trial to pack and start for garrison at
Fort Leavenworth, where we must abandon our un-
conventional life, dress for dinner, struggle with back
hair, and try to get our complexions into condition
again.

Some of our officers had one bright outlook—they
would at last have quarters for their families, and could
begin domestic life again. The men with sweethearts
were going home on leave. The fathers talked of their
children, and wondered if they would recognize the
bronzed and bearded "paternal." We heard the oft-
repeated tales of their brightness, and even now, thinking over those youngsters, they seem to have been very
clever and precocious. Two tiny little urchins were
fighters from the start. Coming into the world with
their fists doubled up, they kept them closed most of
the time when circumstances threw them with each
other. The officers, in a spirit of mischief, incited the
elder to "go for" the younger. They were too young
to do each other harm. I can now see Davie coming
down in front of the quarters, his legs full of swagger,
his tiny face red with rage. Jumping on my godson,
George Yates, he pounded and pommelled the two-year-
and-a-half boy for a few brief moments; but the smaller
of the two rolling uppermost, kept the top place, and
returned the civilities offered. Then the young officers—who, not being fathers, did not look upon this fisti-

cuff as serious—applauded the winner. The under boy in the fight crawled out, and while he ran bawling to his mother this little son of a very brave father shrieked threateningly, in the borrowed language of the frontiersman, "Got a pistol in my boot!" His little fat legs with "low-necked stockings" (as another bright dot dubbed his socks) and the small kid shoes looked anything but warlike. This same George, when he went into the States, and was teased by the children, knew no better threat in retaliation than to say, "I'll put you in the guard-house, I will," which was Choctaw to the civilian children, as they did not know a prison was ever called a guard-house.

The son of one of my friends came in to his mother one day, and said that he had been beaten and kicked by another boy. "Well, what are you going to do about it?" said his military mother; "you are not going to let him get the better of you, are you?" The little son, possibly six years old, not more, replied, energetically, "No, you bet I'm not." "Well, then, after supper go out and find him, and I don't expect you to come in with any story of being worsted in this affair."

All this had gone from the mother's mind until after dinner, when, without explanation, he came to her again, and asked if he should change his clothes. "Why?" she queried. "Because these might get all bloody;" and then she remembered that it was the time appointed for the thrashing of his tormentor.

One of the officers, in pride over his four-year-old,

gave me a description of the tales of the war his son demanded. He had repeated and repeated the same stories time and time again, not being permitted a variation by the exacting child, who knew them all by heart. He said: "The story is a little rough on me; but if any one knows a child, he knows that he wants a plentiful sprinkling of I's, and nothing told in the third person. So I kept on as he demanded, until one day he looked up in my face and said, 'And, father, couldn't you get any one to help you put down the rebellion?'" Instead of tiring of the cunning speeches of the little fellows, we usually asked, as each officer received a letter, "Well, what has 'Guy,' or 'Davie,' or 'George,' or 'Freddie' been getting off now?" And then the missives that devoted husbands carried in their inside pockets were brought out, and some clever speech of the child, written by the fond mother, was read aloud to us.

Before " Taps " sounds I must not neglect to explain one of the calls that fortunately is rarely used. It is the " Rogue's March :"

> " Poor old soldier, poor old soldier,
> Tarred and feathered and sent to —— "—

something that rhymes with

> "Because he would not soldier well."

Court-martial is the usual mode of settling all irregularities, and sentence is pronounced, such as imprisonment, loss of pay, reducing a non-commissioned officer to the ranks, etc. Sometimes, however, the soldier is so absolutely incorrigible and worthless that he is sentenced to lose his hair, and is drummed out of camp. While I was at Leavenworth I saw the execution of this order. The soldier's head was as blue and bald as close shaving could make it, and he marched bareheaded in front of a corps of drummers and fifers before the garrison assembled for parade. I should like to say that he hung his head in shame, but the truth is the audacious fellow, when at the limits of the garrison, leaped into a carriage at the hack stand, pulled on a wig, and waved a hat, which his waiting friend handed him, as he drove out of his military life into that of a civilian.

Occasionally the soldiers of a company rise in wrath over the obstinate determination of a soldier not to be clean, and ask leave to punish him themselves. When men ask permission, and the better men too, the officers know that they will not carry the affair too far. A double line of men is formed to the stream, each one having a switch. The offender is prepared for his compulsory bath, and started down the line. It is an effectual cure for the slovenly. He returns clean, and convinced that it is best to keep so.

But soldiers, clean or otherwise, camp women, officers and their wives, the dogs, the pets, and even the intelligent horses, soon were in a tremor of excitement, for orders had come to break camp, and march to Leavenworth for the winter. Preparations went steadily on. In a few hours we were packed. The wagons were drawn up ready for the tents, and those the soldiers took down and stored away for the march. I sat at some distance from the row of tents, awaiting the bugle-call, " Boots and Saddles," while the eager and excited dogs raced hither and thither among the troopers, and the horses neighed and sniffed the fresh air. Looking back upon a deserted camp is not cheerful : the grass where the tents have stood is trampled, the trenches dug about them to let the water run off from the tent cut the ground into squares ; hay and rubbish are strewn where once it was so trim. Our little arbor in the tree looked lonely enough, and the heap of stones which had formed the foundation was bare and forlorn. The noises that had disturbed me all summer under these rocks were now about to be explained. I had attributed them to rats, to weasels, and, as the night advanced and fears increased, to almost supernatural causes, the sounds were so uncanny ; but no, it was only that a family, seeing something of domestic life above the floor, and being satisfied therewith, had established a hearth-stone of their own below ; but when the floor was removed, and daylight, with prospective storms, let in, a procession, consisting of a mother and seven little soft-furred children, walked out from underneath, to seek other quarters. How it happened that Mrs. Polecat and her progeny had not been discovered by our dogs remains a mystery. It is needless to say that no one disturbed them, or failed to give them permission to do as they wished, and one triumphant woman said : " There ! what did I tell you all the time ? There was something gnawing, rooting, squirming under our tent all summer." That was I.

The officers who served with us that summer have had their service chronicled by a government that keeps records of brave men, but the courageous Eliza and the faithful Henry ought to have a word. Eliza still looks as young as when we ate her good dinners on Big Creek, and though the wife of a colored lawyer in Ohio, she refers to our life out there as among her happiest hours. Henry is janitor in one of the public schools of Topeka, and I hear that his big, tender heart is open still to even the smallest child, for if he sees one running down the street as the bell rings, and knows that he or she is likely to be marked late, he keeps on ringing till the delinquent has reached the door. He finally married his "Mandy," but the following account of his love passages with Eliza I venture to insert, to prove that Big Creek had a romance that summer, though neither the stream nor the romance "ran smooth":

"Miss Libbie, me and Eliza was mighty fond of each other, and off and on we was sparking; but I couldn't say as we was always happy. When she went off down to Leavenworth that time, I begun to hear things she had said 'gainst me, and I got mad. The more I thought about it the madder I got. I concluded I'd go and kill her. I took an ole pistol of the ginnel's, and set to work to oil it, and get the rust off. It took me a right smart time; but I didn't get no ways cool a-doin' it. Then I says to Bishop" (the general's soldier), "off-hand like, would he take keer of my horses. He said yes, and I started. When I got to Fort Harker I heerd more of Eliza's stories, and I biled right over. On the way down I heerd more and more, and when I reached the city of Leavenworth, thar I saw some colored folks we both knew, and such a pack of lies as she had told made me jest jumpin' mad again. I went on out to whar she was staying, bound I'd kill her, and, Miss Libbie, if you'd believe it, the minute I sot eyes on her I forgot it all. I jest melted right down; but pretty soon I fired up again, and I says, 'Miss Eliza Brown, I've cum pretty nigh onto two hundred miles purpose for to kill you.' She flared up, and asked, 'Why?' Then I tole her; but, Miss Libbie, you know how 'tis, I forgot again, and then we kissed and we fought and we loved and we fought and we loved and we kissed, and I jest put up the ol' horse-pistol for keeps."

Eliza and Henry never married. This may be explained on Henry's side by that old Virginia story of a colored swain who said, "Miss Loisa Cheers, I love you a heap, but I don't love you to marry." On Eliza's part it was possibly a case of " were t'other dear charmer away."

As the bugles sent out the last notes of "Boots and Saddles," we guided our horses out of the bend that had sheltered us, and nearly drowned us besides, and looking back to the bit of land almost surrounded with trees, we felt as Henry did towards his Eliza—with all its faults we loved it still. We joined with the band in the regimental song, of return and many a brave heart leaped with joy and said, silently, "Soon I shall be with the girl I left behind me."

THE GIRL I LEFT BEHIND ME.

THE hour was sad I left the maid,
  A ling'ring farewell taking ;
Her sighs and tears my steps delay'd—
  I thought her heart was breaking.
In hurried words her name I bless'd,
  I breathed the vows that bind me,
And to my heart in anguish press'd
  The girl I left behind me.

Then to the East we bore away,
  To win a name in story,
And there, where dawns the sun of day,
  There dawn'd our sun of glory:
Both blaz'd in noon on Alma's height,
  When in the post assign'd me
I shar'd the glory of that fight,
  Sweet girl I left behind me.

Full many a name our banners bore
  Of former deeds of daring,
But they were of the days of yore,
  In which we had no sharing ;
But now *our* laurels freshly won
  With the old ones shall entwin'd be,
Still worthy of our sires each son,
  Sweet girl I left behind me.

The hope of final victory
  Within my bosom burning,
Is mingling with sweet thoughts of thee
  And of my fond returning.
But should I ne'er return again,
  Still worth thy love thou'lt find me ;
Dishonor's breath shall never stain
  The name I'll leave behind me.

The Girl I Left Behind Me.

Moderato.

hour was sad I left the maid, A ling'ring fare-well

tak-ing; Her sighs and tears my steps de - lay'd— I

thought her heart was break-ing.   In   hur-ried words her

name I bless'd, I breath'd the vows that bind   me, And

to my heart in an-guish press'd The girl I left be-

hind me. Then to the East we

bore a - way, To win a name in sto - ry, And

there, where dawns the sun of day, There dawn'd our sun of

glo - ry : Both blaz'd in noon on Al - ma's height, When

in the post as - sign'd me I shar'd the glo - ry

thoughts of thee And of   my fond re - turn - ing. But

days of   yore, In which we had no shar - ing; But

should I ne'er re-turn a - gain, Still worth thy love thou'lt

now, our lau-rels fresh-ly won With the old ones shall en-

find   me; Dis - hon- or's breath shall never stain The

twin'd be, Still wor - thy of our sires each son, Sweet

name I'll leave behind me.

girl   I   left be-hind me.

"Taps," or Extinguish Lights.

Love, good night, must thou go, When the day and the night need thee so? All is well; Speed - eth all to their rest.

CHAPTER XXII.

DANDY.

THERE is still one character in my story of our summer camp who deserves a word, as, since the last chapter was written, he has gone to the heaven which we people who love animals believe is reserved for them. It is of our blithe, faithful, undaunted Dandy that I should like to tell you.

During the Wichita campaign in Kansas and the Indian Territory, in the winter of 1868 and 1869, five hundred horses were sent to the Seventh Cavalry to mount a portion of the regiment. General Custer was in command of the expedition, and the horses were passed in review in front of his tent. Among them he noticed a spirited bay, which he ordered detained at his tent, and, after trying him, decided that he would avail himself of the privilege given to officers, and buy him from the Government. The horse, he discovered, had good blood, though not perfectly proportioned, being too small. He was just within the height required by the quartermaster's requisition; but his fire, his promising powers of endurance, his sound condition, made General Custer think that he would prove equal to the terrible marches, the exposure, and the insufficient forage to which a cavalry horse had to submit.

He was given the name of "Dandy" on the spot, because of his spirited manner, and the little proud peacock airs he never forgot except when he slept.

DANDY.

Dandy had not been long in service before he was subjected to the roughest and hardest life. The soldiers' rations gave out at one time, and the troops lived on the flesh of mules and horses that had died from exhaustion. But Dandy's untiring nerve carried him through. He grew thin from want of forage, but learned, with the other horses, to scrape the snow from the ground in the river valleys, to find little tufts of dried grass, and, failing in this, gnawed the bark from the cottonwood-trees. Nothing seemed to tire him: no day was so cold or so wet that it did not find Dandy full of good cheer.

Test after test was tried on the plucky horse, and he never flagged. An all day's march in the winter, with the blinding snow and tiny particles of ice cutting his face, toiling through depressions in the ground where drifts had accumulated, tugging up declivities to be met on the summit with a keen icy wind that had swept unchecked over hundreds of miles of prairie— all this never took the dance out of his heels, or made his head droop with fatigue. It was this indomitable will that so endeared him to his master. He had a hard gait for a steady march. He never walked, but went on, year in and year out, with a little dancing trot that was most fatiguing. Still, this uncomfortable motion was made up for to General Custer by marvellous powers of endurance and by exceeding good-humor through all vicissitudes.

Our horses were such intimate companions on the plains that we found ourselves as anxious to be *en rapport* with them, and understand their humor, as with those of our friends beside whom we rode. Sometimes we divined as soon as we mounted that the animal under us was sulky or wilful or stubborn, and either we possessed our souls in patience till the ill-humor passed away, or one, more irritable or nervous, fretted at the exhibition of temper, took his horse out of the ranks, and the rest, watching him, said, "Now So-and-so is going to have another 'waltz' with that brute of his, but it's no good fighting anything so fiendish." One can realize, then, what it was to know that there was no variation in the temper of an animal. Imagine any one awakening in the gray dawn to the sound of reveille in a cavalry camp, and, after an ice-cold bath, a luke-warm breakfast, stepping shrinkingly forth into chilly drizzle that the troopers declared had "come to stay." What if all about were silent, or dulled by the cold and damp? Was it not everything to be met by the dancing, joyous motion of a pair of nimble heels, and the softest, most affectionate eyes, while the head turned to rub itself against the arm or shoulder of one the animal loved? Let the elements do their worst — and they attempt every vagary on the plains—that indomitable will and sunshiny disposition of Dandy's triumphed over everything. It was therefore worth while to endure the little choppy motion, which would have been immensely tiresome to many, for the sake of knowing that no day's march could be so long, no storm so violent, as either to fatigue or depress the willing animal. There were those who said that no man, except one with the wonderful powers of endur-ance of General Custer, could have stood the gait.

One of our best riders used to say that there was no worse suffering for a man than to ride a horse that re-fused to come down to a walk. Occasionally it fell to the lot of a soldier to draw from the Government a

horse that had this fault. There was no appeal. The
horse was purchased; he was sound. No horse-trade
could be effected with a citizen, because of the deep
" U. S." branded on the thigh. Sometimes, after a
campaign, an officer can enter a complaint, and ask
to turn in some brute with an irredeemable fault to
the Quartermaster's Department, to be condemned and
sold; but after a campaign was started, it meant a
whole season of jogging misery to the unfortunate
trooper who had fallen heir to such an animal. A
cavalry column marches at the rate of four miles an
hour, and the length of a day's journey varies from
twenty-five to forty miles. After such torture going
on month after month, the troopers would sometimes
cry out in desperation, " For God's sake shoot me, and
leave me behind!"

It was well that Dandy belonged to the commanding officer of his regiment, for he could brook no
horses going before him. If it was unavoidable, he
was flecked with foam and quivering with impatience
in a few moments. It was difficult to keep him beside a horse; he champed his bit, tossed his head, and
pulled furiously on the rein unless he was permitted
to stretch his neck in advance of everything. Then
he became quiet with conquest, and ambled on like a
graceful Andalusian palfrey.

No greater test of Dandy's endurance could have
occurred than a winter's campaign. It was the first
that the regiment had ever attempted at that season of
the year. The success of the expedition reconciled

the men to the hardships; but it was a fearful trial to the whole regiment, man and beast. After the winter was ended, the Seventh Cavalry marched from the Indian Territory to Fort Hays, Kansas, to establish a summer camp. The regiment, from that on, went up and down the State, as well as the adjoining Territories, for several seasons. On one of these marches, a number of years after, when they were traversing a more settled portion of the State, a farmer met, and was about to pass, the column, when General Custer accosted him, asking him about the crops, the ravages of the grasshoppers, then such a pest, and of the growth of the country, in which he was genuinely interested. The farmer turned to ride with him a while, and finally, after eying Dandy sharply, he said:

"Stranger, I'd like to en-quire, if it ain't no offence, where you got your hoss? It's a good un, no mistake."

"You are right," replied the general. "He is as tough as a pine-knot, as willing and spirited as any horse I ever saw." And then he went on to tell him that he thought that he discovered some of these traits when he picked him out of hundreds of animals bought by the quartermaster for the regiment.

"Well, sir," said the frontiersman, "that air hoss once belonged to me. He's got good blood in him. I've got the name of some of his sires at home. I can never get over the selling of him; but, you see, I got hard up, the grasshoppers ate my crops, and, while I was in a tight place, along cum a contractor, and I sold him for $140, the Government price. He was wuth a heap

sight more; but the ready money had to be got somehow, so I let him go."

All General Custer could say was that he was sorry
that he had lost him, but that hardly any price could
tempt him to part with so good a campaigner. He was
then five years old.

Dandy became a great pet with his master. It was
a serious affair to lose a horse on the march, for they
could not be replaced, and consequently the utmost
precautions were taken to lariat or hobble the animals
when the march was over for the day.

Dandy was often not tethered at all. As soon as
the general selected camp he unsaddled and unbridled
him, and turned him loose to graze until the command
came up to pitch the tents. He took a roll or so on
the grass, and grazed about the tent until it was time
to saddle him next morning for the day's march. He
loved the dogs, and permitted all sorts of familiarities from them. Sometimes the stag-hounds, that make
such tremendous leaps, would spring entirely over him
in their antics. He played with them, nipping their
skin to provoke a frolic, and no unexpected attack of
the venturesome dogs was ever met by him with anything but the utmost good-nature. He was a picture
in the midst of the pack of forty, all barking, growling,
scuffling. The grave fox-hounds pressed about his legs
in affection, looking up with luminous, expressive eyes.
The stag-hounds made wild springs in the air, catching
his mane or tail, or jumping to kiss his nose. He tossed
his head, snorted, pranced with delight at all this atten-

tion, set his feet down with excessive caution for fear of hurting a puppy, and was capable of showing more affection in the few mute ways left open to him than people who have the human voice and expressive features at their disposal.

The soldier who took care of him was the strangest contrast to the whole party—dashing cavalryman, mettlesome horse, and rollicking dogs. Indeed, he seemed so much out of place in a cavalry camp that I wanted always to ticket him "Lost, strayed, or stolen." He was slow of speech, thought, and movement, but in affectionate fidelity he was to be trusted even above the gayer and more active trooper. The man lived in a world by himself, with little in common with his comrades, going along a dull, beaten path at snail's pace, while all the wild world of a cavalry camp, with its incessant excitements, its exhilaration, its enthusiasm, sung, shouted, and careered about him. Nothing moved him to a laugh; and if he had whistled I should have sent for the surgeon, thinking he had gone daft. I have a photograph of him standing between and holding with each hand the bridle of Vic, the general's thorough-bred— which was shot in the battle of the Little Big Horn, June 25, 1876—and Dandy. The dogs stand or lie about the group; and the soldier, with his solemn face, looks as if any remark England or America might make about "duty" to him would be superfluous. His horizon encompassed two horses, some dogs, and one yellow-haired officer. He may have had a past—a bald spot on his no longer youthful head spoke of one—but no reference was made to it; nor did he seem to wish for a future in which Dandy, Vic, Blucher, Tuck, and Cardigan (his favorite dogs) and their master were not included.

Dandy enjoyed a hunt above everything. The general could run down a deer with Vic, and for a spirited, quick dash the thorough-bred was best; but Dandy was the old love, and he made such demonstrations of delight over the preparations for the chase that he grew to seem almost human. The officers generally gathered before our quarters, and the horn was sounded as a signal for the kennel gate to be opened. Out swooped the pack, tumbling over each other in their haste, tearing around the house to the horses to have a few preparatory interchanges of animal language. The orderlies holding the horses let them rear and paw the earth; and in the din of the barking, whining dogs, tuning their voices to the horn, the laughter and jovial voices of the officers, the call from the windows and galleries of the women giving a good "send off," there was not an intelligible word. From all this wild scramble, in which dogs, men, and horses seemed involved in a hopeless tangle, the leader extricated himself, and Dandy proudly took the advance. He curveted, danced sidewise, tossed his head and mane, and evinced by every motion that he was born to lead.

Then, when the real work began, he proved that if he was a dandy there was good stuff in him; for he fell to the duty of the hour with a skill and determination that made his master, each time he returned from the chase, pat his neck as he leaped to the ground, and

say, " There never was such another horse created."
The cotton-wood timber along the Missouri River was
in places densely embedded in underbrush, and it took
infinite patience to wend one's way through the thicket;
but Dandy was capital at this. His nerves were in the
wildest state when the deer was spotted.

After the day's sport was ended the horn sounded
from down the valley, and soon the same exuberant
throng poured into the garrison, the dogs leaping and
barking still, the fox-hounds trotting sedately on, covered with burrs, porcupine quills, or cactus, their legs
incased in mud, their rigid tails bleeding from the
sharp thrashing through the thickets; still they gave
tongue with the deep notes of their species. The
horses of the hunters were usually fagged and glad to
hear stable - call; but darting up to the gallery came
the undaunted Dandy, sometimes bearing on his back,
behind the saddle, the game, though the deer was generally too large to admit of using any but a led-horse
to transport it.

If in our rides about the post we saw a gray coyote
skulking along, hiding in the divides or sneaking his
solitary way back to his lair, Dandy spied him also, and
begged for a run. He trembled with the ardor of a
hunter; and it hurt him to see game disappear and he
not chase it. He knew how to gather himself and turn
like a flash when the jack-rabbit " put down its fourth
leg " and doubled on its pursuers. It required such
agile legs as Dandy's to circumvent the active hare.
His lope was too short to take him over the country
23

quickly enough to overtake an antelope, but he could be almost motionless for the moment of loading and firing.

In another chapter of this book I have described Dandy's skill and enthusiasm in buffalo-hunting, and need not repeat it here.

There were many obstructions to smooth going even on the apparently level plains. The buffalo wallow was one. Dandy, coming on these wallows full tilt, learned, if he was going too violently, to veer one side, to leap in and out like a cat. The buffalo trails to water, running in four or more parallel lines, he cleared with a bound. These also are deep ruts, hard and stubborn to the hoof, that have been baked by the sun as is the wallow. He picked his way through a prairie-dog village unguided, and rarely did his hoof sink in the subterraneous traps. His best leaping was over the cactus-beds. These he took with a bound. Dandy was sometimes lent to the wife of one of our officers, and she rode him out to the herd of Government cattle where her husband went on duty. She writes me, " I always started without my stirrup; for it ' was up and away' with Dandy, and I had to find foothold as best I could afterwards."

She was an excellent horsewoman; but her surprise when Dandy took a huge cactus-bed with one leap was something to remember. She said to General Custer, " He shall not catch me again napping;" and he shook and chuckled with amusement, for he had purposely omitted telling her of Dandy's little caper, knowing she would be equal to the situation.

The winter's campaign had been a trying beginning to Dandy's career, but the long, hot summers that followed were a fearful strain on any horse. There was always much trouble about water on the plains. After the rainy season passed the streams went dry, the pools in the buffalo wallows and in the hollows had disappeared, and the whole day of a hot march was spent without so much as a look at water, with possibly the tantalizing mirage floating before their weary eyes all the time. The strongest animals became fagged, their heads drooped with exhaustion, and some dropped by the way to die; still the valiant Dandy kept up.

I do not know whence came all that inexhaustible spring of vitality. In the letters from old friends with us on the frontier that I have received regarding Dandy during the past week each one says, "I never saw him walk." He was in all the campaigns of the regiment for years — in the first Yellowstone campaign, in the Black Hills Expedition, and in the last campaign into the Yellowstone in 1876. As they were starting that spring General Custer said:

"I must take an extra horse this summer in addition to Vic, for Dandy must be favored a little; he begins to show a little let-down in strength."

In the battle of the Little Big Horn, June 25th, he was with the led-horses and was wounded. After the battle he was sent home to me in Monroe, Mich., and I gave him to my father Custer. The horse, so identified with the three sons he had lost, seemed to be a wonderful comfort to him.   I was afraid to have him mount him, for he was then over seventy, and Dandy required every one to be very active who attempted to use him to the saddle.   His journey of over fifteen hundred miles by boat and by cars had not tamed him, and I begged Father Custer to let an officer then with us at least ride him round the block.   At last he yielded, and off Dandy tore through the quiet streets to the amazement of the town.   The old gentleman was unmoved.   He said, "Daughter, I can ride him; there's nothing vicious about him."   And he was right.   It is my belief that he had been studying up his future master.   He let him mount leisurely, and seemed instantly to tame down in gait and manner.   Our father Custer was rather bent in walking, but there was no perceptible curve to his back in riding.   He sat his horse splendidly.   Except for his white hair and flowing, snowy beard, one could hardly imagine so many years had elapsed since he rode after the hounds in his early Virginia and Maryland days.

After leaving the army, Dandy never surprised you by unexpected moves, and it was not necessary to watch for sudden veering to the right and left.   From the life of a gay, dashing cavalry steed he dropped into a steady-going family horse.   The one marked evidence of the old life was displaced when our father Custer took him out for parades.   It soon became a custom for the towns-people to invite the old gentleman and Dandy to head the temperance processions, the Fourth of July celebrations, or any sort of parade the town might inaugurate. He and Dandy were invited to be the guests of Michigan at the State Fair. The invitation was worded, "For Father Custer and his horse Dandy." They led the grand procession that was under the guidance of the marshals of the day. Dandy never for one moment forgot his part. He sidled and ambled and pranced in a gentle sort of teeter, suitable for his aged master, but he scorned to walk like an ordinary every-day horse.

The etiquette of the past generation was to attend all funerals, and Dandy's old master believed that one's friends should be just as carefully attended to the grave as to the altar. Dandy therefore fell into the slow, solemn line, and subdued his step to the occasion. His politics never varied, owing to an unswerving quality in his old master. During the last political campaign his tossing head waved a bandanna through the streets of our town. If it blew in his eyes and interfered with his sight he never showed it, but bore the badge as if it had really been what his owner wanted it to be, a plume of triumph.

Whenever I went home to visit them my father Custer asked, as soon as the welcome was over: "Daughter, would you like to see Dandy? If you would, sit by the front window, and he will be around." When they appeared, Dandy did all the kittening possible in the way of little starts and flourishes, affecting coltish airs, and pretending timidity which was purely fictitious. This pleased the old gentleman, and he called out, as he waved his stove-pipe hat, "You see he isn't an old man's horse yet." I could not help praising my father Custer's firm seat in the saddle, so remarkable in a man between seventy and eighty. My gentle mother Custer, fearing I might plant the seeds of pride even in an old man, said, "Don't say too much to him, daughter; old men might get foolish about their riding." But, nevertheless, my home-coming did not seem complete without the dress parade in front of the house.

During the later years my father Custer has lived on a farm near Monroe, with General Custer's only brother. Dandy, coming in and out of town every day, was obliged to cross a bridge over the River Raisin. Not for worlds would he go over without a little pantomime of sham fright. He minced and hesitated and shied the least bit in the world, arched his neck as if in surprise, and with all these skippy ways looked through the cracks of the boards as if it was the first time that he had ever seen them. Hearing Father Custer's voice, he instantly came down to every-day manners. All the timid girls who were afraid of other horses were willing to go with Father Custer; and many a happy mile has Dandy carried them through the fragrant roads and fields about the "City of Flowers."

Even until this year it has been Father Custer's custom to drive off to the home of one of General Custer's staff, and the thirty miles in a day seemed as nothing to the two veterans. For weeks at a time Dandy gambolled over a rich pasture, kicking up his heels like

a colt when let into it, or made himself comfortable
without being tied in a box-stall, while his master was
enjoying all the hospitality the house afforded. Returning home, they soon started for a forty-mile drive
in another direction.

It has been a common sight in Monroe for years
past to see Dandy quietly standing beside the street
to allow his white-headed owner to dally by the way-
side and carry on a hot political discussion. There
were too many people in the town whom our father
Custer thought needed to be set right in their views,
especially as an election drew near. He would allow
no one to feed or groom his horse, and in consequence
of too many oats the graceful proportions of youth
were fast losing themselves in a real aldermanic outline; but I could not convince our father Custer that
it was not a line of beauty. When he approached the
stable the horse knew his step and whinnied; and he
had the same welcome as he came out to get in the
carriage. The cars stand for a time on the track running through our town, and Father Custer once drove
Dandy's nose almost into the side of a car. In alarm
I asked if he intended to drive over or creep under;
but he quietly answered that he wanted me to see that
the horse was not afraid of anything with him.

"The boys," he added, "had hard work to hold him,
but he knows me; and, daughter, I don't know how I
could have lived without that horse. He's been a comfort to me for thirteen long years."

On a recent Sunday these two comrades went off up

the Raisin for a little time, and all was well.   Life still held one joy for the two—they could go out into the sunshine together, for after all the bereavement of life God's beautiful world remained.

On Monday no whinny of greeting met him as he undid the stable door. For the first time in all his twenty-six years Dandy was ill. All the simple remedies of the farm were administered without avail. Two veterinary surgeons failed to help the suffering beast. He was still the same plucky Dandy. As he never showed a sign of heat, cold, thirst, or hunger in his old soldiering days, so now he met the suffering bravely, only turning his head around to show his appreciation of the presence of the family about him. As General Custer's brother left the stall the poor beast walked after him, rubbing his head against him in affection. The children hardly left him. The mother, with all the maternal tenderness of heart, begged to stay all night in the stable, saying that it seemed cruel to leave him alone.

All day Tuesday our father Custer never left him ; and weeping with grief at his suffering, and the sorrow at recalling all his past, the old man sat hour after hour brushing off the flies and caring for this beloved link with the past.

At night the family went out at twelve, and poor Dandy followed them ; and looking over the half-door of his stall, they saw for the last time his pathetic eyes, dimmed but full of devotion. At four in the morning they went again, and he had fallen, the straw scarcely disturbed about him, showing that he had remained standing until the moment when, thinking he heard the bugle-call "Taps," his light went out forever.

Though this veteran had no muffled sound of drum, no volley fired at his grave, still it was a solemn burying. All day the boy who loved him dug at his grave in the orchard, and the mother and children, suspending work and play, vibrated between the house and the field where the "earthly bed" of their favorite was being prepared.

There, every year, Nature, with all her fidelity, will bury our dear horse in a rosy shower of blossoms which the apple-tree scatters with the least breath of the summer wind.

The silvery head of an old man of eighty-three bends lower this August day, and it is hard to take up his few remaining years without his comrade, the comfort of his bereft life.

BIOGRAPHICAL NOTE

Custer, George Armstrong, 1839–76; American military officer; b. New Rumley, Ohio; graduated at West Point, 1861; served in the Civil War in the Manassas campaign, 1861; the Virginian Peninsula, 1862, as aide-de-camp to McClellan; Maryland campaign, 1862; Rappahannock campaign, 1863; Pennsylvania campaign, 1863; in operations in central Virginia, 1863–64; Richmond campaign, 1864; Shenandoah campaign, 1864–65 brevet major-general for gallantry at Winchester and Cedar Creek and numerous smaller engagements; in command of the cavalry in the pursuit of Lee's army, 1865; in command of the cavalry in the military division of the SW. and Gulf, 1865; chief of cavalry in the Department of Texas, 1865–66; after the war was on W. frontier duty; killed by the Sioux Indians, on the Little Big Horn, Mont.—*From Appleton's New Practical Encyclopedia.*

CUSTER'S FAREWELL ADDRESS TO HIS TROOPS AT THE CLOSE OF THE CIVIL WAR.

HEADQUARTERS THIRD CAVALRY DIVISION,
APPOMATTOX COURT HOUSE, VA., *April* 9, 1865.

Soldiers of the Third Cavalry Division:

With profound gratitude toward the God of battles, by whose blessings our enemies have been humbled and our arms rendered triumphant, your Commanding General avails himself of this his first opportunity to express to you his admiration of the heroic manner in which you have passed through the series of battles which to-day resulted in the surrender of the enemy's entire army.

The record established by your indomitable courage is unparalleled in the annals of war. Your prowess has won for you even the respect and admiration of your enemies. During the past six months, although in most instances confronted by superior numbers, you have captured from the enemy, in open battle, one hundred and eleven pieces of field artillery, sixty-five battle-flags, and upwards of ten thousand prisoners of war, including seven general officers. Within the past ten days, and included in the above, you have captured forty-six pieces of field artillery and thirty-seven battle-flags. You have never lost a gun, never lost a color, and have never been defeated; and notwithstanding the numerous engagements in which you have borne a prominent part, including those memorable battles of the Shenandoah, you have captured every piece of artillery which the enemy has dared to open upon you. The near approach of peace renders it improbable that you will again be called upon to undergo the fatigues of the toilsome march or the exposure of the battle-field; but should the assistance of keen blades, wielded by your sturdy arms, be required to hasten the coming of that glorious peace for which we have been so long contending, the General commanding is proudly confident that, in the future as in the past, every demand will meet with a hearty and willing response.

Let us hope that our work is done, and that, blessed with the comforts of peace, we may be permitted to enjoy the pleasures of home and friends. For our comrades who have fallen, let us ever cherish a grateful remembrance. To the wounded, and to those who languish in Southern prisons, let our heartfelt sympathy be tendered.

And now, speaking for myself alone, when the war is ended and the task of the historian begins—when those deeds of daring, which have rendered the name and fame of the Third Cavalry Division imperishable, are inscribed upon the bright pages of our country's history, I only ask that my name may be written as that of the Commander of the Third Cavalry Division.

G. A. Custer,
Brevet Major General Commanding.

Official:

L. W. Barnhart,

Captain and A. A. A. G.